TOLSTOY
AND THE NOVEL

JOHN BAYLEY

TOLSTOY
AND THE NOVEL

With a new Preface

The University of Chicago Press, Chicago 60637

97 96 95 94 93 92 91 90 89 88   5 4 3 2 1

Library of Congress Cataloging in Publication Data

Bayley, John, 1925–
   Tolstoy and the novel : with a new preface / John Bayley. —
University of Chicago Press ed.
        p.   cm.
   Reprint. Originally published: New York : Viking, 1967, c1966.
   Includes index.
   1. Tolstoy, Leo, graf, 1828–1910—Criticism and interpretation.
I. Title.
PG3385.B38   1988   88–22020
891.73′3—dc19   CIP
ISBN 0–226–03960–9 (pbk.)

CONTENTS

PREFACE, 1988

What is most important about the phenomenon of Tolstoy? I have only recently come to ask myself this question, although I can now see that the answer has always been hidden in the background of *Tolstoy and the Novel*, the book about his work that I wrote more than twenty years ago. Tolstoy is probably our greatest novelist, the man who has given the form its supreme authority. And yet to call him a "novelist", to offer him that professional title, is meaningless, is quite absurd.

Somehow, he wrote these great novels without ever becoming a novelist. He recognised the paradox himself. He maintained that *War and Peace* was not a novel, and even that Russian writers had never really practised the art of the novel as it was understood in the West. *War and Peace* was "what the author wanted to express", in the form in which he felt he could best do so. A great deal follows from this statement of Tolstoy's. It explains what happened to him. It explains why instead of becoming a novelist he became simply "Tolstoy".

Shakespeare died in his early fifties. I think we can imagine him, had he lived longer, continuing to write plays, perhaps another half dozen, perhaps as many as ten or twelve. As it was he had made enough money and preferred to retire from the stage. But he remained a professional, and if the need had arisen he would certainly have considered other subjects and produced more plays. Where the novel is concerned it was the same with Jane Austen, one of Shakespeare's spiritual and literary descendants. She too was a professional, and if she had not died young she would have written more novels, each one no doubt a work of art.

The significance of this similarity is that both Shakespeare and Jane Austen had a kind of innate modesty. They had found the form in which they could express their genius, but the form was bigger than they were, so to speak. Their works were bigger than they were. The reverse is true of Tolstoy. It was both his triumph and his tragedy that he wholly lacked this innate modesty. He was never subdued to the idea of an art. Indeed, when he wrote *What is Art?* he attacked Shakespeare vigorously, and the ground of the attack was really that Shakespeare was an artist. I doubt whether Tolstoy had ever heard of Jane Austen, but if he had he would no doubt have attacked her too. He claimed, perversely, that art's function was to serve mankind, by which he really meant: to serve Tolstoy.

This explains why his novels are so great, and so unlike any others. Not that they are about Tolstoy himself—very much the contrary. They are about Russia, and Russian history, and love and marriage, and what it means to be alive. And for these purposes they *use* the novel form, in the careless way that a great aristocrat uses his money and possessions, his houses and lands. In *Anna Karenina* Tolstoy uses one of the oldest tricks in the business: a double plot, in which one kind of life, one story and sequence of events, is played against another. But it does not strike the reader that this is like a novel. It seems an account of real life.

Tolstoy paid a price for his attitude towards the novel. Using it as he did, he was left wondering whether there was any point in living at all. In his old age he took up a story, that of Hadji Murad, and wrote it as a story just as Shakespeare or Jane Austen might have done. And a friend heard him murmur: "The old man wrote it well." The Russian novelist Gorki was to say that Tolstoy and death were like two bears in one den. They could not live together and one of them had to go. Tolstoy's relation with the novel was much the same, and in that lies its great fascination. The winner: Tolstoy or the Novel? I choose Tolstoy.

John Bayley

St. Catherine's College, Oxford
April 1988

Chronology of Works
examined or mentioned in the Text

Acknowledgements

I am indebted to the Oxford University Press for permission to quote sections from Aylmer Maude's translation of *War and Peace*.

To Dr Theodore Redpath's admirable study of Tolstoy in the series *Modern European Literature and Thought* (Bowes & Bowes) I owe my introduction to the work of some of the Soviet critics I have consulted, notably to N. K. Gudzy's extremely valuable book on Tolstoy's manuscripts and methods of composition, *Kak Rabotal Tolstoy*. I owe a comparable debt to the bibliographical references and the textual and linguistic scholarship of Dr R. F. Christian in his monograph, *Tolstoy's 'War and Peace'* (O.U.P.)

TOLSTOY
AND THE NOVEL

The Russian Background

Life is constantly putting to Russians the question: Where are you?
CHAADAYEV

Two and two still make four, but somehow it seems more lively when it's Russian.
TURGENEV, *Smoke*

I

BARATYNSKY, a poet and guardsman, and a friend of Pushkin, wrote that two qualities were needed for the making of a poet: "the fire of creative imagination and the coldness of controlling reason". From another poet at another time, and in a different country, we might be inclined absent-mindedly to accept this as undoubtedly sound but a little obvious. But Baratynsky was born in 1800, at the threshold of Russia's great literary age. The simplicity of what he says strikes with unexpected force, for it was not only the truth as he saw it, but the truth as it was about to be embodied in the poetry of Pushkin and the novels of Dostoevsky and Tolstoy.

That is the impressive thing about the remarks of nineteenth-century Russian writers—they mean what they say. And they mean what they say in a way that has little to do with literature and literary traditions. Their awakening into self-consciousness strikes us as having a curious purity, as if it occurred simultaneously in every department of living and thinking; a penetrating, unblunted intelligence examining itself, its instincts, sufferings and pleasures; greedily devouring the great bulk of literary matter which the West had amassed on these themes, and assessing it with an almost embarrassing directness. Preoccupied, above all, with ideas, and with ideas as progress. Gogol says: "it is essential that life should take a step forward in the work of a creative artist", and again the phrase seems not the dictum of a man of letters but a sort of hurried practical instruction.

Swaddled in the inertia of its accomplishment, the complacency of its prolongation, Western literature has no comparable critical tone. At our most urgent we still sound literary. "The lyf so short, the craft so long to lerne." Chaucer's tone is already so acquiescent, so resignedly professional. In Russia there was not long to learn: it all had to be done at once. To the English fictional scene in the 1850s it seemed to make little difference if Dickens was saying that the novel was nothing if it was not serious, or Trollope was maintaining that it must end in a feast of sugar plums. Both views dissolve without fuss in the ancient pool of unsurprising precept: that Fancy must be tempered with Judgment; that one must look in one's heart and write; that the sound should be an echo to the sense. By contrast the critical dicta of the Russians seem like telegrams exchanged by revolutionaries after a *coup d'état* has begun, but before it is known whether it will succeed.

If the description of ideas seems so direct and first-hand in nineteenth-century Russia, so does description of objects. In *The Execution of Troppmann* Turgenev is as transparent and objective as Tolstoy ever was. It is significant that Tolstoy wrote *What is Art?* when Russian literature had used its own eyesight and produced its great primary works; when it had caught up with European literature and achieved parity in sophistication and emphasis on technique. Tolstoy is calling for a return not to some primal age-old simplicity but to that of fifty years back. The age of 'nature' in Russian literature was still so close that for Tolstoy—and in him—it was still alive. He saw no need to distinguish between ancient simplicity and modern *simplesse*, between naming things and calling them over for the benefit of the literature class. Because in Pushkin's poetry a nature and a language suddenly light up together, each identifying the other, Russian children may be said to learn things by their Pushkin names. With us, the naming of nature in literature happened too long ago and over too prolonged a period. For an English child the cock and hen are not Chaucer's, or the wind and the rain Shakespeare's, as the goose, the sled, and the snowstorm were named for a Russian child by Pushkin. Though the daffodil was named in English by Shakespeare it was annexed by Wordsworth, who put his romantic trademark on it—the daffodils that *I* saw—and it is this trademark and not the name that is popularly remembered.

Our literary tradition is too cumbered for the best to be the naturally definitive, and for the simplest person to know the best things—that is why Matthew Arnold was so anxious that the best should be isolated and as it were *imposed*, in schools as by critical organisations, upon the public. In France this had been done, but in Russia it did itself. Where Russian children learnt Pushkin's *Winter Evening* (as we can see from Tolstoy's story *Master and Man*), Matthew Arnold found an English classroom reciting some appalling rubbish about 'This native land of mine', by a nineteenth-century versifier.

Arnold admired Tolstoy and wrote one of the first appreciations in English of *Anna Karenina*; and Tolstoy admired Arnold as a critic, giving warm praise twenty years after it was written to his most important theoretical essay, *The Function of Criticism at the Present Time.*

> In our time, when readers are deluged with newspapers, periodicals, books, and by the profusion of advertisements, not only does such criticism seem to me essential, but the whole future culture of our educated world depends on whether such criticism appears and acquires authority . . . criticism which, as Matthew Arnold says, sets itself the task of bringing to the front and pointing out to people all that is best, both in former and in contemporary writers . . . disinterested criticism which understands and loves art and is independent of any party.

Both are conservers in fact, though they might not admit it in so many words—Arnold to the point of being almost a curator. Though for both art is the expression of the religious feeling of its age—Arnold seeing in its highest historical achievements virtually a substitute for Christian dogma—neither Tolstoy nor Arnold show real interest in the radical innovations of form which the spirit of the age may impose upon creative imagination and which become, indeed, the embodiment of that imagination. For Tolstoy, all fashion in form, the whole notion of 'the modern', was evidence of mere restlessness, sterility, the decadence of the clique. Although he says in *What is Art?* (and it is true of his own best work) that a good work of art has its own unique form and individuality, he ignores the implications of this in terms of the difference between one artistic epoch and another; ignores the inconvenient fact that the true imaginative work often only stands out retrospectively, and that no critic can be sure what is great in the art of his own time.

In the Preface to Von Polenz's novel *Der Büttnerbauer*, from which I have quoted above, he asks why "this really artistic production . . . in which the author says what he feels he must say, because he loves what he is speaking about", has not had more recognition? The answer is that the work is conventional. Though the account of a good wife and a brutal husband which Tolstoy praises is certainly edifying and moving, it has no life of its own—the kind of total unconscious originality which informs such scenes in Hardy, for example. Like Arnold's criterion of 'high seriousness', Tolstoy's conception of what is sincere and morally impressive in literature is unavoidably retrospective. Both are saying in effect: great literature has been written, and the good critic knows from it what great literature is like; he must find if he can the same qualities in the work of today, and the writer of today should endeavour to repeat them.

The significance of the parallel between Arnold and Tolstoy is that both give the impression of writing about a *completed* literature. Arnold is most at ease with the classics; and though he proclaims that "the future of literature is immense" he cannot help implying that English literature has also completed its span. So, towards the end of his life does Tolstoy about the Russian. In the same preface he comments on the rapid decline from the greatness of Pushkin to the decadence and triviality of modern Russian poetry. In Russian literature now too, as in others, greatness is in the past, though the past was in his own lifetime.

Arnold's attitude is not untypical of Western literary critics in the nineteenth century and earlier; in Russia Tolstoy's was unique. For all other Russian theorists, greatness was to come. Throughout the nineteenth century the atmosphere of literature and of criticism remains excited, provisional, prospective. There are no accepted standards and no talk of 'disinterestedness' and 'independence of party'—when things are really happening or are going to happen, and literature is in their service, such notions have no meaning. Disinterestedness is for what is dead. All nineteenth-century Russian critics would easily have perceived what their successors mean by 'bourgeois objectivity'. Literature is pushed and pulled about between warring factions and ideologues—Slavophils, revolutionaries, reactionaries, Tolstoyan pacifists—who are agreed on one point: that it is, or can be made to be, of the greatest human and social service; and that writers, as Stalin put it, are the architects of the soul.

When Tolstoy writes disparagingly of critics who "deduce the direction of the movement of our whole society from types depicted by certain writers", and who "express particular economic and political opinions under guise of discussing literature", he is probably referring to Chernyshevsky and Dobrolyubov and their following who, as the literary historian Mirsky says, "regarded literature as texts for utilitarian sermons or as a map of contemporary life, of which the only merit lay in its handiness and accuracy". Taking as their texts the novels of Goncharov and Turgenev, they saw in *Oblomov* or in Turgenev's heroes only the paralysed futility of the old gentry or the ineffectiveness of the liberal progressive; and made no secret of the fact that the authors themselves, as representatives of their class, could not understand the true significance of what they created. No wonder Turgenev referred to the two critics as "the snake and the rattlesnake". Pisarev went further and endeavoured to debunk Pushkin himself. Whereas Belinsky had idealised Pushkin and perceived (rather as the Marxist Lukacs was to do in Tolstoy) the universal appeal and understanding behind the aristocratic exterior, Pisarev argued—and in a sense with equal truth—that Pushkin has all the irresponsibility of the mere artist, and his detachment from questions of social utility.

The great advantage of measuring the achievement of literature by politics and by social progress is that neither writer nor critic will see themselves as epigoni, living on the past and yet paralysed by it. The Russians did not, even after their great epoch was past, for their sense of the destiny of Russia that was to come bore literature, and all the vital confusion of critical opinion about it, along in its train. What mattered was *Russian-ness*, this intoxicating new concept which the critic Grigoriev makes virtually the standard of literary excellence—"if it's Russian, it's good"—and which at the same time had the strong romantic appeal of an idea still in the future and not yet realised. Merezhkovsky can say that "the Russian people has not, so far, found its proper embodiment or type," and can agree with Dostoevsky that when this type arrives it will be as the supreme new European.

> Tolstoy and Dostoevsky are the two great columns, standing apart in the propylaeum of the temple. . . set over against each other in the edifice, incomplete and still obscured by scaffolding, that temple of Russian religion which will be, I believe, the future religion of the whole world. . . .[1]

Already we are prescient of a third comer who is greater than these. Prophetic words: and it would not have troubled Merezhkovsky that the apparition seems to have materialised in neither a religious nor an artistic shape. What mattered was that something was coming to which these two, and others like them, were mere evangelists. This is why the pair did not seem to their contemporaries and successors the climax of a golden age but the beginning of a still more extraordinary one; and why—in spite of all their dissensions—no Russian critic could have written, as Ruskin wrote of the European nineteenth century, that it had become "thoughtfully unproductive of all art—ambitious, industrious, investigative, reflective—and incapable". Even for the aesthetes and decadents at the century's end, art was not separable from the great and strange destiny of Russia; and they were as much absorbed in, and expectant of, that destiny as were the social and revolutionary authors. There was no *Axel's Castle* in Russia; and Sologub's stories or Bely's weird novels, *St Petersburg* and *The Silver Dove*, are of a different order of creation to *A Rebours* or *The Picture of Dorian Gray*. Even the symbolists' doctrines are a part of the national expectation.

Only Tolstoy refused to be expectant. In a sense he hated the future as much as he hated death. For him the Good was con-

---

[1] Merezhkovsky, *Tolstoy as Man and Artist.*

stant and unchanging, and the art that revealed it should be timeless, parabolic, simple. Even as a young man Tolstoy disliked the idea of human and spiritual metamorphosis in response to the pressure of history and of new ideas. For him the destiny of Russia was not apocalyptic and peculiar and her self-awareness, like that of every other people, should be based on the general awareness of "reason, that is, good". The sense of nationality which is none the less so powerful in his work is much more involuntary than with other Russian writers. Like the pride of the body, like war, women's shoulders, or well-set-up guardsmen, one delights in it in spite of oneself. And it is in any case a static, not an emergent thing. It belongs to the present, the present that ideally should be always with us. These attitudes to literature and life distinguish Tolstoy from almost all other vocal Russians of his time.

II

Nineteenth-century Russia sometimes strikes us as being like a school, an exceedingly repressive and old-fashioned one—a military academy perhaps—in which the most brilliant senior boys are submitted to the same humiliating disciplinary processes as the dimmest and most junior pupils. There is Dostoevsky's mock execution and his years in Siberia; Pushkin, forbidden to travel abroad, exiled to his country estate, and finally forced at the age of thirty-five into the humiliating position of a *Kammerjunker* or page, in order that he and his beautiful wife might be kept under the eye of the autocrat in Petersburg. The relation of Pushkin and Herzen to the Tsar Nicholas is like that of a favourite sixth-former in disgrace. As Herzen said of him:

> Nicholas—reflected in every inspector, every school-director, every tutor—confronted the boy at school, in the street, in church, even to some extent in the parental home, stood and stared at him with pewtery unloving eyes . . .

Under Nicholas I—Nicholas *Palka* ('the stick')—Russia was more regimented than Prussia ever was: "half the town in uniform", as Herzen says, "half the town standing at attention, and the whole town taking off its hat".[1] Many writers—Lermontov, Bakunin, down to the Decembrist poet and writer of costume romances, Bestuzhev, who served in a penal battalion and was cut to pieces in a heroic fight with a Caucasian tribe— like Tolstoy himself, served in the army, in Petersburg or garrisoned somewhere in the vast monotony of Russia. Even Goncharov, the creator of Oblomov, was at one point seconded from the civil service to the navy. Nineteenth-century Russian literature echoes with words of command and is full of uniforms, sentries, barracks, and the gambling and dissipation that relieve the tedium of camp life.

"Without despotism", says Pyotr Verkhovensky in *The Devils*, "there can be neither freedom nor equality." There is freedom in the Russian school, but it is the freedom of Hobbes rather than Rousseau, the freedom of a system which exacts the obedience of the flesh rather than the adherence of the will and the spirit. And we feel that the pupils rely on it more than they realise; depend on it for the freedom and boldness of their thought, their unquenchable vitality. Literature, said Belinsky, is a substitute for free institutions in Russia; and Tolstoy in one of his letters is strangely, almost shamelessly, frank about the advantages which a privileged person like himself might enjoy under the system.

> Those Englishmen who come to Russia feel much more free here. At home they are bound by laws which they make themselves through their representatives, and which they obey, imagining all the time that they are free men. Now in this country it was not I who made the laws: consequently I am not bound to obey them—I am a free man.

We raise our eyebrows. Is this the casuistry, the bottomless cynicism, which Conrad saw in the politics of the Russian soul? Yet one takes Tolstoy's point. Any rule which professes to be

---

[1] The Tsars Peter III and Paul were ardent Germanophiles (as was Lenin in a very different way). Russia has always exaggerated and adopted, voluntarily or involuntarily, from her love-hate relation to her influential neighbour. Bakunin's famous confession to the Tsar ("a prodigal, estranged, and perverted son before an indulgent father") shows what Heine called *Deutsche misere*— German abjectness—in its most exuberant Russianised form.

based on co-operative enterprise and the people's will—whether it is the Soviet state or Anglo-Saxon constitutional government —pays for its gain in mutual responsibility a heavy price in hypocrisy. If we are all involved in what we profess to be the best type of government, we have a strong human tendency to ignore the contrast between what it ought to be and what, in detail, it actually is. Entrenched in the wisdom of the British Constitution we were able to gloss over the actual evils of imperialism and *laissez-faire* capitalism; and Tolstoy, perversely enough, held that where such hypocrisy was, any system of government must be contemptible. To him sincerity was far more important than political freedom, and the need that goes with it to compound in some degree for the ruling ethos as a part of oneself. He admired Ruskin, who, because he saw the actual evils of the money state, was equally detached from, and contemptuous of, its political traditions. Tsardom, which as Herzen shows in his brilliant historical analysis,[1] could appeal neither to the old traditions of feudalism nor to the new loyalties of the social contract, was—ironically enough—the perfect milieu for this detachment and this sincerity.

[1] In his commentary on Princess Dashkov's Memoirs at the end of *My Past and Thoughts*. He points out the Russian tendency to regard modern Tsardom as a kind of faceless interim between "the Varangians, the men of Novgorod", and the future. "The turreted walls of the Kremlin screen the flat outlines of the Peter-Paul Fortress from us."

It is a military and civil dictatorship with far more resemblance to the Caesarism of Rome than to a feudal monarchy . . . even to this day it carries the traces of its revolutionary origin. It exists so long as the circumstances that have called it forth remain unaltered and so long as it is true to its destiny . . . but it was not at all a matter of chance; it came in response to the instinctive craving of Russia to develop her forces—how else can its success be explained? The inhuman discipline of Peter the Great and his successors aroused of course horror and loathing, but all that was borne with for the sake of the wide horizons of the new life . . . it has kept its word and created a powerful state. The people love success and strength.

Herzen's analysis is extraordinarily suggestive of what was to come as well as of what was passing. He perceives why a dynamic tyranny is embraced and joyfully endured in Russia, while an autocratic conservatism is rejected. "The oil with which the engines on the new railways are greased will be better for anointing the Tsars at their coronation than the holy unguents of the Uspensky Cathedral."

In Russian literature it produces the famous 'superfluous man'—Pushkin's Onegin, Lermontov's Pechorin, Turgenev's Rudin, even Pierre in *War and Peace*—the hero whose intelligence and aspiration can find nothing to work on and through in the objective social world. There is a good deal in him of the Byronic hero and of Hamlet (Turgenev wrote an influential essay contrasting Hamlet, the ineffective intellectual and *poseur*, with Don Quixote, the single-minded enthusiast), but he also corresponds closely—as Russian heroes have a habit of doing—with an actual type of young man of the period. In Nicholas's military academy there was nothing for such a young man to do; revolt was senseless, reform out of the question: gambling and duelling were the only way out. There is significance in Kozintsev's selection of "Denmark's a prison" as the key phrase for his film version of *Hamlet*. For the Russians, the conditions produced the man, and even when conditions began to change and new types appeared—like the 'sons' of Turgenev's novel and of Dostoevsky's *Devils*—the tradition of the 'superfluous man' remained. We can still recognise him in the Nekhlyudov of Tolstoy's *Resurrection*.

"The superfluous people have made their exit from the stage," says Herzen, "and the embittered will follow them." Literature hardly bears him out. It remains singularly lacking in anger, bitterness, self-importance; in cynicism and time-serving. Herzen himself goes on to claim that

> we have preserved a naive faith in the poet and the writer. We are not used to the thought that it is possible to lie in the spirit and trade in talents. We are not used to the money-grubbers who make profit out of their tears over the people's sufferings, or the traders who turn their sympathy for the proletariat into a well-paid article. And there is a great deal that is good in this confidence, which has not existed for years in Western Europe, and we ought all to try and maintain it.

An extraordinary directness, without cynicism, is characteristic of Pushkin. He is quite lacking in cant, or in that kind of self-display which Byron automatically indulges in. Pushkin himself supplies a reason for this in one of his letters. "Our writers come from the upper class of society. In them aristocratic pride is combined with authors' self-esteem." Byron had the one without the other. Confident in both, Pushkin has no need to show off.

Elsewhere in his letters Pushkin is equally direct on a subject particularly agonising to liberals at many points in history. "We can only pity the Poles," he writes during the Polish insurrection of 1830, "we are too powerful to hate them; the war which is about to begin will be a war of extermination—or at least it ought to be. The love of one's native land, such as it must be for a Polish soul, has always been a gloomy feeling." Brutally direct it may be, yet it has an immediacy and economy of understanding which includes generosity, as we can see in Pushkin's attitude to the Polish poet Mickiewicz. It is this same acceptance of history and fact that we find in Pushkin's poetic masterpiece, *The Bronze Horseman*. In the most depressing situation the Russians did not lose their vitality and explosive force of utterance; they have a kind of weird high spirits in the midst of tyranny and gloom, and Pushkin gives us the reason. Russia was not born for this destiny: Poland was. Mickiewicz is a poet of real gloom, as full of backward sorrows as an Irish bard; but for a Russian gloom is a challenge and a stimulant. We can detect this effervescence, this curious discrepancy between the chill of the words and the ardent vivacity of the tone, in Pushkin's statement at the end of the prologue to *The Bronze Horseman*—*Pechalen budet moi rasskaz*—"mine will be a sad tale". We detect it in the last sentence of one of Gogol's stories —"It is gloomy in this world, gentlemen"—and in the opening words of Dostoevsky's hero from underground—*"Ja chelovek bolnoi, ja zloi chelovek"*—"I am a sick man, a spiteful man".

The vital force that pulsates in these apparently depressing pronouncements reminds us again of the Dotheboys Hall endured by the Russian intelligentsia, and of the comradeship which united them in something resembling pride in the horrors of the old school. Pushkin in fact celebrates in his '19th of October' poems his old school-friends of the Tsarskoe Selo Lyceum, which Alexander I had founded. "On their youthful shoulders", says Herzen, "they carried across the whole kingdom of dead souls the ark in which lay the Russia of the future." Certainly their friendship was of the highest importance to them and to Pushkin; and in its absence of wariness, of self-insulation, and of jealousy (one thinks of Yeats remarking of T. S. Eliot's poetry, "It may be *a* way, but it is not *my* way") it is a kind of friendship seldom found among writers in any age.

So too is their family feeling. We sometimes feel that the first Russian novelists did not so much look in their hearts and write as look at the lives of their mothers and fathers and remember. The *memoir*, whether actual—like Herzen's *My Past and Thoughts*—or invented—Pushkin's *History of the Manor of Goryukhino*, Saltykov-Shchedrin's *Golovlyov Family*—is a seminal form. Aksakov imitated and translated French theatre for years before he found his native inspiration and wrote *Years of Childhood* and *A Family History*. The importance of the family memoir in Tolstoy's development needs no emphasis, though ironically enough it retards as well as matures him. The memoir can have no plot, and his critic and biographer Boris Eykhenbaum points out the absence of plot in the young Tolstoy's work. In a sense he despised it and considered it unnecessary and unnatural, but it is only when he begins to make use of plot in the most conventional sense that his greatest achievement begins.

III

The question of freedom is always important to the writer, and in the Russian situation it is both abstract and urgently practical. Turgenev has the outlook of a liberal European, and he hopes that Russia will come to imitate the European ideal of freedom. But neither Dostoevsky nor Tolstoy would have it so. Dostoevsky included in *The Devils* a venomous sketch of the westernised Turgenev; and in argument with him Tolstoy derided the notion that the champion of Western freedom could possess 'convictions' that really meant something and were not just a device to flatter and support his image of himself. It is the familiar, brutal accusation of the extremist (though Tolstoy's extremism was anti-political) against the well-intentioned liberal, and it made Turgenev very angry.[1] Later in his *Literary*

---

[1] Turgenev's brush with Tolstoy has a possible fictional parallel in *Rudin*, where the hero (often accepted as a kind of self-portrait) wins a similar argument and establishes by casuistry that 'convictions' really do exist. See also Richard Freeborn's excellent *Turgenev: A Study*.

Reminiscences he brought the counter-charge that there was no freedom in *War and Peace*. Tolstoy might well have agreed which shows how temperamentally incomprehensible to one another they were: the word means for them quite different things. For Tolstoy it meant discovering how life intended to imprison one, and going gladly and whole-heartedly into that imprisonment; that is freedom as the survivors of *War and Peace* find it. And Tolstoy took for granted that the writer must submit as much as anyone else; otherwise his writing could have no true human relevance. For Turgenev, on the other hand (as for his admirer Henry James), the writer's personal freedom and non-involvement were required for him to see and to choose what James called his "fictive picture", the "unattached character" who was "endowed with the high attribute of a subject". It is a classic temperamental contrast of the age of the novel, and in this Russian confrontation it appears with a special forcefulness and clarity.

Turgenev is, of course, the exception. In general, the total involvement of Russian writers in their society seems a part of their powerful selfhood, the individuality which has to assert itself and protect itself against the system. Desmond MacCarthy compared Pushkin to a man up to his neck in life but not submerged, always able to see clearly. And it is the same with Tolstoy, whose sense of himself—not as writer, thinker, or sage, but simply *as* himself—is overwhelmingly strong. "As I am, so shall I be," says Pushkin, and Tolstoy echoes him. "As I was at five, so am I now," he said at the end of his life; and like Levin in *Anna Karenina* "he felt that he was himself and did not wish to be anyone else". The egocentricity of the Western romantic writer has nothing in common with this joyful and primitive power of individual existence.

Indeed we might make a distinction, in the context of Russian and Western literature, between the author who writes about himself and his experiences, and the author who *exists*. Gide writes about himself: Tolstoy writes about himself: but with the former we feel the will to create and impose upon us the idea of a unique and significant person; with the latter, only the transparent statement of an existence. It is the same with the comparison, made by Thomas Mann and others, between Goethe and Tolstoy. Both are supreme egotists. But Goethe is absorbed by himself because he is a national genius, a god-like apparition; Tolstoy, because he finds himself experiencing what all other human beings experience. Goethe's self-preoccupation strikes us as perpetually narcissistic, incapable of disturbing its own image; Tolstoy's is the egoism of a man like any other, but immensely *more so*.

When Thomas Mann[1] patronises Tolstoy's moralising and his attempts to disown the flesh, and praises Goethe's majestic and self-justifying development, the soft impeachment is exasperating; and not only because Mann—'the ironic German'—was himself so evidently preoccupied with the Goethean national succession and with himself as the incumbent of Goethean poise. For surely the collapse of the sense of existence in Tolstoy is the surest proof both of how superb and how universal it had been? All of us are subject to such a temporary collapse: Tolstoy experienced it on an overwhelming scale. Tolstoy's embodiment of a kind of universal physical existence would be nothing if it had not been so continually haunted and obsessed by the question of what there was, what there might be, outside himself. A Tolstoy who continued to write novels of the same kind would be an intolerable phenomenon, for his egotism seems to encompass all physical existence. But what grows with it, haunts it, and finally dominates it, is the admission of its limitations, the confrontation of self with what is not self, of life with death. Tolstoy is not ill, not perverse; he plays out in himself, and on his scale, the most universal and inevitable of human dramas. He *is* the state of our existence: he does not, like Goethe, attempt to conquer it and to put himself above it. Ultimately, as Thomas Mann comes near to admitting, Goethe cared for nothing but himself. Tolstoy *was* nothing but himself, and his sense of what awaited him, and what was outside him, is correspondingly more intimate to us all, and more moving.

This fact of existence might be taken as the equivalent in

[1] Thomas Mann, 'Goethe and Tolstoy' (*Essays of Three Decades*).

Russian literature of what Schiller categorised as the *naive*. But in Russia the 'naive' and the 'reflective' periods of literature did not succeed one another, according to Schiller's conception of literary evolution, but occurred simultaneously. Pushkin was well aware of this. He knew how completely his own poetry embodied the genius of a new language; he knew it so well that he did not bother to be 'Russian' in any other than the linguistic sense. He looks towards Europe, and borrows and adapts from it, as if he wished to enshrine Europe in the Russian language and make a new mode of expressing it. In this he reminds us of our own great European poets, of Milton and the Augustans, who saw themselves as carrying into English the classical and European heritage. Pushkin has, so to speak, to be his own Milton and Pope as well as his own Schiller and Byron: he compresses the whole European literary tradition into his poetry, but he is never 'literary', even when he most closely echoes its commonplaces.

It is this which distinguishes him so sharply from the founders of German literature. "German is the only language", he himself remarked, "in which the critics appeared before the authors." Schiller's Law applies most forcibly to Schiller himself. His work is ghostly, reflective; it has no incontrovertibly unique linguistic existence. Where Pushkin takes from the European tradition, Schiller is overshadowed by it. Shakespeare most notably overshadows him: his language, the essence of his imagination, cannot get clear from Shakespeare. Though both Shakespeare and Schiller might be said to cast their shadow over Pushkin's blank-verse drama, *Boris Godunov*, it is the only one of his poems that is so eclipsed; in which the 'naive' existence of language is uncharactered by a foreign intrusion.

Because it has no total and authentic essence of its own, 'reflective' literature and poetry is highly translatable. Tolstoy and Dostoevsky are, as it were, 'naive' in their existence, their Russianness, but 'reflective' in their language. Pushkin casts his shadow over them. For Russians, they can never approach— giants as they are—his status as the great primary author. They owe him more than the foreign reader can easily be aware of: but they also lose, because of him, the seemingly unrepeatable gift of being Russian in speech and European in outlook.

They are far more nationalistic than he. "Great art is national," observes Dr Pevsner, "national art is bad art." Tolstoy and Dostoevsky are not national in this sense, but they are Russian by assertion and intent where Pushkin is naturally so. And, as we shall see, Dostoevsky claims Pushkin for his own purposes as ideologically and spiritually Russian. The paradox is that Pushkin is an untranslatable European, while they are translatable Russians; and that Russia in her isolation at the beginning of the nineteenth century was culturally far closer to Europe than was the awakened nation of the great novelists. The more involved Russia became with Europe, the more she insisted on the separateness of her own cultural status, and the more the exotic flavour of this separateness pleased the rest of Europe.

IV

Compared with Pushkin, both Tolstoy and Dostoevsky protest, and protest too much—there can be no doubt about it. Almost anything can be made out of Pushkin, as out of Shakespeare. His terseness and simplicity yield any number of implications to those who succeed him. Dostoevsky hailed him as a prophet: Gogol borrowed from his swift undeviating stories and transformed them into bizarre and passionate outcries of protest and appeal. In the brief octosyllabics of *The Bronze Horseman* we can see already the historical imagination of *War and Peace*, the same grasp of the relation between human suffering and the tyrant's will, which, in terms of history, is as helpless as its victim. Tolstoy makes the issue explicit, massive, and insistent; but in the end he can "give no other reply to that terrible question"—the question of power and war—than that they are an inevitable part of man's nature. Pushkin's poem does not ask the question and does not seek for an answer; but for all its rapid and sanguine movement, its triumphant brio, it is as heavily weighted as *War and Peace*.

It tells an apparently very different story. A young civil servant, whose betrothed has been drowned in the great flooding of the Neva, goes mad and wanders through Petersburg, past those graceful interminable façades whose Italian symmetry seems to swell to phantasmagorical size in the boundless context

of Russia. When he peered across the river at the height of the
flood to try and make out the cottage where the girl lived, he
could see only the great bronze statue of Peter the Great
towering above the waves. And in his wanderings one night,
when he finds himself again before it, he shakes his fist upward
"at the ruler of half the world", and then runs away in panic
across the square as he sees the statue slowly turn its head
towards him. As he runs all night distractedly about the town he
seems to hear the hooves of the Bronze Horseman at his heels.
"And after that night, whenever the madman passed the statue,
he took off his cap and went by with downcast eyes."

The poem ends with typical abruptness. On a deserted island
in the Neva, visited only by a fisherman to cook his catch or by
a clerk on a Sunday outing, the flood has deposited the wreck
of a cottage. On its threshold the madman's body was found,
and buried out of charity. Pushkin makes no further comment.
In his letters, *à propos* some imperial pronouncement, he remarks
that a tone of irony ill becomes power. And there is no irony
in his poem. His superb eulogy of Petersburg in the prologue—
"I love you, Peter's creation"—is as energetic and straightforward as his account of the madman's end. None the less the
poem failed to pass the censor.

Though Pushkin—always affectionate with his creations—
calls him "my madman", the hero of *The Bronze Horseman* is
not a realised character, as is the other unfortunate clerk who
descends from him—the Akaky Akakyevitch of Gogol's *The
Overcoat*. "There is no need to spell it out" was Pushkin's
dictum: Gogol's genius worked in exactly the opposite way.
He uses Akaky. Belinsky and Dostoevsky ("we have all come
out from under *The Overcoat*") praise Gogol for having exhibited the underdog, the poor victim of the system, the insulted
and injured. It does not seem to have occurred to them to praise
Pushkin for displaying the same things, any more than it occurs
to the critic to praise Shakespeare for displaying the evils of
kingship in *King Lear*. With Belinsky and Gogol begins that
harnessing of Russian literature to social utility which has
continued to this day—both Tolstoy and the Soviets subscribe to
the doctrine of a literature always engaged with human and social
problems, and infecting us so that we see them in the right way.

In *The Overcoat* Gogol makes the right way clear indeed. Marvellous as the story is, and filled with the freedom and gusto of the grotesque, we are none the less conscious of the dead hand of intention, much as we are in Tolstoy's story about the equally unfortunate serf Polikushka. Hardy, it might be said, pursues many of his characters with the same exuberance of bad luck, but there is a difference: it is Hardy's own vision of the world which produces the cruel coincidence, and Hardy is not concerned to impose this vision upon us, only to show us the way things look to him. Gogol and Tolstoy may be said to give coincidence a social status, to imply that it is somehow in league with the regime. In fact, the true story which set Gogol's imagination to work had a happy ending. A poor clerk had made Homeric efforts to save enough to buy a gun to go shooting in the Neva marshes: on his first outing he drops it in the water and loses it: he is heartbroken, but his colleagues club together to get him enough to buy another one. The story is not merely true but also, so to speak, Pushkinian. Life, for Pushkin, is quite heartbreaking enough without laying it on too thick. We may suppose him to have felt a certain amusement at what Gogol made of the episode, perhaps the same amusement that induced him to parody, in his own story *The Station Master*, the type of the poor girl betrayed by the heartless hussar; and to give to a tale about such a girl an unexpectedly happy and yet logical ending.

Still, Pushkin himself suggested the theme of *Dead Souls* to Gogol, and his sympathetic genius is visible in *The Overcoat*. Both poem and story break off on an enigmatic note. How did the madman's corpse come to be where it was found? Is the 'ghost' at the end of the tale that of Akaky, or is it simply the robber still at his business of stealing overcoats? Both Gogol's story and Tolstoy's *Polikushka* have endings whose inconsequence—comically weird in the first case and movingly simple in the other—redeem the rather ruthless determinism of their plots. But *The Bronze Horseman* remains on an altogether different level of art. It is in the grandest sense a disinterested poem, perhaps the first and last Russian masterpiece which neither engages itself automatically with the current theories and ideals of the Russian intelligentsia, nor self-consciously refrains from doing so. Pushkin, like Shakespeare (we imagine), had above all the sense of a job to do and a job done. "I look at a finished poem of mine as a cobbler looks at a pair of boots: I sell for profit." Each poem presented to him a fresh problem in imaginative seizure and technical execution. He is bound neither by the continuity of ideology and obsession, nor by absorption in his own spiritual development. For him there is only one criterion for the poet—*Dovolyen?*—is he himself satisfied? If so, then let the *narod* desecrate his altar in their ignorance or enthusiasm. He cares nothing for their opinion, nor for the Tsar's.

In attempting to invoke, with his engaging doctrine of 'aesthetic bliss', the Horatian innocence of Pushkin, his great admirer Vladimir Nabokov only shows how impossible it is for an artist to do so today. Though they precede him in time, Byron and Keats were no more able to hold Pushkin's view of art than Tolstoy and Gorky were to be. It depends on his over-lordship of Russian statement—with all that this implies—and his position in history, on a threshold of language but an inheritor of social and historic tradition. In deliberately taking the same kind of stand, a Nabokov or a Robert Graves enclose themselves, for better or worse, within a certain kind of aesthetic pale. In the nineteenth century, Pushkin's aesthetic should be that of a minor writer, but his art is that of one of the greatest and most spacious. Time has buried the paradox, in Russia as in the rest of Europe—perhaps temporarily, perhaps for ever. Only once in a language (so one would suppose) can the aesthetic viewpoint have the authority and the inclusiveness of great art. Perhaps in Africa, where Pushkin was proud to claim his own ancestors, the miracle will come round again.

v

However that may be, the literature that follows Pushkin certainly pulls out every last social and national implication from the compact folds of his verse. Gogol and Dostoevsky both take up the image of Russia as a galloping horse, forced by Peter's iron bridle to the very edge of the abyss. At the end of *Dead Souls* Gogol expands it into his famous vision of the

Russian *troika* in its mad career; and in *The Brothers Karamazov* Mitya's counsel rhetorically pictures the same headlong *troika*— the terror, disgust, and admiration of other lands. Both novelists seem a little flabby and shrill compared to Pushkin, but there is no denying the power of the vision. The Petersburg brought to life in *The Bronze Horseman* continues to exercise an equal fascination over Gogol and Dostoevsky. But for them it has nothing of the graceful, martial exuberance of Pushkin's prologue—of gilt spires shining in the long nocturnal daylight; of cannon saluting the birth of an heir to the throne, and the breaking up of the blue ice on the Neva; of feasting and sleigh-riding. For them, as for Andrei Bely, its last imaginative celebrant before the Revolution, it is a creation of dreams and phantoms. This too is in Pushkin. The Tsar who planted the city in the marshes was dreaming gigantically of Dresden, London and Rome: the hero of the poem, clinging to one of the great stone lions in Peter's square and gazing wildly across the waves to where his beloved lives—was he dreaming too? Was his humble idea of making a home as phantasmal as Peter's mighty one? Is all life a dream? Pushkin throws off the question without further comment. But it remains one that can hardly fail to occur to the visitor to Petersburg, even today.

And again Gogol makes the dream more explicit. In *Nevsky Prospekt*, the girl of the hero's dreams, seen tripping along the great street in all the glamour of the dream city, turns out to be an ordinary prostitute: and the hero kills himself. The romantic vision in early Russian fiction is remarkably urbanised and localised. "Do we ever get what we want?" asks Gogol, with a characteristic gastronomic image—"one can order whatever he wants and has a tiny mouth: another has a mouth the size of the War Office Arch and has to remain satisfied with a dinner of potatoes." We meet the Petersburg prostitute again in Dostoevsky's *Notes from Underground*—the solemn, hopeless girl who disappears out of the hero's life into the falling sleet— and again in the Sonia of *Crime and Punishment*.

Dostoevsky is usually the least topographical of authors, but Petersburg gets under even his skin, and the bridges, the façades and the embankments, become a part of Raskolnikov's peripatetic nightmare after the murder of the old money-lender.

Indeed the atmosphere of the capital enables Dostoevsky to make the book so hallucinatory, and to mingle so disturbingly actual with mental events. Has the whole sequence of decision and action, terror and confession, happened in the hero's mind? Both Raskolnikov and his creator find it difficult to remember that the crime has occurred in fact: its true dimension is in the world of fantasy, where Dostoevsky's previous hero of *Notes from Underground* had his less hypothetical and hence ultimately more disturbing being. But in *Crime and Punishment* the Western genre of criminal melodrama is effectively naturalised in the mental and spiritual townscape of Petersburg.

In Dickens's fog-ridden London and Victor Hugo's grotesque Paris there is a relation almost acceptable and snug between the architectural setting and the mood. In Peter's city the proportions of the age of reason are weirdly discrepant with the tyranny of the visionary will. The paradox weighs on the hero of Pisemsky's novel *A Thousand Souls*, who—fresh from the homely geniality of Moscow—feels his spirits sink to zero in the great capital he had so much longed to see. He walks once or twice round Falconnet's imperious statue; gazes at the Winter Palace and at St Isaac's Cathedral; but "these sights had the most irritating effect on him", and there came over him the great Petersburg *cafard*, the inability to tell the real from the unreal, or to distinguish his perplexed interior alienation from his external surroundings.

Tolstoy alone resists the siren charms of Petersburg. It is a most significant fact. 'The Seer of the Flesh' would have no truck with these metropolitan hallucinations. True, *War and Peace* begins in Petersburg: the window-ledge on which Dolokhov sits to drink his bottle of rum, and win his bet, was doubtless one with an elegant pediment, on some big house beside the Moika; but we cannot place it from the narrative, whose extreme reality seems to depend upon keeping the topography of the phantom city at arm's length. Moscow is real: we know where the Rostovs' house is, and we share Nicholas's impatience to be home as he sees the familar landmarks; we are present at the English club banquet, and in the Kremlin courtyard where Petya cheers the Tsar and manages to seize his bit of biscuit. Of the Karenin's house in Petersburg we have no such apprehension; though we see the imperial villages outside the town, with the race-course, the wooden dachas, and the cold green foliage of the northern summer. Only in *Resurrection* does Tolstoy suddenly show us the classic Pushkinian vista of Neva, Winter Palace, and Admiralty spire; and he does it for a macabre reason. We have just been into the Peter and Paul Fortress; seen the Governor doing table-turning with his A.D.C., and heard him assure us that the prisoners are well-treated "and soon become fat and very quiet". After this, even the perspective of the ghost city seems a return to what is sane and alive.

Tolstoy's shunning of Petersburg is the more marked in contrast with its fascination for other writers. For the size of Russia does not produce in fiction a corresponding topographical diversity—perhaps a society as rigidly compartmented and centralised as that created by Peter was bound to produce a corresponding centralisation of literary themes. There were, too, important social reasons for Tolstoy's neglect of Peter's capital, which we must touch on later, but the most crucial thing is his rejection of it as the headquarters of native artifice, of literary succession and aspiration. Every town in Shakespeare's plays, as has been said, is London, and almost every great French and English writer has something of the same relation to the capital. But Russia had two capitals: and Pushkin is a Petersburg, Tolstoy a Moscow, man.

Inevitable Comparisons

*. . . Tolstoy, who seems to have been given to the world for the special
purpose of being contrasted with Dostoevsky.*

D. S. MIRSKY, *A History of Russian Literature*

I

ONE might, though with a different intention, make the
same distinction between Dostoevsky and Tolstoy. Raskolnikov and the Underground Man haunt the capital of the spirit:
Stiva Oblonsky and old Count Rostov, those two sanctifiers of
the flesh, preside over Moscow. But more instructive are the
ways in which his two great legatees react to Pushkin himself,
for nothing sets them more subtly apart than their attitude to
the primary Russian author. Tolstoy distrusts—it may be even
resents—Pushkin, but regards him as a fact of nature, set apart.
Dostoevsky annexes him and makes use of him.

It is observed in *Mansfield Park* that the English don't have
to know they know Shakespeare—he is in their blood. In *Anna
Karenina* both Stiva and Levin quote Pushkin; and the cheerfully
ignorant Stiva, misremembering Pushkin's anacreontic version of
how to recognise people in love, has him as much 'in the blood'
as does the Tolstoyan Levin. Levin, who has led the same kind
of sexual life as Tolstoy (though as we never see this happening
it is not entirely easy to believe) finds his remorse before him
in Pushkin's words—"I tremble and curse, but cannot wash
out the bitter lines". Both find the words without the poet's
name; and their breasts, as Dr Johnson would say, return the
universal echo.

Dostoevsky, on the other hand, took upon himself the role of
epiphanist: he will show forth Pushkin's secret. It is said that he
liked reciting *The Prophet*, his voice rising to a thrilling scream
on the last line—"Burn hearts of men with the word!" It is a
terrifying and exhilarating poem, in which Pushkin embodies
the *prophetness* of the prophet, so to speak, as Blake embodies

31

the tigerishness of the tiger. We are not told what he is pro-
phesying about. He may bring peace or blood, enlightenment
and truth, or tyranny, obfuscation and darkness. But Dostoevsky
ignores this. For him Pushkin was a great prophet whose
message was still not understood. In consequence his famous
Pushkin Address tells us much about Dostoevsky, rather as
Coleridge on *Hamlet* tells us much about Coleridge. Pushkin,
like Shakespeare, is universal, so this is as it should be—in
listening to his descendants we cannot help learning about him—
but whereas for Tolstoy Pushkin is in the Russian bloodstream
and his influence omnipresent and unavoidable, to Dostoevsky
he has a secret which his heirs must solve, and a message they
must reveal. For Dostoevsky, Pushkin was as Nietzsche or
Marx—one who foresaw what truth will be—and, specifically,
one who foresaw what Russian truth would be.

"Pushkin appeared", says Dostoevsky in his Address, "at the
very inception of our true selfconsciousness." He not only
understood and felt with the Russian *narod*, but he divined and
expressed its peculiar *narodnost*, its 'people's truth'. But the
phrase 'true self-consciousness' is equivocal, like so many of
Dostoevsky's phrases. Does it mean what the Russian people
involuntarily are, or what—now they have suddenly sprung into
awareness—they can be persuaded to think they are? For Dostoevsky the latter sense is what matters: for Tolstoy, the former.
War and Peace is the great celebration of how the Russian
people manifested itself, and *is*. But for Dostoevsky the national
identity is a process of continued indoctrination, of continual
becoming. Pushkin began the process. Tolstoy, Dostoevsky
more than once implies, has attempted to arrest it. In his diary
he refers to his contemporary's greatest work as "nothing more
than historical pictures of times long past".

Yet ironically enough the craze to *be* Russian, which made
Dostoevsky's revelation of Pushkin's 'Russian truth' so much
acclaimed by the intellectuals, now belongs more uncompromis-
ingly to the past than the state of *being* Russian celebrated by
Tolstoy. And how light-hearted, by comparison with Dosto-
evsky's insistence, is Pushkin's own vision—"There it smells of
Russia!"—in the magical prologue to *Ruslan and Lyudmila*.
That is Russian in the sense in which *The Canterbury Tales* and

A Midsummer Night's Dream are English, not in the conscious and combative sense in which Dostoevsky claims Pushkin as a national prophet. Pushkin uses the new national adjective with an unselfconscious joy, and a simplicity almost mischievous. "How fresh is a Russian girl's cheek in the powder of snow!" No nineteenth-century English poet—as we can see from Wordsworth's Dover sonnet, which provoked Keats to a parody—could have used 'English' here without seeming either weighty or coy.

A German poet would be still worse. The phrase *'We Germans'*—so unbearably complacent and claustrophobic—alters its whole scope when it becomes in the nineteenth-century novel *'We Russians'*. In spite of the Slavophils, the discovery of being Russian did not mean the assertion of a limiting and defensive ethnic awareness. Yet like the discovery of other kinds of nationality, the process is inevitably retrospective: we cannot say *Russian* without looking back. The Russians had scarcely invented themselves before the period of invention was over, before 'the present time'—with all it implies of contradiction and disappearance—intervened. We know what the Germans are like and what the French—they have always been so—but for Europe the Russians are isolated by the very completeness and rapidity of their historical and literary self-realisation.

And nowhere is our sense of isolation and completeness more marked than in our reading of Tolstoy. His genius and his temperament enabled him to capture the nineteenth-century self-identification of Russia and liberate it in the vast enclosure of his own solipsism. This solipsism, this sense of Tolstoy *being* the great world he writes about, must have struck every reader of his novels. He can possess it because its identity—though not its existence—is so new and yet so complete in every part: in Tolstoy it is fixed at once into clearness, detail and tranquillity. His use of the word *Russian* has a magisterial subjectivity which we hardly think of questioning. No one could be less prophetic than Tolstoy, yet no one could be less accused of insulating himself to look back upon and write about the good old days. For there *were* no good old days: they were mute, bestial and inglorious. The good old days had just sprung into existence under the pen of the writer, becoming at the same moment past and present. The unique and grand attraction of Tolstoy's writing is the morning freshness of a morning already and irrevocably in the past. When he attempts to look forward, to be provisional—as in *Resurrection*—he is unconvincing. It is precisely Dostoevsky's strength, on the other hand, to be provisional; to insist on the dynamism of the new Russian identity, its progress onward to higher things.

II

No wonder Dostoevsky's audience was so enthusiastic. There is nothing more bracing than the assurance that all questions—even the ones that great artists pose in their works—can be solved; that we are all moving, and in the right direction.

> Everywhere in Pushkin there sounds a faith in the Russian character, in its spiritual might . . .
>
> > *With hope for all the good and glory*
> > *I look ahead, devoid of fear,*
>
> says the poet himself, referring to another subject; yet these words are directly applicable to his entire national creative work.

Dostoevsky is one of those engaging and valuable critics who are not to be put off by the mere context of an author's meaning: he left such considerations to the more sober and scholarly lecture of Turgenev. He has an insatiable appetite for historical generalisations and significant types, like the 'superfluous man'.

> He is an alien in his own country; for a whole century he has been unaccustomed to work; he is devoid of culture; he has fulfilled strange and unaccountable obligations associated with this or that of the fourteen classes into which Russian educated society is divided.

Aleko, the hero of Pushkin's poem *The Gipsies*, is the prime example of such a man, and in him was "discerned and ingeniously noted that unhappy wanderer in his native land, that traditional Russian sufferer detached from the people, who appeared in our society *as a historical necessity*". (My italics.)

Expelled from 'the fourteen classes', an exile from the

school, Aleko lives among the gipsies of Moldavia and marries a gipsy girl. But she is unfaithful to him; he kills her and her lover, and is cast out by the tribe and left utterly alone. The poem ends characteristically on this full stop, but what went wrong, demands Dostoevsky? It is that Aleko was proud; he would not "submit himself to humble communion with the people". It is the same with Eugene Onegin. He cannot love Tatiana, who for Dostoevsky symbolises the *narod*, "firmly standing on her own soil". He cannot love at all, for he is a mere creation of fashion and history; and Dostoevsky singles out the stanza in which Tatiana examines his empty room and follows the marks in the margins of his books, becoming aware that he is nothing but a parody. Again Pushkin draws no conclusion: he has folded 'my Tatiana' and 'my Onegin' deeply into the stuff of life—and not merely Russian life—and he is well aware that real women and parody men often marry and do well enough, and vice versa. But Dostoevsky is not deterred. Onegin must shed his parodic identity; by contact with the people he must become as strong, as instinctive, and as humble as Tatiana herself. Only so can he be saved. And he *must* be saved, else for what reason has Russia become conscious of her destiny?

Destiny!—Dostoevsky goes on to claim that Pushkin could embody not only Russia's, but that of other nations as well. Shakespeare, Cervantes, Schiller—yes, "but please point to even one of these geniuses who possessed such a universal susceptibility as Pushkin".

> Even the greatest of the European poets were never able to embody in themselves with such potency as Pushkin the genius of an alien people—their spirit, its hidden depth, its longing for its predestination. In dealing with foreign nations it may be said, on the contrary, that the European poets reincarnated in them their own nationality, interpreting them from their own national point of view. Even in Shakespeare, his Italians, for instance, are almost invariably Englishmen. Pushkin alone—among all world poets—possesses the faculty of completely reincarnating in himself an alien nationality.

This is a critical point of the greatest interest, in relation tno only to Pushkin but to all nineteenth-century Russian literature, particularly Tolstoy. Coming after other literatures, Pushkin and his successors were able to perceive in them and extract from them their 'feel', combining it with the directness of the Russian language and attitude to life. It is thus that Tolstoy extracts the 'feel' of Rousseau and Voltaire. Pushkin expressed his sense of Europe and her art in poetry because he could not experience it in fact, like many educated Russians of today who stagger us by their minute and loving knowledge of patterns of European life which they know only from books. But in drawing our attention to this Pushkinian capability, Dostoevsky has ingeniously confused the 'feel' of a national literature with the destiny of its nation, and universal literary susceptibility and appeal with a future of universal brotherhood. Pushkin's poem *The Feast of the Plague* certainly shows a wonderful intuition of the feel of English lyric at its best, but it is a surprise to be informed by Dostoevsky that in this lyric Pushkin discerns "the anguish of British genius . . . its suffering presentiment of its future". How ominously he dotes on the future! "To become a genuine and all-round Russian means, perhaps, to become brother to all men, *a universal man*, if you please. Oh, the peoples of Europe have no idea how dear they are to us! . . . Future Russians will comprehend that to become a genuine Russian means to seek finally to reconcile all European controversies, to show the solution of European anguish in our all-humanitarian and all-unifying Russian soul." The peoples of Europe might perhaps hang back a little at the prospect of this sublime fraternal ingestion, for Dostoevsky is not a wholly reassuring champion of universal harmony.

None the less the Pushkin Address is a remarkable document, and particularly suggestive of the kinds of use which Tolstoy and Dostoevsky could make of their predecessor. "All these artistic treasures and gems of creative insight were left by our great poet as mere landmarks for future artists and workers in the same realm." If the inspiration for Dostoevsky is Pushkin's flair for national diagnosis, for Tolstoy it is his generalising power, his 'universal susceptibility'. As Natasha and Pierre, Tatiana and Onegin acquire a wider and more universal appeal: as Raskolnikov and his sister they form another chapter in the development of a national type. Of course this is a crude over-simplification, but it conveys something of the difference between the two novelists' attitude to their characters, and to the influences which have been present at their begetting.

In his admirable notes to Pushkin's *Eugene Onegin*, Nabokov points out how strangely alienated Onegin is before his duel with Lensky.

> His behaviour has an uncanny dream-like quality, as if he had been infected by Tatiana's recent nightmare. . . . When Lensky falls, one almost expects Onegin to wake (as Tatiana does) and realise that it has all been a dream.

It is this dream-like state of alienation, this suspension of the ordinary process of moral habit, which Dostoevsky seizes on as the characteristic of the superfluous man most promising for fictional development. For us Russians, says Dostoevsky, the alienation from moral habit is the beginning of spiritual life, the promise of the future. It proceeds from some unsatisfied longing. And a sentence in the Address shows us exactly how the idea of Raskolnikov may have come into Dostoevsky's mind. Onegin, he says, killed Lensky in the duel out of mere spleen, "which may have been an outgrowth of a longing for some universal ideal: this is so typical of us, so plausible". What Pushkin intriguingly and sensitively renders as a psychological fact, Dostoevsky exploits as a sign of the times. For in killing the old money-lender Raskolnikov, too, had a longing for "some universal ideal", some outlet for feeling and action which the age denies him. He is at the mercy of his own power of abstraction, crushed beneath it "like a man under a stone".

Dostoevsky gives to the Superfluous Man a new and formidable intelligence—his own—and a sour, penetrating, obsessive talent for introspection. He becomes the Underground Man ("underfloor man" perhaps conveys more of the punning sense inherent in the Russian *podpolnii chelovek*) or in the cant term of our own day, the Outsider. But in spite of the immense vitality which Dostoevsky puts into his 'underfloor' heroes he cannot save them by uniting them with the people, though they are evolved in order to show how necessary and inevitable is that solution to their problems, "Now a new history commences," he tells us at the end of *Crime and Punishment*, and "unknown realities of life". In the Siberian plain, dotted with the black tents of the nomads (even here Dostoevsky seems to be remembering the last scene of *The Gipsies*) Raskolnikov and Sonia embrace. "This may well form the theme of a new tale"—but it is a tale which Dostoevsky was never able to write. We might compare the very similar end of *Resurrection*, and contrast both with Pushkin's own abrupt leave-taking of his Superfluous Men —Aleko in the deserted steppe, and Onegin back in the dream city of Petersburg. In spite of Dostoevsky's claim that Pushkin's characters are the landmarks by which his successors measure their own creative progress, neither he nor Tolstoy can in fact continue beyond the point where Pushkin breaks off, except by imposing on the traditional character their own notions of how to find salvation.

Pushkin stops where his artistic conception of the work bids him stop; Dostoevsky and Tolstoy (it is one of the many points where the resemblance between them is more significant than the contrast) pursue us with assertion and argument which often remain unendorsed by their imaginative vision. At the level of polemic both are determined optimists about mankind; but this kind of bustling optimism, so especially typical of Dostoevsky, does not come from the sources of their creative power. His militant and millennial cheerfulness, his conviction that all will be well when the Slavs are united "and Constantinople is ours", must always startle and embarrass Dostoevsky's Western admirers. For it is not Dostoevsky the civic theorist and zealous national reformer who has had so much influence on our fiction: it is the Dostoevsky who in a mood of bitter satire created the underfloor man, the man who does not mind if the world "drowns in blood" so long as he can drink his tea. "In the Russian land there are no *fools*," says the underfloor man, there is no one who believes in "the great and the beautiful" just because he has been told it exists. European fiction has hastened to discover and to celebrate this isolated man, who views all social assumptions and ideals with the total scepticism born of his isolation. And the American novel continues, in spectacular and often tedious convulsions, to rid itself of its last national assumptions about "the great and the beautiful" society. Fools are out: anti-heroes, outsiders, the pointless, the alienated, the displaced, the Ginger Men—are in.

There is a certain poetic justice in the fact that Dostoevsky's corrosive satire on the underfloor man should have fathered such a progeny, for his intellectual purpose in the work was fatally compromised by his own emotional powers. Something rather similar happened to Swift in the last book of *Gulliver's Travels*. Dostoevsky intended to blast scientific determinism and expose a social evil, a man "born in a chemical retort, not in the womb of nature", a man who cannot even honestly dislike his fellows but "derives that dislike from books". In fact he created a new and ominous hero. The negative qualities of this hero were to be swallowed up in union with the people, and in the 'unknown realities' of the love which Raskolnikov is on the brink of at the end of *Crime and Punishment*. But even Dostoevsky could not realise this possibility imaginatively—it is the negative qualities that become positive ones and carry down to us their penetrating and fertilising exuberance. *"I am a sick man, a spiteful man."* It is this vitality which lives on when the populist solution has become a mere historical curiosity. This naked self, which Dostoevsky so intensely apprehended, has become the undying worm of fiction. For if the early novel saw the individual as part of the social whole, the post-Dostoevsky novel has come to represent his awareness of himself as a solitary being, who wishes to dream and to act "as he *likes*, and not necessarily as reason and self-interest would have him do". Reason and self-interest are merely the agents of social pressure and conformity. And the novel—supremely—has become a refuge from such pressures.

Dostoevsky would be outraged to hear it. But there is nothing illogical about the process, nor about the part he plays in it. Though the underfloor man is a comment on the educated and superfluous Russian—all pseudo-scientific theory and no natural social instinct—he is also Dostoevsky himself. And Dostoevsky was not a nice man: he was *zloi chelovek*. It is the resources of his self-knowledge that we find in his hero, the knowledge of how pleasurable humiliation is, and cruelty, and even the groans that one utters with the toothache. And there is the further reason—the political one—for the great and disconcerting power of the portrait. When, under tyranny, one becomes fully selfconscious, it is to find one is alone, and free. One has not made the laws: one can do what one likes: and freedom is terror—the kind of terror the underfloor man inspires in our civic breasts.

Again we remember Tolstoy's curious remark about the Englishman discovering true freedom in Russia. Yet this freedom, the mental anarchy of the intelligent slave, the utter cynicism which Conrad held to be the real truth in the Russian soul—such freedom can lead to madness, to the kind of collapse which Herzen in his memoirs records of Granovsky and other of his university friends. We remember the hero of Pushkin's poem, condemned to total freedom by the disaster which befalls him, and wandering with only one object left on his horizon—the Bronze Horseman whose iron will has made him what he is. The underfloor man has a very similar relation—done in terms of the comic grotesque—with an officer who simply walks through him every time they meet on the Nevsky, and who is for months the only object in his life. The underfloor man is determined the officer shall notice him, and at last, after many abortive attempts, he nerves himself to stand the push and to push back. "Again he did not appear even to have noticed me, and yet I felt certain that he was shamming. To this day I am sure of it." But his idol is stationed elsewhere, and fourteen years later the underfloor man still recalls him with the regret of a lover.

Isolation and obsession, then, are the logical results of this freedom *à la Russe*, for Tolstoy no less than for Dostoevsky. But where Dostoevsky can not only exult in them imaginatively but create new types and dramas out of their victims, for Tolstoy they produce a situation too serious to be made use of in fiction. Ironically enough, Tolstoy may be said to have suffered the Russian extremity more keenly than Dostoevsky, because he cannot turn it into imagination and idea. He can write a *Confession*; he can guard himself with a system and a way of life; but he cannot ease his confrontation of life in the reflections of an Ivan, the fable of a Stavrogin and a Grand Inquisitor. His Prince Andrew is like a superfluous man, but is not one. He is not representative or the development of a type; he becomes real to us only through his own unique social and family situation. It is a curious fact that Tolstoy comes closest to making use of Russian themes, to exhibiting a specific and characteristic Russian literary development, in two stories which are terrible and powerful and yet failures: *The Kreutzer Sonata* and *The Death of Ivan Ilyich*. They are failures because their heroes do not seem at home in the world into which Tolstoy has forced them; whereas Dostoevsky's heroes, no more powerfully and obsessively conceived, are as at home in theirs as fish in water. The shorter, the more abrupt Tolstoy's invention of a world, the less real: he increases in his own sort of reality the more he goes on, the further he extends the ramifications of his art and his tale. Dostoevsky, on the other hand, becomes more fantastic and more literary the further he develops his characters; with scandal, disaster and *dénouement* ever more artfully contrived and piled up. Like those of many good detective stories, his characters begin in the world of fact and contingency and end in that of dramatic convention, of marvellous mental solution.

Only the hero of *Notes from Underground* remains throughout at—so to speak—a Tolstoyan level of reality; at a level where his isolation and its consequences strike us as just *so,* just as they would be in life, and not as Dostoevsky contrived them. This is what is so impressive about the original underfloor man: he seems to exist as inevitably in his setting as the Rostovs in theirs. The underfloor men in our fiction today have participation in society *withheld* from them by their creators, whereas their original historically did not have it. There is an odd sense here in which the Russians and ourselves have changed places. Our novelists try to create imaginatively the climate that in nineteenth-century Russia existed politically. Their characters have freedom in Tolstoy's sense—they have not made the laws —they are free to smash the lavatory pan or to sit in the dust-bin. Modern Soviet fictional characters, on the other hand, do not possess political freedom in Tolstoy's sense but are seen as an implicated and responsible part of the body politic. And it may be that fiction flourishes best, or at least most rankly, where communal responsibility and mutuality are not directly required of us?

III

It is difficult to emphasise too much Tolstoy's casual remark about Russian and English freedom, for a great pillow of honest irresponsibility lay always ready to receive the strenuous and committed posture of the Russian nineteenth-century novel. The philosopher Shestov, whom Mirsky calls Tolstoy's most perceptive critic, observes that Tolstoy calmly preaches anarchy because he knows beyond all doubt that he will not be obeyed. As for Dostoevsky, whose prophecies are so unremittingly rapacious—all *"Russland, Russland über alles"*—" only those listened to him", says Shestov, "who without his voice would have marched on Constantinople, oppressed the Poles, and made ready the sufferings that are necessary to the soul of the peasant". Had it not been so, he might have found himself in the position of the Prophet in the Russian fairy-tale whose head was struck off by the Prince—"whereupon the people became quiet and went home". Historically, Shestov is right. There is something very engaging in the spectacle of this wise Jew from Kiev (his real name was Schwartzmann) quietly putting the mighty seers of Russia in their place.

Like his masters, Dostoevsky never got to Constantinople; he never succeeded in rehabilitating his characters in the world and in 'the true realities' of the *narod*. But his failure as a prophet of regeneration is his success as a dramatist of good and evil. Critics[1] have pointed out how much his plots owe to an inspired use of the conventions of drama and melodrama, to Hugo and Eugene Sue as well as to Shakespeare and Schiller. Indeed it seems to me likely that when in *Crime and Punishment* Svidrigailov lures Raskolnikov's sister to his room, Dostoevsky is making use of the *Measure for Measure* situation (familiar to him from Pushkin's rendering of it in his poem *Angelo*) of a sister blackmailed into giving her virtue in return for her brother's safety. Dostoevsky's treatment of this is in his stagiest vein—abetted by the first English translators, Svidrigailov all but tells the proud beauty to scream her loudest—but his truest dramatic effects carry no suggestion of actors on the boards.

[1] E.g. V. Ivanov in *Freedom and the Tragic Life*, and especially G. Steiner, *Tolstoy or Dostoevsky*.

They illustrate rather what might be called 'the Timon effect'. Shakespeare's Timon puts himself outside humanity. But within this savage negation there resides the undefiled human knowledge, the image of the good as only the great writer can convey it.

> *Put armour on thine ears and on thine eyes*
> *Whose proof nor yells of mothers, maids, nor babes,*
> *Nor sight of priests in holy vestments bleeding,*
> *Shall pierce a jot.*

The ferocity shows its opposite with agonising certainty. Satan in *Paradise Lost* moves us for the same reason: not because he is a hero and a rebel, but because he alone in the poem is invested with the idiom to convey dramatically what goodness is, because he is aware of the rent in his nature which separates him from "pleasures not for him ordained", so that he must cry out "Evil, be thou my good". Hamlet's tirades against his mother and Ophelia have the same perversity, and Byron—a great Timon lover—occasionally achieves the effect. His bitter poem on hearing that his wife was ill conveys in spite of himself a yearning for reconciliation, affection and "the common good of life," as great as that of the underfloor man when the despised Lise came to see him. Lermontov, whose understanding of Byron was more deeply intuitive than that of any other Russian author, Pushkin included, dramatises through Pechorin—the 'Hero of Our Time'—a comparable impression.

This satanic division or rent in their nature—the *nadryv* as Dostoevsky calls it—this is what separates his characters so completely from those of Tolstoy. When crisis or alienation comes to one of Tolstoy's characters it comes from outside, like a thief reconnoitring and breaking into an orderly house. Whereas Dostoevsky's can live with—and even live *by*—the cracks and contradictions in themselves, to be penetrated by the outside world is for Tolstoy's people the supreme anguish, a catastrophe not to be healed or overcome. In terms of the construction of a novel, the dramatic principle of the *nadryv* is replaced in Tolstoy by the static principle of *samodovolnost*—self-sufficiency, or self-esteem. When that is gone, the Tolstoyan character is lost indeed.

This self-sufficiency is something that we shall be remarking continually in the study of Tolstoy's novels. Strangely enough, it is just because they are so solipsistic that his people live so easily in a totally realistic environment and among all the random detail of life. When their environment becomes unified and makes sense, it is a sinister thing: it makes sense *against* them, enters them to tell them they must die, and presents itself to them in a singular, coherent, and therefore insupportable, form. Conversely, the dramatically unified world of Dostoevsky permits his characters to exist as aspects of it, as extensions of its thought, passion, idea.

But we must not emphasise this evident contrast too much. The resemblance between the great pair is as revealing as the contrast. In his brilliant analysis of Dostoevsky's dramatic method George Steiner observes that "the dramatist works with Occam's razor; nothing is preserved beyond strict necessity and pertinence". Yet to say that Shakespeare (whom Steiner compares here with Dostoevsky) works thus would be misleading, and Dostoevsky, too, continually exceeds or is unaware of the kind of self-limitation implied. Both have the supreme power of gratuitous creation, of proliferating kinds of reality in excess of dramatic requirement, and even apparently incompatible with what we suppose to be the totality of that requirement.

Take the scene already referred to in *Crime and Punishment*, when Svidrigailov lures Dounia to his room and confronts her pistol, urging her to shoot him or submit to him. The melodrama is apparently total, and typical of Dostoevsky, except for one thing. Svidrigailov is comically in error about Dounia; he supposes that she is a character like himself, a Dostoevskyan character. She is not! Her reactions and motives are not of a piece with the emotional and intelligential life of the drama—descended as she is from Pushkin's Tatiana, she is as real and as forthright as her, or as Tolstoy's Natasha. Svidrigailov is obsessed by her as Raskolnikov is by the prostitute Sonia. Both men involuntarily crave the girls' love as a benediction that will join them again to the human race. But whereas Sonia knows her part, so to speak, and is wholly subdued to the Dostoevskyan atmosphere, Dounia does not. At first it seems she does: she fires one chamber of the revolver, misses, and when Svidrigailov comes to point-blank range she shudders, flings it away and submits to his caress.

> "You refuse to fire!" exclaimed Svidrigailov amazed, breathing slowly. The fear of death was perhaps not the heaviest burden of which he felt his mind freed; yet he would have had difficulty in explaining the nature of the relief he experienced.

So perhaps would Dostoevsky, but the scene—one of the most effective of all his dramatic tableaux—does it for him. Svidrigailov thinks, which would be logical in the Dostoevskyan dimension he inhabits, that she can't shoot because she loves him, because she has submitted to the logic of his world. The reality is different. She can't shoot him, but no, she does not love him—why should she?—her emotions do not work in her author's way. For Svidrigailov this revelation of her difference is a moment of final emptiness and absurdity. He releases her, and goes out to shoot himself The whole episode carries instant conviction, and is no less moving for being so weirdly comic. It is far more convincing than the salvation of Raskolnikov by Sonia, though the one could not exist without the other—to that extent and in so odd a way is dramatic unity preserved. Dostoevsky's helpless mastery in the lesser drama seems to depend on his conscious schematisation in the major one.

The gruesome success of Svidrigailov—the man who is 'nothing in particular'—as a character owes much to his relation to the solid and quite 'other' figure of Dounia. He is perhaps the nearest that Dostoevsky came to a satire on one of his own characters. To my mind, the scene is more subtly satisfying than the famous confrontation in *The Idiot* between Nastasia Filippovna and her suitors. There the drama has the fiery purity of Racine—all are melted into one vision of man's heart—but Dostoevsky was a novelist, and it is when he calls up the power of individualisation which the novelist wields that he is at his most moving. The climactic meeting of the underfloor man with the prostitute Lise has something of the same wry, factual hopelessness that marks the encounter of Dounia and Svidrigailov. The underfloor man is deeply pitied by Lise; he hates her for it, and when he has wept in her arms defends himself by putting money in her hand. She goes without a word, and he feels an instant desire to run after her.

> The air was so still that snow was falling almost perpendicularly, and forming a thick coverlet upon the pavements of the deserted streets. Not a sound was there to be heard, not a soul to be seen. The street-lamps seemed to be burning with a curious sort of dimness. Running a couple of hundred paces to the nearest corner, I stopped.
>
> Where could she have got to? And why was I running after her at all?
>
> Ah, why indeed? To go upon my knees to her, to weep out tears of repentance, to kiss her feet, to ask of her pardon? Yes, all these things, I, at that instant, longed to do. My breast seemed to be burning with a longing to do them.
>
> "Yet what good would it do us?" Should I not be hating her tomorrow for the very reason that tonight I had kissed her feet? . . . Surely things are best as they are?" I continued as I regained my room and set myself to drown with fancies the terrible aching of my heart. . . . Never before or since have I suffered, have I repented, as I did then.
>
> Yet I still believe that at the very moment when I left my rooms to go in pursuit of her I was aware that I should return after going two hundred paces!

Dostoevsky never rendered his peculiar vision so authentically and so movingly as he does here, unless at the more purely visionary moment in *The Brothers Karamazov* when Mitya wakes from his 'good dream'. The secret of the thing is its unexpectedness. With what triumphant irony Dostoevsky justifies his contempt for idealistic notions of "the great and the beautiful", and yet with what uncanny force the reality of these things declares itself through all the 'fancies' of the underfloor man! It is a remarkable instance of the Timon effect. And like other instances of that effect it transcends drama—its impact is only incidentally dramatic. There is no suggestion, as there is in Dostoevsky's later novels, of the big scene and the manœuvred climax. Dramatic art is always prone to patterns of repetition, as phrases like "the tragic hero" show, and the contriving of its climax usually precedes and determines (Shakespeare is again the exception) the reality of those who take part in it. Pyotr Verkhovensky and Kirillov in *The Possessed* exist in order to be fused in the final nightmare of their last meeting: they have no freedom outside it. But the climax of the underfloor man's story is not like this. Its complete authenticity is vouched for by the fact that it is an unwilled and accidental event, and yet an event whose significance is overwhelming.

IV

Totally individual units as they are, Tolstoy's characters never repeat a dramatic pattern. Their point is themselves, as Tolstoy himself observed that the meaning of a work of art is its own totality. Their names, even, *are* themselves without *meaning* themselves. They have none of the mysterious or grotesque suggestibility of Dostoevsky's or Gogol's names. Raskolnikov means a schismatic, an 'old believer'; Gogol's Sobakevitch is based on the Russian word for a dog; Smerdyakov and Korobochka sound meaningful and 'right' even to Western ears. Tolstoy's names, on the other hand, are often the simplest possible adaptations from those of real people—Oblonsky from Obolensky, Bolkonsky from Volkonsky. Count Rostov starts life simply as Count Tolstoy. Any significance they possess is social and historical, not literary, whereas Dostoevsky's names in his first drafts often reveal a literary antecedent.

When he refers in his notes to Stavrogin as his 'Prince Harry', Dostoevsky recalls one of the most enigmatic of Shakespeare's characters, about whose nature critics will always speculate as they do about Stavrogin's. None the less the association is misleading, for Shakespeare's Hal is a person and a prince before he is a mere cleft for interpretation—Stavrogin is not. Hal's nature is both determined and indicated by his public role—Stavrogin exists in a void. We owe Hal to Shakespeare's creative instinct in reconciling traditional pictures of the ideal prince with his own complex empirical understanding of what men of power were like. We owe Stavrogin to Dostoevsky's preoccupation with the abstract enigma of the man of power, to whom all who meet him are inexorably drawn, and on whom they depend as even Verkhovensky depends upon Stavrogin. Dostoevsky goes for the *geistliches Geheimnis*, the essential mystery of the man: Shakespeare is innocent of the notion involved. Both treat the character dramatically but there is a world of difference in their dramatic approach. Dostoevsky is on the whole an example of the theory of drama pronounced by Lukacs and echoed by George Steiner, that "any trait of character not strictly relevant to the living dynamics of collision must be judged superfluous". But Shakespeare is not, and in this respect at least he is closer to Tolstoy than he is to Dostoevsky.

Dostoevsky's *dramatis personae* depend on a secret. What is Stavrogin's and what Prince Myshkin's, who were one and the same at an early stage of Dostoevsky's creative process? For Dostoevsky, as for numerous lesser dramatic technicians, such a secret is the essence of drama. Dostoevsky proclaimed that Pushkin had a secret which he died without revealing: he has the same attitude towards the poet as to literary figures of the past—Hamlet, Don Quixote, Prince Hal. Their secret is to be explored and set forth in his own characters. Yet his very mastery of the dramatic mode is weakened by this preoccupation with its formulae. The secret can, so to speak, burst—in one of the great climactic scandals—but it can never be solved. What exactly is the matter with Stavrogin and Myshkin? What was to be the *nadryv* that would open in the shining nature of Alyosha? We never find out. We cannot. For the secret is not in themselves but in the attitude of their narrator. For him, only the nature divided by the unspeakable secret of its inner lust and irrationality can convey an image of the good: those who are good themselves and in each other—like Pierre and Natasha—merely embody it, and are thus undramatic, unresonant, null. Dostoevsky vulgarised this conviction into a formula, that of the great sinner who sins his way to God, or—for in Dostoevsky's theology the two are virtually the same thing—the intellectual rationalist who becomes reunited with the people in Christ. As we have seen, neither of these things was ever brought about, though in the last years of Dostoevsky's life Alyosha was the hero chosen for his supreme attempt at it.

Yet none of Dostoevsky's dramatic characters succeed in conveying his vision of the good in the only terms in which we can in practice understand it—the terms of observed daily behaviour. Dramatically we have only flashes of it, sudden visions, like Mitya's great moment after the dream. Only in the underfloor man do we have it *in toto*, in terms of complete and fascinated intimacy. He is Dostoevsky's greatest triumph. And it is highly significant that the voice from under the floorboards ends up with something very like a body, bestowed on him by Lise in the intensity of her embrace. Like the dying Invisible Man he becomes visible in her arms, for this is perhaps the only embrace in Dostoevsky's novels with any physical substance in it. I have already remarked on his unexpected hints of self-examination and self-mockery. The fact that Father Zossima, in *The Brothers Karamazov*, not only stinks after death, but stinks worse than might have been expected, may be another instance of it. Dostoevsky's humour is not always conventionally grotesque, but valiant and unexpected. We see it again in the presentation of Father Ferapont, almost Tolstoyan in its balance of analysis and amusement. It is almost as if the body, ignored so long by Dostoevsky, were reasserting itself.

Is the lack of convincing being in Stavrogin and others due not to their supposed depths—the notion of 'profundity' in an author's characters rarely stands up to examination—but to their lack of physical existence? Tolstoy would probably have thought so. The only work of Dostoevsky he admired unreservedly was *The House of the Dead*, where the convicts all have substance, real legs with real chains on them. Indeed it looks as if his recognition of this kind of reality shut off for Dostoevsky the possibility of entering this outer man, and dramatising the soul of his being. The many marvellous portraits in *The House of the Dead* all depend on his frank ignorance of what their subjects are 'really like'. Because we *see* Gazin, the convict who has raped and murdered children, there is no point in asking why he has done what he has done: he is just made that way. It is because we do not see Stavrogin that the whole apparatus of his conscience and his past can be created and caressed as if they were hypothetical things, which Dostoevsky depended on being able to create in order to make sense of the world. Bodies, physical extensions in space, are sufficient to themselves in *The House of the Dead*, where Dostoevsky shows how marvellously aware he can be of them, significantly preferring the incomprehensible common criminals to the intellectually accessible political prisoners.

All Tolstoy's characters begin with a body, often conjured into solidity before us by one insistent touch of physical description; and sometimes (like the Little Princess) they end with nothing else. Sometimes, as occurs in real life, we begin to take the body for granted, hardly noticing it at all in our interest in what is happening inside the mind. But the body is always there, always quite separate from other bodies, and because so separated, isolated also in its mental awareness. There is none of the intuitive communion which makes Dostoevsky's exchanges so dramatic. The Tolstoyan body is a far more opaque and mysterious thing than the Dostoevskyan 'secret'. And this sturdy selfhood is also, in numerous and individual ways, highly selfconscious. Tolstoy's characters are physically aware of themselves, as Tolstoy became aware of himself at three years old when his hands stroked with pleasure the slippery sides of the wooden tub in which he was being bathed; our enjoyment of them largely proceeds from the intensity of the satisfaction which they feel in being themselves.

We shall find this *samodovolnost*, this self-sufficiency, everywhere in his novels, but particularly in *War and Peace*. Everywhere we shall find references to his characters being pleased with themselves. It is the condition of their vitality—deprived of it, they cease to exist. It is neither formulated nor approved; it is simply an attribute of life, of the fully sentient being. Yet to say it is not approved is to stretch the facts: of course Tolstoy is wholly on its side; he cannot help endorsing it; it is an aspect of his own huge confidence in himself and his own being. This confidence is deeply aristocratic, not so much in the class sense—though that of course comes into it—but in the sense in which complete self-sufficiency is the most aristocratic of feelings, the feeling which may unite king and beggar; and which does in fact unite Pierre, who is revelling in his new-found consciousness of it, with the simple soldier Karataev, who possesses it unknowingly. Most of Tolstoy's women—and especially Natasha—possess this *samodovolnost* in its most potent form. No one is more aware than Tolstoy that young girls, however seemingly innocent and unaware, have an intense physical selfconsciousness —the most mesmerising part of their charm. (Young men possess it too, but in them it is less charming to other men, though Tolstoy conveys it with equal potency). I suspect that much of the resentment that some readers feel for Tolstoy's heroic characters—and particularly Natasha—is due to their calm invincible aristocratic conceit. She does not condescend to be intelligent, says Pierre admiringly of Natasha. And of course they do not trouble to assert themselves, to exhibit any kind of earned or cultivated superiority. Like one of Henry James's grand ladies they only seem absently, maddeningly conscious "of keeping, at every moment of their lives, every advantage". That advantage is their physical individuality.

v

Dostoevsky, we feel, lives with his characters in a state of mutual light and darkness, awaking with a start to listen to them as if they were expositions and ideas, propelling them hither and thither while remaining at the same time at their beck and call. He is a sorcerer's apprentice, a sleep-walker like Dickens, from whom he learned so much. And yet, as we have seen, he is capable of recognising and respecting the sheer physical intractibility of his creations—Dounia, the underfloor man. Like Shakespeare, he can have it both ways. Does Tolstoy? I think one must admit that he does not. When his persons have no continuous and confident apprehension of themselves they are—so to speak—at the mercy of their creator. It may be that Dostoevsky possesses a theoretically greater creative range.

For just because Tolstoy's characters are isolated, they are isolated *with* Tolstoy. Dostoevsky never speaks of his characters possessively: Tolstoy (and Pushkin) frequently do. It is an odd thing that Dostoevsky's climaxes should so often seem contrived, and yet his persons so little in his possession. The murder of Shatov in *The Possessed*, for instance, though painful, is not moving—it has been too carefully laid on for too long past. If Dostoevsky told us that he did not know it would happen, we should not believe him, though we half believe Tolstoy when he tells us it was not his conscious intention that Anna should throw herself under the train, as we half believe Pushkin when he says: "my Tatiana has gone and got married—I should never have thought it of her". Tolstoy and Pushkin possess their characters though they do not control them: with Dostoevsky it usually seems the other way round.

We see the predicament of Tolstoy when unable to recognise a character most clearly in the case of Platon Karataev in *War and Peace*. Tolstoy actually seems almost nervous as he tries to endow him with physical independence, emphasising again and again his *roundness* (the roundness of the single unit shows its separation from other units) his voice and his smell. But the attempt here defeats itself. It is essential that Karataev should be unaware of himself as "the unfathomable, rounded, eternal personification of the spirit of simplicity and truth", for that unawareness is the whole ground of Pierre's admiration for him; yet without such an awareness he cannot have a life of his own, independent of Tolstoy. The emphasis on roundness, smell, and so forth, are fatal here, because they are not aspects of his own *samodovolnost* but imposed on him from outside. The simplest of Tolstoy's characters, when they come off, are not nobly unconscious of themselves but, on the contrary, full of a sense of what it means to be them. A scene in *Resurrection* shows us two peasants—an old man and woman—in conversation with the hero. Both are slyly aware of his uneasiness, and of themselves in relation to him. " 'How do we get on?—we get on very badly', the old man drawled, as if it gave him pleasure", and "the old woman seemed to pride herself on the way she behaved with a gentleman".

The prisoners who are shot just before we meet Karataev are the same sort of men as he, but they are intensely real because they are unable to understand or believe what is going to happen to them—"they could not believe it because they alone knew what their life meant to them, and so they neither understood nor believed that it could be taken from them". "They alone knew what their life meant to them"—that is the point, and that is the secret of how Tolstoy gives them their freedom. Because I am a unit I alone know what life in my body means to me. Tolstoy normally has the strongest sense of this, yet only one detail in the description of Karataev really impresses us as acknowledging it. Pierre is aware that Karataev would not miss him in the least, and that he, Pierre, would not mind their separation either. This makes us realise that if we don't think that Karataev comes off, it is not—so to speak—his fault, but Tolstoy's and our own. What we think is no concern of Karataev's—we have simply been taking a disproportionate interest in him. That even Karataev lives in the context of this large reality, which never disintegrates when we poke and probe it, shows how little Tolstoyan reality is affected by something 'not coming off'. At no point do we have to remember—as we have to even in Dostoevsky—that we are reading a novel, and this goes some way towards explaining our acceptance of Tolstoy's personal tyranny, his abstract sententiousness and his overbearing clarity.

For in spite of—or perhaps because of—his stance of authority, Tolstoy defines his concept of freedom, for himself and for others, very clearly. At the end of *War and Peace* he tells us that "Reason gives expression to the laws of inevitability. Consciousness gives expression to the essence of freedom." Freedom is consciousness of our physical being. "A man having no freedom cannot be conceived of except as deprived of life." "Consciousness says: 'I alone am, and all that exists is but me. . .'."

"Freedom not limited by anything", Tolstoy goes on, "is the essence of life in man's consciousness. Freedom is the thing examined. Inevitability is what examines. Freedom is the content. Inevitability is the form."

> Only by separating the two sources of cognition, related to one another as form to content, do we get the mutually exclusive and separately incomprehensible conceptions of freedom and inevitability. Only by uniting them do we get a clear conception of man's life.

The argument is clear. Yet what stays with us of it is the premise: "I alone am, and all that exists is but me". "Solipsism", says Shestov dryly, "dogged Tolstoy already in early youth, but at the time he did not know what to do with the impertinent oppressive idea, so he ignored it. Finally, he came to it. The older a man becomes, the more he learns how to make use of impertinent ideas."

None the less, a conception of art is implicit in Tolstoy's words that is much truer to the achievement of his novels than his own official theory of art was to be. To the great Tolstoyan creator, "all that exists is but me", and yet "inevitability is the form". In order to make his audience swallow the first, he must convince them of the second. Tolstoy's world is in the fullest sense that of the solipsistic consciousness, and that of external inevitability. In how many post-Tolstoyan novelists (Hemingway is one example) are we not aware of the primacy of the first consideration—"all that exists is but me"—and the total neglect of the second? The more we read Tolstoy, the more we become aware of the clear and harmonious relation of the two kinds of cognition, and of the sense of liberation—of his world and hence of ourselves—that follows from it. The greatest art is something of a trick—the happy yet laborious coincidence that constitutes a trick. In the world of *War and Peace* we feel that everything happens as it has to happen, but also as everyone wants it to happen: freedom and inevitability are in complete accord, and this majestic illusion worked by art "calms and satisfies us", in Matthew Arnold's phrase, "as nothing else can".

But should art calm and satisfy us? Neither Tolstoy nor Dostoevsky —indeed hardly any Russian author—would have bothered to entertain the notion. In spite of his admiration for Schopenhauer, Tolstoy never consciously thought of the world of art as the world of calm, of emancipation from the will. For him freedom was an aspect of vitality, of being fully committed to existence—*Zhizn*, life with a capital L, is invoked almost as often by the great Russian authors as it is by modern critics—it did not mean abdication and repose. Tolstoy and Dostoevsky are at one here, though to Dostoevsky the nature of freedom is of course very different. The underfloor man tells us that he once belonged to a leading club and "cultivated the art of self-respect"; and this self-respect is virtually a petrified bourgeois form of Tolstoy's aristocratic self-sufficiency. Freedom for Dostoevsky is a terrifying and unpredictable thing, a release of desires like that of the crippled girl in *The Brothers Karamazov*, who wants to crucify a little boy and sit opposite him eating pineapple compote. Tolstoy, the rationalist and admirer of Kant, assigns the highest role to reason, and to freedom as the sphere in which it moves. Dostoevsky, oddly enough, would have agreed with Hume that it "is, and ought only to be, the slave of the passions".

> See here: reason is an excellent thing—I do not deny that for a moment, but reason is reason and no more . . . whereas volition is a manifestation of all life (that is to say, of human life as a whole, with reason and every other sort of appendage included). It is true that, in this particular manifestation of it, human life is a sorry failure; yet it nevertheless is life, and not the mere working-out of a square root.

These comments by the underfloor man might almost have been written in refutation of the Tolstoy who wrote

> Freedom apart from necessity, that is, apart from the laws of reason that define it, differs in no way from gravitation, or heat or the force that makes things grow. . . .

Differs in no way, that is, from the constant, predictable movements and cycles of earthly affairs. For Tolstoy, the impulses of freedom are as regular and universal as the harvest: for Dostoevsky they are as eccentric and random as a shower of meteorites. Tolstoy, too, wishes to equate scientific and natural law; the solipsistic isolation of the individual is for him no different from any other natural phenomenon, chartable according to "the laws of reason that define it". For Dostoevsky the mad volition of the individual must lead to God, for it can lead nowhere else.

Tolstoy's desire to assign and tidy up the limits of freedom and necessity means nothing to Dostoevsky. At one in the spirit with his characters, he is no more free than they are: the concept of a character's freedom and the consequent liberation of the reader, so definable and straightforward in Tolstoy's world, is irrelevant in Dostoevsky's. Freedom in Tolstoy begins with separateness, with bodies not impinging upon one another, and art begins with our awareness of other peoples's bodies; of the Little Princess's upper lip; of Veslovsky's fat legs, and his habit of sitting with one of them doubled under him: of Anna's new habit, noticed by Dolly, of screwing up her eyes "as if she were blinking at her life so as not to see it all".

This closed, completed and assigned quality in Tolstoy's art might be a limiting and ultimately a desolating thing, as it is with so many writers who both start, as he does, with such definition, and finish too. The similar observations he made in actual life were often, one feels, both crude and ruthless. His remark about Turgenev "waggling his democratic haunches" annoys one intensely, because it is so difficult ever afterwards not to think of it when thinking of Turgenev. We are trapped by Tolstoy's outrageously sure touch on a characteristic physical impression. Yet his characters come off better than his friends; they are too large for this limiting cruelty. After meeting Vronsky, Anna may not recover from her sudden apprehension of how large and protruding are Karenin's ears, but we can, and do. Karenin goes on, his ears forgotten, to become one of the most subtly perceived personalities in the book, because one of its most physically *lived with* personalities. It is worth noting in this context that D. H. Lawrence, who has so much of Tolstoy's extraordinary power of description by what seems almost physical seizure, never goes on to live with the person whom he has seized. His creative power is as abstract as Tolstoy's is physical: he rejects those whom he dislikes with a savage fastidiousness. Moreover, he neither has nor wishes to have Tolstoy's immense worldly knowledge. His numerous unsympathetic portraits leave us finally incredulous, because they refuse to admit the existence of the actual self-coherent world in which the victim lives. Given length and time, Tolstoy's bulk of worldly curiosity and understanding redeems the impression which his definitive penetration at first seems to impose on him. Logically his method should lead us into a closed world, and yet his world stays open.

For however positive and authoritative it may appear to be, in the dimension of *War and Peace* and *Anna Karenina* no analysis is ever complete. Definitive assertion never closes off a person or episode, but gives them a further surge of unexpected vitality. Thus at the moment when Prince Andrew declares his love for Natasha, "he held her hands, looked into her eyes, and did not find in his heart his former love for her". The moment, so entirely convincing, is yet not deadly, because it is not dwelt on as a literary point or a psychological demonstration. It is not done for reasons anything like those of Sartre, who makes his lover say "I don't love you" when he had been about to say "I love you". Instead of the sensations he had become accustomed to think of as love, Prince Andrew now felt pity, fear, "and an oppressive yet joyful sense of the duty that now bound him to her for ever". One positive sensation has been succeeded by another, nor is this the end of the process—there is no end. The same kind of thing occurs in *Anna Karenina*, after the marriage of Kitty and Levin. After describing all their entrancing and novel sensations Tolstoy calmly observes that they were never afterwards able to look back upon this time without feelings of depression and shame. This makes the truth of the idyll not less but more valid, in terms of their natures and of the society they live in, and it is so clear and invigorating that we receive it with the same sort of delight.

VI

No one who is not interested in himself can be interested in a great novel, and in Tolstoy we experience in greater measure than in any other novelist the recognition of ourselves that leads to increased self-knowledge. Moreover, the relation between the self—our own and Tolstoy's—and the rest of society is never self-excluding: he never puts us and himself outside the world he writes of. Few novelists evade some sort of concealment and composition with the reader when they are describing a social order. Evelyn Waugh's narrator in *Brideshead Revisited*, for instance, gives no sign of recognising how immensely important to him is the social life he describes to us, and what obsessional anxieties it causes him. Self-knowledge is withheld from us and therefore suspended in us; and a kind of death, which Tolstoy is pitiless in revealing, occurs in a society whose members are unable to examine their pretensions to be what they are. It is the society of *The Death of Ivan Ilyich*. Another kind of narrative evasion, effective and adroit but none the less serving also to equivocate the relation between author and reader, can be found in Anthony Powell's series *The Music of Time*. These narrators are excused any open effort at self-knowledge, and we are excused it with them, by a literary arrangement that in its unspoken intent to avoid difficulty resembles a social one. What we are offered instead is a dubious kind of detachment, a front seat at the social show.

Both authors probably inherit this transaction from the great example of Proust, whose whole vast social structure exists ultimately only to give his narrator a point and a past. By remembering it all he disassociates himself from it, and this puts us outside it at two removes, which in a sense is where we want to be. We are outside Proust, who is himself outside the world of his novel. With Tolstoy this cannot happen. The sort of technical disingenuousness by which the novelist puts himself and us in a favoured relation to the novel and the world it describes is quite alien to him. It is Tolstoy, his character, and ourselves, who are simultaneously making the gaffe at the ball, who thought no gentleman wore those kind of gloves, who are snubbed when patronising the cabman with confidences. We seem as vulnerable as his characters and himself; and as Tolstoy never achieved invulnerability, so we never do.

This almost disconcerting simplicity comes from Tolstoy's massive and casual assumption that the world is as he sees it, and as he says it is. He needs no theory about how to see the world and how to convey its reality. Though he was to become engrossed, as we shall see, in the detailed technical problems of the novelist, he never for a moment required the support of a primary conviction about the Novel. The theoretical implications of this form of creation meant nothing to him. Has it become, as august theorists like Lukacs incline to believe, the characteristic art form of *alienation*, of the individual's sense of divorce from his surroundings and from the world at large? Is its whole typical notion of, and interest in, separate individuals a reflection of our attempt to find compensation in art for the loss of a state in which the individual knew his surroundings by belonging to them, and not by surveying them from outside?

It may be so, but Tolstoy shows not the faintest interest in such questions. It may be, indeed, that the great period of novel-writing is over when the novelist begins to ask them, and others like them. All novelists with an implied or stated theory about the Novel's relation to life are certainly alienated—the theoretical term fits here—by this very fact: by necessity or choice they put themselves on the outside looking in; they consider what kind of structure it is they are going to make out of what they can see of the world. Their isolation impels them to a theory about the nature of life itself. "What is it, life?" Virginia Woolf is continually asking. The impression of opaque glitter which her novels give us, of words as things, seems the result of this very search for transparency. She creates because she is unable to be, and her creations cannot therefore, to most persons, appear as an adequate representation of being.

Although, as I shall argue in the last chapter, Pasternak's novel *Dr Zhivago* seems to me to draw its life and truth from an unconscious resurrection of the Tolstoyan tradition, there is no doubt that Pasternak himself started out—like so many other modern novelists—from a theory about the nature of reality, a theory different indeed from that of Virginia Woolf and other more recent novelists, but resembling theirs in that its effect is to substitute a structure for a transparency. He rejects—so he is reported as saying—the inherent causality of the nineteenth-century novel (we remember Virginia Woolf's denial that reality could be adequately represented in a sequential narrative of the Arnold Bennett type).

> For me reality lies not there, but in the multiplicity of the universe. ... Nature is much richer in coincidences than is our imagination. ... Of course I made the coincidences on purpose ... just as I purposely did not fully characterise the people in the book. For I wanted to get away from the idea of causality. The innovation of the book lies precisely in this conception of reality.[1]

One wonders what Tolstoy would have made of this. I think what would have baffled him most is the implication that the novelist has it in his power to characterise or not to characterise, to give or withhold—in the interest of his own conception of reality—physical being from the persons he creates. For Tolstoy this would have seemed like being able to have or not to have the function of the parts of one's own body, to consign one's liver or one's power of locomotion to non-existence if it suited one. For him the creation of a character was not a voluntary act—a controlled shaping of abstract material—but an involuntary process, a recognition, like stubbing a toe or shaking a hand. Once given, such an act of recognition could not be with-

---

[1] Ralph Matlaw, *A Visit with Pasternak.*

drawn—the body of the creation, its mere mass and extension, is there, and there at every moment.

There are qualifications to be made here which have cropped up already and will do so in greater detail in the next chapter. But always when comparing Tolstoy with other novelists we find ourselves returning again and again to this point, and being forced to repeat it at the risk of tedium, because it is the key to our understanding of his unique status in fiction. Tolstoy's solipsism is, ironically enough, the answer to the novelist's problem of abstraction and alienation. He identifies in his own body all the other bodies of the world. ·

There is irony too in the fact that many craftsmanlike novelists let it be known with a certain pride that when making a novel they first imagine *people*. Turgenev certainly did so, as we shall see when we come in the next chapter to discuss Russian ideas on the form of the Novel, and so in a sense did his fellow-craftsman Henry James. To Tolstoy the claim, with its accompanying admission that the novelist works with his mind's eye, would have seemed quite irrelevant. However his own creations achieve their impression of physical life it is not by these means. All novels can do is to present an illusion of life, but Turgenev and James so evidently begin from the premise that it is an illusion, and that their characters dissolve into and obtain significance from their creator's mental life. Required as we are to believe none the less in the reality of such characters, we may begin in our own minds to speculate about their hypothetical physical existence, and thus we disturb the whole convention of plausibility inside which the novelist is working. I find, for example, that I cannot help trying to supply Isabel Archer, the heroine of Henry James's *The Portrait of a Lady*, with the primary biological being with which James has so obviously not endowed her. What did she like in bed? what did she like to eat? These are not wholly impertinent queries, for we feel there is an answer to them in the case of Emma Bovary and Emma Wood-house, and even in that of other James heroines, though the author has not needed or wanted to supply it. But with James's *Portrait* it is no use, because at moments of eating or making love there *is* no Isabel Archer—she does not exist. The same is true of E. M. Forster's Mrs Moore, or Conrad's Lord Jim—we feel that the mind that has created them is not able or willing to concede their existence outside its own imaginative requirement of them.

We might object that it is difficult to accept the truth of this requirement where mere passive, corroborative, actuality is lacking. But the more crucial objection, I feel, is that these bodiless characters often inhabit fictions which are faithful to time as we experience it in life, and yet can offer no corresponding physical continuity. Of all novelists Tolstoy is the most faithful to the rigorous requirement which the imitation of continuity imposes on the novelist, but which so many are compelled to ignore by their reluctance or inability to sustain the burden of physical being in their creative vision. I am not claiming unique honours for the Tolstoyan power of keeping the body continuously before us—many minor writers exercise it with varying degrees of success and for many great ones it is irrelevant. As we have seen, Dostoevsky uses it at times with a special uncanny and dramatic force, and at other times not at all. Falstaff most certainly has a body, Hamlet perhaps has not—both are equally real. But for Tolstoy the body is the indispensable premise of fictional reality. And this means, amongst other things, that in his world we never feel that different kinds of reality have got mixed up, or have conjured up their own limitations, so that they reveal the necessities of artifice and the inescapable fact of fiction.

"Not a novel . . ." *War and Peace*

What can be older than the relations of married couples, of parents to children, of children to parents; the relations of men to their fellow-countrymen and to foreigners, to an invasion, to defence, to property, to the land . . .?

TOLSTOY, *What is Art?*

To enjoy a novel we must feel surrounded by it on all sides: it cannot exist as a more or less conspicuous thing among the rest of things.

ORTEGA Y GASSET

1. *Forms*

MOST great novels succeed by being absolutely individual. They not only show us a way of looking at the world but make us feel—at least for a time—that this is what the world is really like. At later readings we realise, often with no diminishment of pleasure or admiration, that this is what Sterne or Stendhal or Lawrence see the world as being like. While conceding the truth of what they offer we remain aware of the large area outside them.

In the West this idea of the novel has come to be taken for granted, almost unconsciously. As I suggested at the end of the last chapter, novelists themselves tacitly allow, sometimes even assert, the limitations which their status as novelists require of their view of life. When Stendhal speaks of the novelist as "the mirror in the roadway" he is, one feels, giving in to the *notion* of the novel, recognising its shifting but positive status, as unreservedly as is Henry James in his Prefaces, D. H. Lawrence in his comments on the novel's function, or Michel Butor in his programme for an entirely new type of fiction. The newer the fiction, the more revolutionary, the more it unconsciously depends on the novel as an idea; somewhat in the way in which undergraduates in the old days unconsciously revealed by their wish to steal policemen's helmets their acceptance of the status and sanctity of the Force. In the novels of Jean Genet, for instance, do we not recognise the wholly French fictional tradition on which they depend for their novelty and—in Gide's phrase—their *nouvelles choses à dire?*

Although Tolstoy said that he had learnt from Stendhal how to describe war, the *mot* about "the mirror in the roadway" would have meant nothing to him, as neither would that other equally irritating status phrase—"une tranche de vie". Such phrases offer a background to Tolstoy's comment on the un-freedom of those who live under laws of their own making in a western constitutional government. The novelists who invent these phrases, like the M.P.s who pass the laws, are making sticks for their own backs, blinkers for themselves and their fellows. But in Russia there is no obligation to support the idea of the novel, and on at least four occasions Tolstoy observes that this idea has never acquired any real status or meaning in Russian literature. When he makes critical remarks about fiction—and in the course of his life he made a good number—they are seldom about the form of the novel, its constitution and mode of government so to speak, but about the people in it and the man behind it.

"Anyone writing a novel", he says in his essay on Maupassant, "must have a clear and firm idea as to what is good and bad in life." We can press the political parallel further, and say that in the West novelists acquire their individuality, their air of being different from other novelists, precisely *because* they have submitted themselves to laws of their own making, just as the citizens who submit themselves to the laws of a free country are different in opinions, outlook, and so forth. For Tolstoy, difference begins further back, in the heart and in the body.

When the first draft of *War and Peace*, entitled *1805*, began to appear in *The Russian Messenger*, Tolstoy would not allow the editor to call it a novel, although, being almost entirely about family life in high society, it was much more like a conventional novel than the final project turned out to be; and incidentally much more like a first sketch of the ideal novel which Percy Lubbock felt could be separated out of the great mass of *War and Peace*. In the cancelled preface of a later draft, Tolstoy says that what he wrote would not fit into any category "whether novel, short story, poem, or history"; and in the Foreword to the first serial version of *1805*, which also remained unused, he says that "in publishing the beginning of my projected work, I do not promise a continuation or conclusion". (We remember that Dickens and Hardy, in their serials, had to invent further instalments and a *dénouement*, come what might.) "We Russians," he goes on, "generally speaking, do not know how to write novels in the sense in which this genre is understood in Europe." An even more decisive statement of his attitude is the article *Some Words about 'War and Peace'*, which appeared in *Russian Archive* after the first three volumes had been published.

> What is *War and Peace*? It is not a novel, even less is it a poem, and still less a historical chronicle. *War and Peace* is what the author wished and was able to express in the form in which it is expressed. Such an announcement of disregard for conventional form in an artistic production might seem presumptuous were it premeditated, and were there not precedents for it. But the history of Russian literature since the time of Pushkin not merely affords many examples of such deviations from European forms, but does not offer a single example of the contrary. From Gogol's *Dead Souls* to Dostoevsky's *House of the Dead*, in the recent period of Russian literature, there is not a single artistic prose work, rising at all above mediocrity, which quite fits into the form of a novel, epic, or story.

As Tolstoy was later to put it to Goldenweiser, "a good work of art can in its entirety be expressed only by itself". Where *War and Peace* is concerned, the question of *genre* is irrelevant, and it is this that has bothered Western admirers of the novel as a form, both theorists and exponents. "What is *War and Peace* about?" asks Percy Lubbock, who goes on to suggest that Tolstoy was unaware of the fact that he was writing two novels at once. One might as well say that in *Hamlet* Shakespeare did not realise that he was writing a comedy and a tragedy at once. To understand Tolstoy's relation to the novel one must drop all preconceptions about its form, for the Russians make use of that form without adopting it like a constitution and putting themselves under its rule. *War and Peace*, as we shall see, is filled with the conventions, and even the *clichés*, of the Western novel, but they are never allowed to get out of hand and dictate its development or inform its underlying assumptions.

Henry James could not admit to the citizenship of novelists anyone who would not exercise his electoral rights in the parliament of form, and as a novelist he virtually writes Tolstoy off. But of course he understands very well the issues involved. "Really, universally, relations end nowhere, and the exquisite problem of the artist is eternally but to draw, by a geometry of his own, the circle within which they shall happily *appear* to do so."[1] Relations in *War and Peace* certainly do not stop anywhere, and yet Tolstoy is not evidently concerned to mount any kind of exquisite geometry on their behalf. So little do the relations of Pierre, with us and with his world, stop, that they may be said never to have started. So many of the important things of his life have taken place outside the action of the book, gigantic though it is. Technically, he has important affinities with a Dostoevskyan hero, for instance Prince Myshkin, who also arrives from outside, from Switzerland, with the most formative years of his life behind him and never referred to.

Pierre seems always on the verge of actually living, in contrast with the immense and unconscious life of Natasha, and it is this contrast which gives its extraordinary breadth of reality to *War and Peace* as a macrocosm of human consciousness. For do we not in fact, in life, simultaneously perceive ourselves as living and as not living?—as persons endlessly about to begin, surveying life from the wings, and also as persons fully and physically engaged in the operations of life—cooking, writing letters, making love, and so forth? Consciousness is, so to speak, capable both of more and of less than being alive. And it is this paradox which succeeds in Pierre and Natasha and spells their relation to the rest of the book.

Compare them with some of the most memorable of James's characters—for instance Isabel Archer in *The Portrait of a Lady* or Charlotte Stant in *The Golden Bowl*—and the question of 'where relations stop,' in James and in Tolstoy becomes clearer. The circle in which they are suspended—the two women—gives them their reality: but if we try to think what would have happened to Isabel on her return to Rome, or to Charlotte in America, we have to give up. James in fact has invoked, and consciously invoked, the dramatic principle: no one is quite real

[1] Preface to *Roderick Hudson*.

except in relation to the others, and when the circle is completed, then "all smiles stop together". Yet James has tried to have it both ways, like the great artist he is, and nearly succeeded. We *can* think what would have happened to these women and at least to Charlotte—almost he invites us to do so—but only if we are prepared to accept the domination of the dramatic circle. We may think, that is, but we will not think very far; for there is nothing further of crucial importance, of real and continuing interest, to be thought about. In Tolstoy, on the other hand, we feel that after 1500 pages or so he is just starting, when the novel ends, on some very interesting things about Pierre, which he will never tell us about, but which we can continue to speculate on for ourselves.

Among the great Russian novelists Turgenev alone, perhaps, took on the constitutional responsibilities of a Western novelist, and Henry James honours him for it far above Tolstoy. Many of Turgenev's observations about the craft—"I have never started from *ideas* but always from *images*"[1] and "The public does not need you, but you need the public"—might almost have been made by James himself in one of his more candid moments. Turgenev tried to praise Tolstoy by saying that "you are becoming free—free from your own views and prejudices"— free, that is, in the Western novelist's way which Tolstoy detested—detached from life and obedient only to form. Tolstoy retaliated by including Turgenev's *A Sportsman's Sketches*— "the best thing he ever wrote"—in his catalogue of Russian masterpieces that are not novels. The inference is plain. Turgenev is for Tolstoy only a great writer when, like other Russians, he has "created his own form", a form "completely original", not when he is being a "novelist".

2. Histories

Pushkin's tale, *The Captain's Daughter*, which describes the great rebellion of Pugachev in 1773, during Catherine's reign,

---

[1] Tolstoy, as I implied in the last chapter, does not care where he starts from or how crude his first conception is. In the first plans for *War and Peace* Count Rostov is called Count *Prostoy*—the word *prostoy* means simple, open, honest—and there is no doubt that the Rostov family stood for these things in Tolstoy's first conception. Only in the final version do they *embody* them.

is the first imagined relation of an episode from Russian history, but it is no more a historical novel than is *War and Peace*. It strikes us at first as a rather baffling work, with nothing very memorable about it. Tolstoy himself commented, as if uneasily, on its bareness, and observes that writers cannot be so straightforward and simple any more. Certainly Pushkin's way of imagining the past is the very opposite of Tolstoy's. *War and Peace* has a remarkable appearance of simplicity, but this simplicity is the result of an emphasis so uniform and so multitudinous that we sometimes feel that there is nothing left for us to think or to say, and that we cannot notice anything that Tolstoy has not. The simplicity of Tolstoy is overpowering: that of Pushkin is neither enigmatic nor evasive, but rapid and light. He writes about the past as if he were writing a letter home about his recent experiences. The horrors of the rebellion cause him neither to heighten, nor deliberately to lower, his style. And he is just as prepared to 'comment' as Tolstoy himself, though he does it through the narrator, who composes the book as a memoir. The Captain, Commandant of a fortress in the rebel country, is interrogating a Bashkir.

The Bashkir crossed the threshold with difficulty (he was wearing fetters) and, taking off his tall cap, stood by the door. I glanced at him and shuddered. I shall never forget that man. He seemed to be over seventy. He had neither nose nor ears. His head was shaven; instead of a beard, a few grey hairs stuck out; he was small, thin and bent, but his narrow eyes still had a gleam in them.

"Aha," said the Commandant, recognising by the terrible marks one of the rebels punished in 1741. "I see you are an old wolf and have been in our snares. Rebelling must be an old game to you, to judge by the look of your head. Come nearer; tell me, who sent you?"

The old Bashkir was silent and gazed at the Commandant with an utterly senseless expression.

"Why don't you speak?" Ivan Kuzmich went on. "Don't you understand Russian? Yulay, ask him in your language who sent him to our fortress."

Yulay repeated Ivan Kuzmich's question in Tartar. But the Bashkir looked at him with the same expression and did not answer a word.

"Very well," the Commandant said. "I will make you speak!

Lads, take off his stupid striped gown and streak his back. Mind you do it thoroughly, Yulay!''

Two soldiers began undressing the Bashkir. The unfortunate man's face expressed anxiety. He looked about him like some wild creature caught by children. But when the old man was made to put his hands round the soldier's neck and was lifted off the ground and Yulay brandished the whip, the Bashkir groaned in a weak, imploring voice, and, nodding his head, opened his mouth in which a short stump could be seen instead of a tongue.

When I recall that this happened in my lifetime, and that now I have lived to see the gentle reign of the Emperor Alexander, I cannot but marvel at the rapid progress of enlightenment and the diffusion of humane principles. Young man! If ever my notes fall into your hands, remember that the best and most permanent changes are those due to the softening of manners and morals, and not to any violent upheavals.

It was a shock to all of us.

The tone of the commentary, and the lack of exaggerated horror, are exactly right. In his late story, *Hadji Murad*, Tolstoy has the same unobtrusive brilliance of description, but—too intent on the art that conceals art—he is careful to avoid the commentary, and so he does not achieve the historical naturalness and anonymity of this narrative. He is too careful in a literary way— almost a Western way—to avoid being shocked. The only sentence to which art can be seen to have contributed here is the comparison of the frightened Bashkir to "some wild creature caught by children".

Yet the passage gives us an insight, too, into the reason why all the great nineteenth-century Russians are so good on their history. They feel continuingly in touch with it—horrors and all—in a direct and homely way. They neither romanticise it nor cut themselves off from it, but are soberly thankful (as Shakespeare and the Elizabethans were thankful) if they are spared a repetition in their own time of the same sort of events. Scott subtitled his account of the '45 " 'Tis Sixty Years Since", and Pushkin was almost exactly the same distance in time from Pugachev, but their attitudes to the rebellion they describe could hardly be more different. Pushkin borrows greatly from Scott. He makes his hero—like Waverley—appear to join the opposite side, and then be accused of treason by his own; and he lifts from *The Heart of Midlothian* the scene in which the captain's daughter goes to the Empress Catherine at Tsarskoe Selo to plead for the hero's life. But he does not borrow Scott's presentation of rebellion as Romance, safely situated in the past and hence to be seen—in contrast to the prosaic present—as something delightful and picturesque. Nor does he see the past as something over and done with, and thus the novelist's preserve. Unemphatically placed as it is, the comment of the narrator in the penultimate chapter—"God save us from seeing a Russian revolt, senseless and merciless!"—strikes like a hammerblow. It is a comment out of Shakespeare's histories, not Scott's novels.

Tolstoy also borrows from Scott, in particular from the device of coincidence as used in historical romance ("Great God! Can it really be Sir Hubert, my own father?") without which the enormous wheels of *War and Peace* could hardly continue to revolve. Tolstoy avails himself of coincidence without drawing attention to it. It is a convenience, and not, as it has become in that distinguished descendant of Tolstoy's novel—*Dr Zhivago* —a quasi-symbolic method. Princess Mary's rescue by Nicholas Rostov, and Pierre's by Dolokhov, are obvious instances, and Tolstoy's easy and natural use of the device makes a satisfying contrast to the expanse of the book, the *versts* that stretch away from us in every direction. It also shows us that the obverse of this boundless geographical space is the narrow dimension of a self-contained class; the rulers of *War and Peace*, its *deux cents familles*, are in fact all known to one another (we are told half-way through that Pierre "knew everyone in Moscow and St Petersburg") and meet all over Russia as if at a *soirée* or a club.[1] Kutuzov and Andrew's father are old comrades in arms; Kutuzov is an admirer of Pierre's wife; and hence Andrew gets

---

[1] A particularly engaging example occurs when Colonel Denisov (who is based on the real life guerilla leader, D. V. Davydov) goes to Kutuzov with his plan for attacking the French.

"I give my word of honour as a Russian officer," said Denisov, "that I can break Napoleon's line of communication."

"What relation are you to Intendant-General Kiril Andreevich Denisov?" asked Kutuzov, interrupting him.

"He is my uncle, your Serene Highness."

"Ah, we were friends," said Kutuzov cordially.

the *entrée* to Austerlitz and Pierre to Borodino—and we with them.

Yet Tolstoy's domestication by coincidence gives us an indication why we have from *The Captain's Daughter* a more authentic feel of history than from *War and Peace*. Pushkin respects history, and is content to study it and to exercise his intelligence upon it: to Tolstoy it represents a kind of personal challenge—it must be attacked, absorbed, taken over. And in *Some Words about 'War and Peace'* Tolstoy reveals the two ways in which this takeover of history is to be achieved. First, human characteristics are invariable, and "in those days also people loved, envied, sought truth and virtue, and were carried away by passion"—i.e. all the things I feel were felt by people in the past, and consequently they are all really *me*. Second, "There was the same complex mental and moral life among the upper classes, who were in some instances even more refined than now"—i.e. my own class (which chiefly interests me) and which was even more important then, enjoyed collectively the conviction that I myself do now: that everything stems from and depends upon our own existence. To paraphrase in this way is, of course, unfair, but I am not really misrepresenting Tolstoy. All his historical theories, with their extraordinary interest, authority and illumination, do depend upon these two swift annexatory steps, after which his historical period is at his feet, as Europe was at Napoleon's.

Let us return for a moment to the extract from *The Captain's Daughter* quoted above. The day after the events described, the fortress is taken by Pugachev, and the old Bashkir sits astride the gallows and handles the rope while the Commandant and his lieutenant are hanged. Nothing is said about the Bashkir's sentiments, or whether this was his revenge on the Russian colonial methods the Commandant stood for, and whether it pleased him. The hero, Ensign Grinyov, is himself about to be hanged, but is saved by the intervention of his old servant; he sees the Commandant's wife killed, and finally "having eaten my supper with great relish, went to sleep on a bare floor, exhausted both in mind and body". Next day he observes in passing some rebels pulling off and appropriating the boots of the hanged men.

I have unavoidably given these details more emphasis than they have in the text: the point is that this conveys exactly what the hero's reaction to such events would have been at that time. It is not necessarily Pushkin's reaction, but he has imagined— so lightly and completely that it hardly looks like imagination at all: it is more like Defoe and Richardson than Scott—the reactions of a young man of Grinyov's upbringing, right down to the fervent plea that manners and methods may continue to soften and improve. Now let us take a comparable episode in *War and Peace*, the shooting of the alleged incendiarists by the French in Moscow. Pierre, like Grinyov, is waiting—as he thinks—for execution; and his eye registers with nightmare vividness the appearance and behaviour of the people round him. He ceases to be any sort of character at all, but is merely a vehicle for the overpowering precision of Tolstoyan detail, and Tolstoy concedes this by saying "he lost the power of thinking and understanding. He could only hear and see." But here Tolstoy is not being quite truthful. Pierre is also to feel an immense and generalised incredulity and horror, which his creator compels the other participants to share. "On the faces of all the Russians, and of the French soldiers and officers without exception, he read the same dismay, horror, and conflict that were in his own heart." Even the fact that he has himself been saved means nothing to him.

> The fifth prisoner, the one next to Pierre, was led away—alone. Pierre did not understand that he was saved, that he and the rest had been brought there only to witness the execution. With ever-growing horror, and no sense of joy or relief, he gazed at what was taking place. The fifth man was the factory lad in the loose cloak. The moment they laid hands on him, he sprang aside in terror and clutched at Pierre. (Pierre shuddered and shook himself free.) The lad was unable to walk. They dragged him along holding him up under the arms, and he screamed. When they got him to the post he grew quiet, as if he had suddenly understood something. Whether he understood that screaming was useless, or whether he thought it incredible that men should kill him, at any rate he took his stand at the post, waiting to be blindfolded like the others, and like a wounded animal looked around him with glittering eyes.
>
> Pierre was no longer able to turn away and close his eyes. His curiosity and agitation, like that of the whole crowd, reached the

highest pitch at this fifth murder. Like the others this fifth man seemed calm; he wrapped his loose cloak closer and rubbed one bare foot with the other.

When they began to blindfold him he himself adjusted the knot which hurt the back of his head; then when they propped him against the bloodstained post, he leaned back and, not being comfortable in that position, straightened himself, adjusted his feet, and leaned back again more comfortably. Pierre did not take his eyes from him and did not miss his slightest movement.

Probably a word of command was given and was followed by the reports of eight muskets; but try as he would Pierre could not afterwards remember having heard the slightest sound of the shots. He only saw how the workman suddenly sank down on the cords that held him, how blood showed itself in two places, how the ropes slackened under the weight of the hanging body, and how the workman sat down, his head hanging unnaturally and one leg bent under him. Pierre ran up to the post. No one hindered him. Pale frightened people were doing something around the workman. The lower jaw of an old Frenchman with a thick moustache trembled as he untied the ropes. The body collapsed. The soldiers dragged it awkwardly from the post and began pushing it into the pit.

They all plainly and certainly knew that they were criminals who must hide the traces of their guilt as quickly as possible.

The concluding comment is not that of a man of the age, but that of Tolstoy himself (it shows, incidentally, how impossible it is to separate Tolstoy the moralist from Tolstoy the novelist at any stage of life) and though the description is one of almost mesmeric horror, yet it is surely somehow not completely moving, or satisfactory. This has nothing to do with the moral comment however. I think the explanation is that it is not seen by a real character, or rather by a character who retains his reality at this moment. It is at such moments that we are aware of Pierre's lack of a body, and of a past—the two things are connected—and we are also aware of Tolstoy's need for such a person, with these assets, at these moments. If any member of the Rostov or Bolkonsky families had been the spectator, the scene would have been very different. It would have been anchored firmly to the whole selfhood of such a spectator, as are the deeds of the guerrillas which Petya hears about in their camp. The sights that Ensign Grinyov saw in the fortress are

likewise unobtrusively connected with the sense of him established for us in the first few pages of *The Captain's Daughter*:
how when a child on an autumn day he watched his mother
making jam with honey while his father read the Court Calen-
dar; how he made a kite out of a map of the world while his
French tutor was sleeping off the effects of vodka—and so forth.

The point is that a character like this makes us aware of the
necessary multiplicity of human response, of the fact that even at
such a scene some of the soldiers and spectators must in the
nature of things have been bored, phlegmatic, or actively and
enjoyingly curious. But Tolstoy wants to achieve a dramatic and
metaphoric *unity* of response, as if we were all absorbed in a
tragic spectacle; to reduce the multiplicity of reaction to one
sensation—the sensation that he had himself felt on witnessing
a public execution in Paris. For this purpose Pierre is his chosen
instrument. He never *becomes* Tolstoy, but at these moments his
carefully constructed physical self—his corpulence, spectacles,
good-natured hang-dog look, etc.—become as it were the physical equivalent of Tolstoy's powerful abstract singlemindedness
—they are there not to give Pierre a true self, but to persuade
us that the truths we are being told are as solid as the flesh,
and are identified with it. We find the same sort of physical
counterpart of an insistent Tolstoyan point in Karataev's *roundness*. It is one of the strange artificialities of this seemingly so
natural book that Tolstoy can juggle with the flesh as with truth
and reason, forcing it to conform to the same kind of willed
simplicity.

For Pierre's size and corpulence, Karataev's roundness, are
not true characteristics of the flesh, the flesh that dominates
the life of Tolstoy's novels. The process makes us realise how
little a sense of the flesh has to do with description of physical
appearance. It is more a question of intuitive and involuntary
sympathy. Theoretically, we know much more about the appearance of Pierre and Karataev than about, say, that of Nicholas
Rostov and Anatole Kuragin. But it is the latter whom we know
in the flesh. And bad characters, like Napoleon and Anatole,
retain the sympathy of the flesh. Napoleon, snorting and grunt-
ing with pleasure as he is massaged with a brush by his valet;
unable to taste the punch on the evening before Borodino

because of his cold; above all, at Austerlitz, when "his face wore that special look of confident, self-complacent happiness that one sees on the face of a boy happily in love"—the tone is overtly objective, satirical, even disgusted, but in fact Tolstoy cannot withhold his intuitive sympathy with, and understanding of, the body. Physically we feel as convinced by, and as *comfortable* with, these two, as we feel physically uncommitted with Pierre and Karataev.

> Anatole was not quick-witted, nor ready or eloquent in conversation, but he had the faculty, so invaluable in society, of composure and imperturbable self possession. If a man lacking in self-confidence remains dumb on a first introduction and betrays a consciousness of the impropriety of such silence and an anxiety to find something to say, the effect is bad. But Anatole was dumb, swung his foot, and smilingly examined the Princess's hair. It was evident that he could be silent in this way for a very long time. "If anyone finds this silence inconvenient, let him talk, but I don't want to," he seemed to say.

Inside Anatole, as it were, we "sit with arms akimbo before a table on the corner of which he smilingly and absentmindedly fixed his large and handsome eye"; we feel his sensations at the sight of the pretty Mlle Bourrienne; and when his "large white plump leg" is cut off in the operating tent after Borodino, we seem to feel the pang in our own bodies.

But with Prince Andrew, who is lying wounded in the same tent, we have no bodily communication.

> After the sufferings he had been enduring Prince Andrew enjoyed a blissful feeling such as he had not experienced for a long time. All the best and happiest moments of his life—especially his earliest childhood, when he used to be undressed and put to bed, and when leaning over him his nurse sang him to sleep and he, burying his head in the pillow, felt happy in the mere consciousness of life—returned to his memory, not merely as something past but as something present.

We assent completely, but it is from our own experience, not from our knowledge of Prince Andrew. Like Pierre, he does not have a true body: there is this difference between both of them and the other characters, and it is not a difference we can simply put down to their being aspects of Tolstoy himself. The difference is not total, as we shall see, but it is significant, for no other novel can show such different and apparently incompatible kinds of character living together. It is as if Becky Sharp and David Copperfield, Waverley and Tom Jones and Tristram Shandy, together with Onegin and Julien Sorel, Rousseau's Emile and Voltaire's Candide and Goethe's Wilhelm Meister and many more, were all meeting in the same book, taking part in the same plot, communicating freely with one another. For in addition to drawing on his own unparalleled resources of family and class experience, Tolstoy has borrowed every type of character from every kind of novel: not only does he know a lot of people at first-hand—he has absorbed all the artificial ways of describing them.

Moreover, his genius insensibly persuades us that we do actually in life apprehend people in all these different ways, the ways imagined by each kind of novel, so that we feel that Pierre and Andrew are bound to be seekers and questioners because the one has no past and the other no roots in life, forgetting that Tolstoy has deprived them of these things precisely in order that they should conform to the fictional, *Bildungsroman*, type of the seeker. Andrew is a son from a *Bildungsroman* with a father from a historical novel, from Scott or *The Captain's Daughter*. Old Bolkonsky (who was closely modelled on Tolstoy's own grandfather, together with recollections he had heard about Field-Marshal Kamensky) is entirely accessible to us, as much in what we imagine of his old military days, "in the hot nights of the Crimea", as in what we see of his patriarchal life at Bald Hills. But his son, as does happen in life, is distant. We receive vivid perceptions through him (see the childhood passage) but they remain generalised Tolstoy: they are not connected specifically with him. What was he like as a child at Bald Hills? When did he meet the Little Princess, and how did his courtship of her proceed?

We share this uncertainty about Andrew with Natasha, and— more significantly—with her mother. Embedded in life, the Rostovs cannot really believe that the marriage will take place, any more than they can believe they will die. When Natasha sings, her mother remembers her own youth and reflects that "there was something unnatural and dreadful in this impending marriage of Natasha and Prince Andrew". It is like a marriage of life with death.

3. Deaths

Like Death, Andrew remains a stranger to the Rostovs. They cannot see him as a complete being any more than we can—any more than his own son can on the last page of the novel. He has become a symbolic figure, by insensible stages and without any apparent intention on Tolstoy's part. Natasha fights for his life, as life struggles against death, and when he dies old Count Rostov—that champion of the flesh—has to realise death too, and is never the same again. Not only death is symbolised in him, but dissatisfaction, aspiration, change, all the cravings of the spirit, all the changes that undermine the solid kingdom of the flesh, the ball, the supper, the bedroom. Tolstoy's distrust of the spirit, and of the changes it makes, appears in how he handles Andrew, and how he confines him with the greatest skill and naturalness to a particular *enclave*.

This naturalness conceals Tolstoy's laborious and uncertain construction of Andrew, which is intimately connected with the construction of the whole plot. First he was to have died at Austerlitz. Tolstoy decided to keep him alive, but that it was a risk to do so is shown by the uncertainty and hesitations of the ensuing drafts. His attitude of controlled exasperation towards the Little Princess was originally one of settled rudeness, culminating in a burst of fury when she receives a *billet* from Anatole. His rudeness is that of Lermontov's Pechorin and Pushkin's Onegin; it must have been difficult to head him off from being a figure of that kind. When he first sees Natasha he is bewitched because she is in fancy dress as a boy (an incident later transferred to Nicholas and Sonya) but in another version he takes no notice of her at all. Tolstoy's bother is to avoid nailing down Andrew with the kinds of *aperçu* he is so good at: he must not be open to the usual Tolstoyan 'discoveries'. (It would be out of the question, for instance, for Pierre to perceive that Andrew doesn't *really* care about the beauties of nature, as the 'I' of *Boyhood and Youth* suddenly realises about his great friend and hero Nekhlyudov who is something of a Prince

Andrew figure.) Such stages of illumination would be all wrong, as would be any particular aspect of Natasha (fancy dress, etc.) which would reveal something further about him by their attraction for him. Her attraction must be symbolic of life itself.

At last Tolstoy—remembering an experience of his own—hit on the way to convey this. Andrew hears Natasha and Sonya talking together at night as they lean out of the window below his, and in this way her reality—her sense of her family and her happy sense of herself that make up this reality—comes before him in the right abstract and ideal way, in a way that could not have been conveyed by Natasha herself in a direct confrontation with him. Natasha's own reactions presented an equal difficulty. In one version she is made to tell Sonya that Prince Andrew was such a charming creature that she has never seen and could never imagine anyone comparable! This clearly will not do, and neither will another version in which she says she doesn't like him, that "there is something proud, something dry about him". In the final version the magical ball takes over, and removes the need for any coherent comment from her. Indeed, Tolstoy ingeniously increases her reality by this method, implying her readiness for life that can take even the shadowy Prince Andrew in its stride; that is then dashed by the prospect of a year's delay; and finally pours itself helplessly into an infatuation with a 'real man' (real both for us and for her)—Anatole Kuragin.

Natasha's mode of love presents a marked contrast with that of Pushkin's Tatiana, so often compared with her as the same type of vital Russian heroine. Natasha's love is generalised, founded on her own sense of herself and—less consciously—on her almost explosive expectancy, her need not to be *wasted*. Onegin, whom Tatiana loves, is like Andrew an unintimate figure, but for quite different reasons. He gets what reality he has from the delighted scrutiny of Pushkin, and the devoted scrutiny of Tatiana. His own consciousness is nothing. As Nabokov observes, "Onegin grows fluid and flaccid as soon as he starts to feel, as soon as he departs from the existence he had acquired trom his maker in terms of colourful parody". Significantly, Natasha's love is solipsistic, in herself, typical of Tolstoyan *samodovolnost*: it does not need to know its object, and its object is correspondingly unknowable in terms of objective scrutiny. But when Tatiana sees the marks that Onegin's fingernail has scratched in the margins of his books, and realises that he is nothing but a parody, a creature of intellectual and social fashion—it does not destroy her love for him, it actually increases it! Finding the loved person's underlinings in a book is almost as intimate as watching them asleep. The two heroines are alike in the vigour of their affections, but it is a very different kind of affection for all that. In Onegin, Pushkin presents an *object* for us to enjoy, and for his heroine to love. In Andrew, Tolstoy creates the symbolic figure of a spectator of life, in the presence of whom Natasha can show what life there is in herself.

Andrew is created for death. He looks towards death as something true and real at last; and after all the false starts, alterations and reprieves, he achieves his right end. Of course this is something of a Tolstoyan *post hoc ergo propter hoc*, but it is a fact that all the characters in *War and Peace*—from the greatest to the least—get exactly what their natures require. The book is a massive feat of arbitration, arrived at after countless checks and deliberations: though its huge scale gives an effect of all the random inevitability of life, it also satisfies an ideal. It is an immensely audacious and successful attempt to compel the whole area of living to acknowledge the rule of art, proportion, of what is 'right'. What Henry James deprecatingly called "a wonderful mass of life" is in fact a highly complex patterning of human fulfilment, an allotment of fates on earth as authoritative as Dante's in the world to come. It is significant that the first drafts of the novel carried the title "All's well that ends well".

In his old age Tolstoy said, "when the characters in novels and stories do what from their spiritual nature they are unable to do, it is a terrible thing". To live, as the novel understands and conveys life, is what Prince Andrew would not have been able to do. It is impossible to imagine him developing a relation with Natasha, or communicating with her as Pierre and Natasha communicate in the last pages of the novel. For him Natasha represents life. It is his destiny as a character to conceptualise what others embody. He perceives through metaphor and symbol, as he sees the great oak-tree, apparently bare and dead, coming again into leaf. A much more moving instance of this, to my mind, than the rather grandiloquent image of the oak-tree, is his glimpse of the two little girls as he visits the abandoned house at Bald Hills on his retreat with his regiment.

> ... two little girls, running out from the hot-house carrying in their skirts plums they had plucked from the trees there, came upon Prince Andrew. On seeing the young master, the elder one, with frightened look, clutched her younger companion by the hand and hid with her behind a birch tree, not stopping to pick up some green plums they had dropped.
>
> Prince Andrew turned away with startled haste, unwilling to let them see that they had been observed. He was sorry for the pretty frightened little girl, was afraid of looking at her, and yet felt an irresistible desire to do so. A new sensation of comfort and relief came over him when, seeing these girls, he realized the existence of other human interests entirely aloof from his own and just as legitimate as those that occupied him. Evidently these girls passionately desired one thing—to carry away and eat those green plums without being caught—and Prince Andrew shared their wish for the success of their enterprise. He could not resist looking at them once more. Believing their danger past, they sprang from their ambush, and chirruping something in their shrill little voices and holding up their skirts, their bare little sunburnt feet scampered merrily and quickly across the meadow grass.

We can see from this passage exactly why Andrew 'loved' Natasha—it resembles the scene where he hears the two of them talking by the window—and why the word 'love' in the novel has no meaning of its own apart from the continuous demands and rights of life. He loves the idea of life more than the actuality. When he rejoins his soldiers he finds them splashing about naked in a pond, and he is revolted at the sight of "all that healthy white flesh", doomed to the chances of war. Nor do we ever have a greater sense, by contrast, of what life means, than when Andrew, after all his intimations of death, "the presence of which he had felt continually all his life"—in the clouds above the battlefield of Austerlitz and in the birch-tree field before Borodino—confronts Natasha and the Princess Mary on his deathbed.

> In one thin, translucently white hand he held a handkerchief, while with the other he stroked the delicate moustache he had grown, moving his fingers slowly. His eyes gazed at them as they entered.

On seeing his face and meeting his eyes Princess Mary's pace suddenly slackened, she felt her tears dry up and her sobs ceased. She suddenly felt guilty and grew timid on catching the expression of his face and eyes.

"But in what am I to blame?" she asked herself. "Because you are alive and thinking of the living, while I . . ." his cold stern look replied.

In the deep gaze that seemed to look not outwards but inwards there was an almost hostile expression as he slowly regarded his sister and Natasha.

I have suggested that Andrew is not subject to 'discoveries', and to Tolstoy's intimate kinds of examination, but this is not entirely true. Tolstoy's genius for character, as comprehensive and apparently involuntary as Shakespeare's, and with far more opportunity for detailed development than Shakespeare has within the limits of a play, could not avoid Andrew's becoming more than a centre of reflection and of symbol. The sheer worldliness of Tolstoy's observation keeps breaking in. We learn, for example, that Andrew befriends Boris, whom he does not much care for, because it gives him an apparently disinterested motive for remaining in touch with the inner ring where preferment is organised and high-level gossip exchanged. And Tolstoy notes that his exasperated criticism of the Russian military leadership both masks and gives an outlet to the tormenting jealousy that he feels about Natasha and Kuragin. But these are perceptions that could relate to someone else: they are not wholly him. What is? I observed that the scene with the two little girls reveals his attitude to life, and so it does; but the deeper and less demonstrated veracity in it is Andrew's *niceness*, a basic quality that we recognise and respond to here, though we have hardly met it before at first-hand. In the same way the deathbed quotation above shows something else about him that we recognise—in spite of the change in him he is still the same man who used to treat the Little Princess with such cold sarcasm. The life he disliked in her he is fond of in his sister and adores in Natasha, but now that it is time to leave it his manner is much the same as of old. Though he has only grown a moustache on his deathbed we seem to recognise that coldly fastidious gesture of stroking it.

"There, you see how strangely fate has brought us together," said he, breaking the silence and pointing to Natasha. "She looks after me all the time."

Princess Mary heard him and did not understand how he could say such a thing. He, the sensitive, tender Prince Andrew, how could he say that, before her whom he loved and who loved him? Had he expected to live he could not have said those words in that offensively cold tone. If he had not known that he was dying, how could he have failed to pity her and how could he speak like that in her presence? The only explanation was that he was indifferent, because something else, much more important, had been revealed to him.

The conversation was cold and disconnected, and continually broke off.

"Mary came by way of Ryazan," said Natasha.

Prince Andrew did not notice that she called his sister *Mary*, and only after calling her so in his presence did Natasha notice it herself.

"Really?" he asked.

"They told her that all Moscow has been burnt down, and that . . ."

Natasha stopped. It was impossible to talk. It was plain he was making an effort to listen, but could not do so.

"Yes, they say it's burnt," he said. "It's a great pity," and he gazed straight before him absently stroking his moustache with his fingers.

"And so you have met Count Nicholas, Mary?" Prince Andrew suddenly said, evidently wishing to speak pleasantly to them. "He wrote here that he took a great liking to you," he went on simply and calmly, evidently unable to understand all the complex significance his words had for living people.

Apart from the theme of death, the passage is full of the multitudinous meaning—like the significance of Natasha's use of the name *Mary*—which has been building up throughout the book. It is checked once by Tolstoy's remark—"he was indifferent because something else, much more important, had been revealed to him". Certainly Andrew may think so, but Tolstoy announces the fact with just a shade too much determination: the surface of almost helpless mastery is disturbed. For where death is concerned, Tolstoy in *War and Peace* was under the spell of Schopenhauer. Life is a sleep and death an awakening. "An awakening from life came to Prince Andrew together with his awakening from sleep. And compared to the duration of life it did not seem to him slower than an awakening from sleep compared to the duration of a dream." As Shestov points out, the second sentence comes almost verbatim from *The World as Will and Idea*. In Andrew, Tolstoy has deliberately created the man who fits this conception of death. With his usual confidence Tolstoy annexes death through Andrew, to show that it must *be* something because life is so much something. Yet life and death cannot understand one another.

> —"Shall I live? What do you think?"
> "I am sure of it!—sure!" Natasha almost shouted, taking hold of both his hands in a passionate movement.

Natasha "almost shouts" her belief because she can do nothing else—she cannot believe in anything but life. Even when after the last change in Andrew she sees he is dying, she goes about "with a buoyant step"—a phrase twice repeated. This has a deep tragic propriety, for the two are fulfilling their whole natures. Only old Count Rostov is touching. He cries for himself at Andrew's death, because he "knows he must shortly take the same terrible step"; and he knows this because his old assurance —his *samodovolnost*—has gone.

> He had been a brisk, cheerful, self-assured old man, now he seemed a pitiful, bewildered person . . . he continually looked round as if asking everybody if he was doing the right thing. After the destruction of Moscow and of his property, thrown out of his accustomed groove, he seemed to have lost the sense of his own significance and to feel there was no longer a place for him in life.

As Isaiah Berlin points out, Tolstoy's conception of history resembles in many ways that of Marx, whom he had never heard of at the time he was writing *War and Peace*, and this applies to his sense of personal history as well as the history of nations. His imaginative grasp of the individual life is such that freedom does indeed become the recognition of one's personal necessity, and 'to each according to his needs' is not only the ideal of society but seems in *War and Peace* the law of life and death.

The rightness of death in *War and Peace*—one might almost say its good taste—makes a remarkable contrast with *The Death of Ivan Ilyich.* To Ivan Ilyich's relatives his death is in deplorable taste, and his friends' reaction to it is that "Ivan Ilyich has made a mess of things—not like you and me". Why this change? The biographies show us what happened to Tolstoy: how after the enormous creative effort of *War and Peace* his mind (to borrow one of his metaphors) went on turning itself round and round like a screw with a stripped thread. There is nothing surprising about this: it follows like the night the day. With all his natural genius and his immense advantages—no writer ever had more—Tolstoy had achieved simultaneously his most prolonged and most sublime imagination of life, and a fulfilment of his desires in home and marriage which coincided with that imagination. In spite of studying Greek and beginning to write another historical novel he could not distract himself from a growing terror of that very fullness of life, that apparent coincidence with all its aspects, which he had attained. It began to suggest to him, as to the hero of *The Memoirs of a Madman*, that death is the only real thing, and death ought not to exist.

Tolstoy had always been fascinated by death, but as a means of analysing and enquiring into life. He used it as a touchstone for evaluating people: their responses to it show what they are like. This is particularly true of his first book, *Childhood*. There the death of the narrator's mother acts almost as a catalyst that precipitates his perceptions about the other members of the household and about himself.

> I felt a kind of enjoyment in knowing I was unhappy, and I tried to stimulate my sense of unhappiness.

At the funeral he is most aware of the discomfort of his clothes, and keeps "stealthily observing all the people who were present".

> My father stood at the head of the coffin. He was as white as a sheet and obviously had difficulty in restraining his tears. His tall figure in a black frock-coat, his pale expressive face, and his movements, graceful and assured as ever when he crossed himself, bowed, touching the floor with his fingers, took a candle from the priest's hand, or approached the coffin, were extremely effective; but, I don't know why, I did not like him being able to show himself off so effectively at that moment.

The same beady eye watches the reactions of the rest of the family. Only two pass the test. One is his mother's old nurse Natalya Savishna—"with clasped hands and eyes raised to heaven she was not weeping but praying"—the other is a five-year-old child, whose reaction at the sight of the corpse is a scream of fear so terrible that the narrator never forgot it.

The little girl's reaction to death is as instinctive as that of Natasha to life. And Natalya Savishna is equally unselfconscious. She tells the narrator that his mother's soul is above their head at that moment waiting to enter heaven, "as though she were relating quite ordinary things which she had seen herself, and concerning which it could never enter anyone's head to doubt". Then the butler comes in to ask for stores which the old woman is reluctant to hand over.

> I was struck by the change from the touching emotion with which she had been speaking to me to this captiousness and concern over petty trifles. . . . Grief had taken such a hold of her that she did not find it necessary to conceal that she was nevertheless able to attend to everyday matters; she would not even have understood how such an idea could occur to anyone.
>
> Self-conceit is a sentiment entirely incompatible with genuine sorrow, and yet it is so firmly engrafted on human nature that even the most profound sorrow can seldom expel it altogether. Vanity in sorrow expresses itself by a desire to appear either stricken with grief or unhappy or brave: and this ignoble desire which we do not acknowledge but which hardly ever leaves us even in the deepest trouble robs our grief of its strength, dignity and sincerity. But Natalya Savishna was so utterly stricken by her unhappiness that not a single desire lingered in her soul and she went on living only from habit.

Childhood, Boyhood and Youth was one of the non-novels which Tolstoy singled out as characteristic of the Russian indifference to the form. So was *War and Peace*, and Tolstoy would probably have called *Ivan Ilyich* another. But the early and the late works have much more in common with each other than either has with *War and Peace*, and this emerges most clearly in the use Tolstoy makes of death. In the stories it is an occasion for dogma, because it reveals—as pitilessly as Tolstoy wishes himself to reveal—human egoism, triviality and insincerity. Thus we have in *Childhood* not only the brilliant and sympathetic observation of the old nurse, but also the unmistakably enjoying tone—both Gallic and Olympian—of the commentary. Death is an occasion for vitality. This relish is replaced in *Ivan Ilyich* by the compulsion to confront and outface death itself, but the survivors are to be examined and judged by the same inflexible criterion—are they sincere? In *War and Peace* the question of sincerity does not arise. Death is a solution and a reconciliation, an episode in continuity. It is illuminating to compare the narrator of *Childhood's* catalogue of the modes of grief observed at his mother's funeral with the account in *War and Peace* of how the Rostov family and Princess Mary respond to Andrew's death. In the first, there is one centre of analysis and judgment: in the second, the crudity of this analysis is softened, dissipated among the survivors, so that we have an exact balance between narration and participation in which judgment by externals no longer applies. This is a clumsy way of conveying our impression that Andrew's death is moving, and that of the young narrator's mother merely interesting. The narrator reveres his old nurse for *not* being interested, but this reverence does not affect the narrative tone.

The bounding vitality of *Childhood* does not of course oppress us as we are oppressed in *Ivan Ilyich*, but the presence of Tolstoy in it is so overwhelming that we experience something of the same difficulty in seeing past him, as it were, to the people he is describing. Indeed the nature of the work requires that we should not. It is as if we had come to stay with an acquaintance, who introduces us to his familiar circle so masterfully and rapidly that we are too dazzled to form any opinion of our own. In *War and Peace* we seem to belong to the family in our own right.

It is only when Tolstoy subdues himself by plotting an artificial continuity for his characters that he releases our own independent and coherent response to them. For it is an ironic fact that only by caring enough about them to invent a story for them does Tolstoy as a writer create 'real'—that is to say fully and fictionally realised—characters. If he does not, they can only have the static, incoherent, meaningless reality of people we meet briefly in life. *Childhood, Boyhood and Youth* is full of such meetings. After his own mother has died, the narrator goes to call on a young friend and meets his mother.

My answers to her enquiries about my relations evidently aroused her melancholy interest, as if while hearing me she sadly recalled happier times. Her son had gone out somewhere. She looked at me silently for a minute or two and suddenly burst into tears. I sat before her and could not imagine what to say or do. She continued to weep without looking at me. At first I felt sorry for her, then I wondered whether I ought not to try to console her, and how to do it; but finally I became vexed that she should place me in such an awkward situation.

"Oh, God! How absurd it is to keep on crying! I loved your mother so, we were such friends . . . we . . . and . . . ."

She found her handkerchief, covered her face with it, and continued to cry. My position was again an awkward one and continued to be so for a good while. I felt vexed and yet sorry for her. Her tears seemed sincere, but I thought that she was not crying so much about my mother as because she herself was not happy now, and things had been much better in those days.

We have an immediate sense of the shrewdness and truth of the narrator's perception, but neither he nor we are likely to meet the lady again, and so the perception vanishes, as such things do in life, in a dull feeling of discouragement and discomfort. It is precisely because the thing is so like life that our interest droops and our curiosity seems futile, even impertinent. Tolstoy has not the knack, as Chekhov has, of raising the random and the hapless to the level of art and sharing it with us there. In order to understand people with love, and to present them so that they are thus understood by us, he needs plot on the scale with which he deploys it in *War and Peace*, and he needs to use on the same scale the conventions which the novel has always used.

The method of *Childhood, Boyhood and Youth* has much in common with the method of Tolstoy's first recorded composition, *An Account of Yesterday*, which was to set out exactly what had happened to him for the past twenty-four hours. The conception has remarkable and startling affinities with fictional experiments in our own century. And as with those experiments the chief technical difficulty is the presence of the author, not as a personality but as an impresario and contriver. The conventions of the novel do at least offer an escape route for the author from his art, a ladder by which he can enter and leave his creation at will. There is a great difference between the personality of

Tolstoy as it appears in *War and Peace* and *Anna*, and his presence as innovator, analyst and note-taker in *Childhood, Boyhood and Youth*. It is curious that *David Copperfield*, which Tolstoy much admired and which has in its first half so much of the primal vividness of *Childhood*,[1] combines both a novel and also the *Childhood* type of a work *sui generis*. Like Tolstoy, Dickens needed the conventions of the novel; but unlike him he was quite prepared to use them to keep in motion a work which had reached the logical end of its own peculiar being; for with the hero's arrival at his Aunt Betsy Trotwood's house *David Copperfield* as such ends, and a novel with the same title takes over. There is a hesitation, a period of flatness when we say goodbye to David and to the private Dickens with whom he is so closely identified, and then the more characteristic and official vitality of a Dickens novel takes over and begins to absorb and entertain us in a different way. Tolstoy never attempts this peculiarly Dickensian audacity of swapping horses in midstream, but the example of *David Copperfield* shows what a gap exists between the world and the method of *Childhood* and that of *War and Peace*—a gap only insecurely bridged by the transitional attempt of *The Cossacks*, in which Olenin is a poor substitute for the narrator of *Childhood* since he has not achieved the objectively plotted status of Andrew and Pierre.

Death in *Childhood* is a meaningless catastrophe and an occasion of absorbing interest; it is meaningless because the victim has had no life in the story and only serves the perceptions of the narrator. But when the art of the novel is called in, death becomes part of a plot; and acquires in Tolstoy's handling a natural rightness to go with this artificial one. Such are the deaths of Andrew, of Petya and Karataev, and of Hadji Murad in Tolstoy's last story. In these there is no Tolstoyan spectator concerned to analyse and to learn from the reactions of the survivors. It is significant that the moving death in *Childhood*,

---

[1] It was appearing in the Russian periodical *Sovremennik* while Tolstoy was meditating his own book. At least one touch—David's curiosity about his own grief after his mother's death, and his pride in it before his schoolfellows—may possibly have suggested an analysis of the same state of mind to Tolstoy.

that of the old nurse Natalya Savishna, is not entrusted to the reactions of the narrator but takes place while he is away. Simply told, it is as moving in its mildness as the death of the Virgin in Mantegna's picture. That of the old chieftain, Hadji Murad, is a fine physical achievement, like the climax of a sporting event. Nowhere else does Tolstoy follow the last moments of the dying so attentively and yet with such scrupulous honesty.

> He did not move but still he felt.
>
> When Hadji Aga, who was the first to reach him, struck him on the head with a large dagger, it seemed to Hadji Murad that someone was striking him with a hammer and he could not understand who was doing it or why. That was his last consciousness of any connection with his body. He felt nothing more and his enemies kicked and hacked at what had no longer anything in common with him.

Nothing, if one comes to think of it, can be more daringly presumptuous on the writer's part than to put himself inside a dying man and describe his last moments of life. Tolstoy does it with Ivan Ilyich as well as with Hadji Murad. But whereas he makes no attempt to explain or to own the latter, the former is his creature entirely. And one of the signs of possession is the determined use of metaphor in his last moments: he is not even allowed to die in his own way. To die is (apparently) to lose the awareness of oneself, and this is what Hadji Murad does, but Tolstoy assumes and retains awareness on Ivan Ilyich's behalf. He is thrust into "the black bag", and "he felt that his agony was due to his being thrust into that black hole and still more to his not being able to get right into it. He was hindered from getting into it by the conviction that his life had been a good one." But at last he fell through the hole, "and there at the bottom was a light".

> What had happened to him was like the sensation one sometimes experiences in a railway carriage where one thinks one is going backwards while one is really going forwards and suddenly becomes aware of the real direction.

As he has done before, Tolstoy alternates the metaphor used for the sensations of the dying with description of what the spectators saw. The account makes a great initial impact, but is not, I think, ultimately moving by Tolstoy's highest standards. We are deeply impressed by our first reading of *Ivan Ilyich*, and our expectations, remaining high, are surely disappointed when we read it again. The description is too weighted, the power too authoritative. But the account of Andrew's death—seen as it is by persons whom we have gradually come to know so well because they are involved in the true and yet artificial continuity of a story—increases its power to move us at each reading. And this in spite of the fact that the process of Andrew's death is so like that of Ivan Ilyich in the telling, and, in so far as this is confident and metaphorical, almost equally unconvincing. Andrew's dream, in which he feels death as a monster forcing its way through a door which he tries in vain to hold shut, is surely a nightmare of the healthy and alive, not of the dying? The dream does not seem his but Tolstoy's; the author's metaphors and figures of speech have the property of removing the individuality of what is happening. Perhaps apprehending this, Tolstoy usually distrusts them, as one feels he would have distrusted Turgenev's graphic metaphor in *On the Eve*.

> Death is like a fisherman who has caught a fish in his net and leaves it for a time in the water. The fish still swims about, but the net surrounds it, and the fisherman will take it when he wishes.

How many of us, as individuals, actually feel ourselves in this position? And it is as individuals, not as metaphors, that we die.

So Andrew dies, but Ivan Ilyich does not. Ivan Ilyich is a very ordinary man. Tolstoy emphasises this continually, but he also emphasises that as a result of his approaching death Ivan Ilyich ceased to be ordinary. And this change is not natural but arbitrary and forced. The background is filled in with pungent and detailed observation in Tolstoy's most effective style—the furniture and decoration of an upper-middle-class flat in the Petersburg of the '80s is brilliantly described—but it is not affectionate detail, like the description of the Bergs' party in *War and Peace*. That Ivan Ilyich should have his slight but fatal accident when adjusting the folds of the curtain on a step-ladder is grimly effective, for interior decoration is perhaps more subject than most human activities to the law which Tolstoy holds here to be typical of all activity except saving one's soul—the law of diminishing returns. When the curtains are adjusted they cease to interest and distract and one must find some other interest and distraction, but Tolstoy ignores the fact that Ivan Ilyich—like most ordinary mortals—is quite capable of finding one. He will not have it that human life, even at its most aimless level, is usually self-renewing. And though we can believe that the sick man would sometimes have hated his wife for being well, he would not have hated her the whole time, "with his whole soul". Sometimes at least he would cling to her as something familiar, human and once physically loved, but Tolstoy became convinced in his later years that what was once physically loved must become for that very reason physically repellent.

It is not so much this, however, nor the implications of the statement that "his life had been most simple, most ordinary, and therefore most terrible" that falsify the tale. No one is more able than Tolstoy to interest and impress us by what he asserts; and there is an almost complete harmony in *War and Peace* between the narrative and didactic sides, as between all the other disparate elements. Nor can we object to Tolstoy's contempt for doctors, a contempt as much in evidence in *War and Peace* and *Anna Karenina* as it is here. No, it is when he imputes all these things to Ivan Ilyich himself that we cease to assent. His death is bound to be painful, but not in this terrible gloating way. In fact, Ivan Ilyich's reaction to his fate has at first the simpleness and naturalness of the great open world of self-conceit which Tolstoy knew so well, the world of *War and Peace* in which solipsism is in reasonable accord with mutuality.

The syllogism he had learnt from Kiezewetter's Logic: "Caius is a man, men are mortal, therefore Caius is mortal", had always seemed to him correct as applied to Caius, but certainly not as applied to himself. That Caius—man in the abstract—was mortal, was perfectly correct, but he was not Caius, not an abstract man, but a creature quite quite separate from all others. He had been little Vanya, with a mamma and a papa, with Mitya and Volodya, with the toys, a coachman and a nurse, afterwards with Katenka and with all the joys, griefs, and delights of childhood, boyhood, and youth. What did Caius know of the smell of that striped leather ball Vanya had been so fond of? Had Caius kissed his mother's hand like that, and did the silk of her dress rustle so for Caius? Had he rioted like that at school when the pastry was bad? Had Caius been in love like that? Could Caius preside at a session as he did? "Caius really was mortal, and it was right for him to die; but for me, little Vanya, Ivan Ilych, with all my thoughts and emotions, it's altogether a different matter. It cannot be that I ought to die. That would be too terrible."

We remember Nicholas's sensation at the battle of Schön Grabern. "Can they be coming at me? And why? To kill me? *Me*, whom everyone is so fond of? He remembered his mother's love for him, and his family's, and his friends', and the enemy's intention to kill him seemed impossible." It is this sensation, surely, and not "the conviction that his life has been a good one", that makes death dreadful to Ivan Ilyich? And we know that this sensation would persist until, numbed by physically suffering, he would disappear among such scraps of recollection from his childhood as Tolstoy gives him ("the taste of French plums and how they wrinkle the mouth up")—disappear without other dignity than the right and proper one of being himself. That dignity requires that his death should take place on the same level as "the visitings, the curtains, the sturgeon for dinner", because these were the materials of his life. He is not Prince Andrew. We feel for him as we might for an animal compelled by its master to perform some unnatural trick.

Shestov observed that before Tolstoy's conversion he described life as an enchanted ballroom: after it, as a torture chamber. And Mirsky adds that the first fifty years of his life might be imaged in Natasha going to her first dance and the last thirty by Ivan Ilyich and his black bag. But we are more concerned with what happened to his creations than with what happened to him, and at any time during his writing life he was liable to take over his characters in the interests of some fixed idea. We see it happening in *War and Peace*, with Karataev and Prince Andrew, as we see it happening in early stories like *Strider* and *Polikushka*. Though the process is not so thorough-going as with *The Kreutzer Sonata, Resurrection*, or *Ivan Ilyich*, it is essentially the same. But it is easy to forget that Tolstoy is quite capable of choosing *exactly the right person* to carry the message or illustrate the parable, and when this happens we are hardly more aware of the use which is being made of him than if—like Stiva or Denisov—he seemed an entirely free person.

This happens in *Master and Man*, written a few years after *Ivan Ilyich*. Brekhunov, a merchant proud of his ability to drive a hard bargain, sets out by sleigh with his servant Nikita on an urgent business trip. A snowstorm blows up, and the two take refuge with a well-off peasant family. Tolstoy's sensitivity to person and thing was never greater, and the pair of travellers and the family they shelter with appear before us as vividly as do Dron and Alpatych in *War and Peace*, or the merchant who cheats Stiva in *Anna Karenina*. As the pair leave—the merchant being determined to push on—the son of the house guides them on their way, cheerfully shouting quotations from Pushkin's poem *Winter Evening*—

> *Storms with darkness hide the sky,*
> *Snowy circles wheeling wild. . . .*

which he has read in his school primer. Tolstoy does not bother to give author or title—any Russian reading his story would know the poem by heart. The comedy of this (and Tolstoy's humour, though uncertain and captious, is always something to reckon with) is connected with the fact that his view of poetry— even Pushkin's—was not high. We remember how in *Childhood* the narrator is ashamed to have written a birthday poem for his grandmother in which the form forces him to express what he feels to be insincerities (". . . why did I write a lie? Of course it is only poetry, but I needn't have done *that*") and how the falsity of the relation between Boris and Julie Karagina is expressed by the album verses they write to one another. The humour here is connected with description and reality: it echoes more subtly the grim and emphatic contrast in *Ivan Ilyich* between the false appearance of life—curtain choosing and sturgeon for dinner—and the real issue of life and death. A poem about a snowstorm is one thing—a snowstorm itself is another: a snowstorm can kill. Yet the contrast is not harshly asserted. Tolstoy also clearly finds it admirable that the young man should have enjoyed and learnt such apt words for what nature is doing. Education increases happiness and self-esteem—those

powers that rule over the world of *War and Peace*—and worldly
happiness and self-esteem are not rejected here.

> Young Petrushka did not think of danger. He knew the road and
> the whole district so well, and the lines about "snowy circles
> wheeling wild" described what was happening so aptly that they
> made him feel good.

Having shown them the road, he goes back. But the two travellers have soon lost their way again. They are not alarmed, they
huddle in their coats (Brekhunov's is much thicker than his
servant's) and rest the horse. Tolstoy goes on steadily with
detail after detail, none of them particularly frightening. (In his
conversations with Goldenweiser he commented on a story by
Andreyev that it seemed to be saying hopefully to the reader:
"Are you frightened now?—are you frightened now?") Brekhunov thinks about his business, manages to light a cigarette
("he was very glad he had managed to do what he wanted")
and finally contrives to read his watch, thinking it must be near
dawn. It is ten past twelve. Nikita is asleep. Still not seriously
alarmed, but now too restive to remain quiet, Brekhunov
manages to mount the horse and makes off to try and find a
house. Whether, if he did, he would have come back for Nikita
remains an open question—probably not. He feels exasperated
with his servant for not having, as he has, something to plan
and to live for.

> Suddenly a dark patch showed up in front of him. His heart beat
> with joy, and he rode towards the object, already seeing in imagin-
> ation the walls of village houses. But the dark patch was not
> stationary, it kept moving; and it was not a village but some tall
> stalks of wormwood sticking up through the snow on the boundary
> between two fields, and desperately tossing about under the pressure
> of the wind which beat it all to one side and whistled through it.

The sight gives him (and us) the first real feeling of terror. He
struggles on and again he thinks he sees the village, but it is the
same line of wormwood, tormented by the wind. He has gone
in a circle. Eventually he finds himself back at the sledge and the
sleeping Nikita, who wakes up and groans that he is dying.

> Vasili Andreevich stood silent and motionless for half a minute.
> Then suddenly, with the same resolution with which he used to

strike hands when making a good purchase, he took a step back and turning up his sleeves began raking the snow off Nikita and out of the sledge. Having done this he hurriedly undid his girdle, opened out his fur coat, and having pushed Nikita down, lay down on top of him, covering him not only with his fur coat but with the whole of his body, which glowed with warmth. After pushing the skirts of his coat between Nikita and the sides of the sledge, and holding down its hem with his knees, Vasili Andreevich lay like that face down, with his head pressed against the front of the sledge. Here he no longer heard the horse's movements or the whistling of the wind, but only Nikita's breathing. At first and for a long time Nikita lay motionless, then he sighed deeply and moved.

"There, and you say you are dying! Lie still and get warm, that's our way . . ." began Vasili Andreevich.

But to his great surprise he could say no more, for tears came to his eyes and his lower jaw began to quiver rapidly. He stopped speaking and only gulped down the risings in his throat. "Seems I was badly frightened and have gone quite weak," he thought. But this weakness was not only not unpleasant, but gave him a peculiar joy such as he had never felt before.

"That's our way!" he said to himself, experiencing a strange and solemn tenderness. He lay like that for a long time, wiping his eyes on the fur of his coat and tucking under his knee the right skirt, which the wind kept turning up.

But he longed so passionately to tell somebody of his joyful condition that he said: "Nikita!"

"It's comfortable, warm!" came a voice from beneath.

"There, you see, friend, I was going to perish. And you would have been frozen, and I should have . . ."

But again his jaws began to quiver and his eyes to fill with tears, and he could say no more. . . .

Nikita kept him warm from below, and his fur coats from above. . . .

"No fear, we shan't lose him this time!" he said to himself, referring to his getting the peasant warm with the same boastfulness with which he spoke of his buying and selling.

When they are found the next day, Brekhunov is dead, but Nikita is just alive and recovers. "When he found he was still in this world he was sorry rather than glad, especially when he found that the toes on both his feet were frozen".

This account misses the quiet and methodical accumulation of detail which is such a feature of the tale (the detail in Tolstoy's early story *The Snowstorm* is equally vivid but lacks this method) and I am not sure that *Master and Man* is not the most impressive story, in terms of his own theory of art, which Tolstoy ever wrote. The motives of the merchant, his business-like vigour and his desire to share his self-satisfaction with someone else, as if it were a bargain; the obvious calculation that in keeping Nikita warm he will keep himself warm too—all this makes the impulse to help the servant both moving and convincing. The moral of the story works without strain because the nature and personality of Brekhunov is fully established and he is allowed to remain true to it throughout.

Mirsky observes that Brekhunov's death, like Ivan Ilyich's, "evokes nothing but the most ultimate horror and anguish", but here he is surely wrong. It is not, after all, the actual death of Ivan Ilyich that evokes these feelings but rather the way he is thrust into it by Tolstoy. One can quote his own words against him—"when characters do what from their spiritual nature they are unable to do, it is a terrible thing". Brekhunov's death, which entirely belongs to him, is not in the least horrifying, but deeply moving and also, in a not at all macabre sense, funny. It makes us want to laugh and cry—a ghastly formula when used deliberately in a blurb or in praise of Russian soulfulness, but here neither more nor less than the truth. In general we feel about Tolstoy's humour that he is not concerned with it himself, and probably rather despises the notion, but that it comes out from under his hand involuntarily when his narrative is at its best.

4. *Lives*

In *Master and Man* we have one of the best small-scale examples of how the narrative is unfolded and given the density which is also typical of *War and Peace*. Closely connected with the way Tolstoy uses character or lets it go free is his use—in the same sense—of detail. He was both censured and admired in his lifetime for the tendency to put in everything about everything, from the grease on the wheel of the cart to the fingernails of the regimental doctor's wife. Turgenev told him that one couldn't really spend ten pages describing what N. N. did with his hand. At their best, Tolstoy's details strike us neither as selected for a particular purpose nor accumulated at random, but as a sign of a vast organism in progress, like the multiplicity of wrinkles on a moving elephant's back. Instead of paralysing narrative they seem only to enlarge its movement. In a sense they do serve a purpose though—they prevent Tolstoy's own purpose becoming too evident. When we see the point, in a limited sense, of one of his details, we begin to feel hunted at once. Thus in *Ivan Ilyich* a friend comes in to see the widow after the funeral and sits down on a springy pouffe.

> Praskovya Fedorovna had been on the point of warning him to take another seat, but felt that such a warning was out of keeping with her present condition and so changed her mind. As he sat down on the pouffe Peter Ivanovich recalled how Ivan Ilych had arranged this room and had consulted him regarding this pink cretonne with green leaves. The whole room was full of furniture and knick-knacks, and on her way to the sofa the lace of the widow's black shawl caught on the carved edge of the table. Peter Ivanovich rose to detach it, and the springs of the pouffe, relieved of his weight, rose also and gave him a push. The widow began detaching her shawl herself, and Peter Ivanovich again sat down, suppressing the rebellious springs of the pouffe under him. But the widow had not quite freed herself and Peter Ivanovich got up again, and again the pouffe rebelled and even creaked. When this was all over she took out a clean cambric handkerchief and began to weep. The episode with the shawl and the struggle with the pouffe had cooled Peter Ivanovich's emotions and he sat there with a sullen look on his face.

This is not funny but merely determined. Such illustrative intentions are the stock in trade of lesser writers, and it is astonishing that the author of *Childhood*, on the one hand, and of *Master and Man* on the other, should resort to them. But it must be admitted that this uncertainty of touch—whether deliberate, as when he has the didactic bit between his teeth, or simply inadvertent— is very characteristic of Tolstoy. So vast an organism cannot be expected to have good taste. In the passage which describes the abandoned garden at Bald Hills and the little girls taking the plums, an old peasant is described as sitting on a garden seat "like a fly impassive on the face of a loved one who is dead". It is a simile worthy of a tenth-rate romantic poet or a precocious sixth-form essay. Yet only a few lines later we have the entirely Tolstoyan comparison of the mass of soldiers bathing in the pond to "carp stuffed into a watering-can".

One might contrast both with this characteristically elegant simile of Turgenev at the beginning of *First Love*. "My fancies fluttered round the same images like martins round a bell tower at dawn." This is poetic and charming and we remember it: indeed we already start to remember it, as it were, when we first read it. It seems to promise and contain too much of the plot, not drawing attention to itself unduly, but suggesting that what is to come is already there—fixed and taken care of. And this is in general true of Turgenev's descriptive felicities. They imply that the author is a fixed point, and that the work of art—like a yo-yo—will unroll itself away from him to the length of its string and then coil itself back to him again. Tolstoy is not a fixed point; he is constantly on the move, carrying us with him. His delight in the object in itself, and his copiousness in recording it, is like that of a man in a train who does not want to miss anything as he goes past, carried onward by forces greater than his own sense of words. Railway journeys are always memorable in Tolstoy, like Anna's from Moscow to Petersburg, or the start of Nekhlyudov's journey to Siberia. All his details and perceptions depend on this steady onward movement, which is never arrested throughout his long life.

Most of the tactics and devices to which we take objection—but never the didactic interludes, which are very much a part of the onward flow—seem to be outside this movement, not holding it up but merely extrinsic to it. We do not find such a movement in Dostoevsky, where the patterns are repetitive and dramatically fulfilled. We do find it in D. H. Lawrence, but we often feel with him that there is not enough space in front of us, that we shall soon be going round and round. In front of Tolstoy infinite space seems to extend, and the magical resonance in Russian literature of the troika, the clattering hooves, the onrushing train—all seem to merge into his onward movement. He never joins in the 'Whither?' of other Russian writers; he seems to value above all stability, enduringness, the past . . . and yet his progress seems always more massive and more assured than theirs.

Like the current of life itself he is difficult to remember. What was I doing last Thursday week? When did I last see Timokhin? When did the Old Prince first become so fond of Mlle Bourrienne? These seem questions of the same kind. People who have read *War and Peace* more than once, and enjoyed it immensely, can often scarcely remember a thing about it. Yet the same persons can recall the plots of Thackeray and Trollope; what was said by Dickens's characters and what George Eliot said about hers; and every letter and conversation in Jane Austen. Odd questions about the processes of art are raised by the category of great writers we remember, and that of still greater writers we do not. We remember best, perhaps, when we have ourselves to do some interpreting; when the intelligence is fully engaged in the effort of complex appreciation. We remember, in fact, our own powers of perception and sensitivity as much as those of the author. This does not happen with Tolstoy. Enjoyment of *War and Peace* is particularly pure because it is immediate, and no challenge is offered to our talent for modification, for perceiving—as Mill said about Kant— "what poor Tolstoy would be at". As no other author, Tolstoy makes the critic feel how superfluous his office can be.

This then is the chief effect of life in Tolstoy. But the set pieces, the high spots—surely we remember them? If they were complete in themselves we should remember more, but they are never rounded off and presented as moments in time. An abridged version of *War and Peace*, the desirability of which was hinted by critics like Percy Lubbock, would be intolerable. This is not too strong a word, for when Natasha is singing the song at Uncle's, or Nicholas is at the hunt, the essence of idyll pumped into the air is already dangerously strong. Enriched still further it could become overpowering, even sickly. At moments like this we remember how daring is the egoism of the great book, how exclusive in terms of class and privilege. Russia belonged to Tolstoy because Russia belonged, literally, to his class. The possession of the past in which he was so assured is an early equivalent of that enormous, delirious, communal sense of possession which—far more than the revolutionary programme of the Bolshevik leaders—animated the mass of the people in 1917 and ensured the success of the revolution. Tolstoy's instinctive "Russia belongs to me" was ultimately to be echoed by the old worker crying out in the streets with incredulous joy, "All Petrograd, all Russia belong to *me!*" The immense confidence of *War and Peace* depends on the truth of the earlier claim, a truth so explicit and overwhelming that it finally had to give way to the later one. Whatever the defects of the new system, a visit to Russia convinces one that Russians have still not got over the joy of feeling they own their country, as Tolstoy owned his.

5. *'Understanding', and 'Making it Strange'*

The primitive vitality in this sense of possession reminds us of childhood, and almost everything in *War and Peace* springs out of the childhood world and returns to it for judgment. It is the source of life and sensation, the setting of the idyll. The idyll has all the capacity of childish appetite—'more, more yet'—Anatole Kuragin shouting for *more* troikas, *more* champagne, *more* gipsy music reminds us of the piercing, senseless cry of ecstasy which the small Natasha used to utter. Kuragin's is the spoilt version of that eagerness which keeps every stage of Natasha's life in correspondence with her life as a child—her marital communication with Pierre echoes the communication between children in the family. This depends upon *understanding*, a particularly Tolstoyan quality, which he explains in *Youth*.

> Apart from the general faculties, which are more or less developed according to the individual, of intellect, sensibility and artistic feeling, there exists a special capacity that is more or less developed in different circles of society and especially in families, which I call mutual *understanding*. The essence of this capacity lies in an agreed sense of proportion and an accepted and identical outlook on things. Two members of the same set or the same family possessing this faculty can always allow an expression of feeling up to a certain point beyond which they both see only empty phrases. Simultaneously both perceive where commendation ends and irony begins, where enthusiasm ceases and pretence takes its place—all of which may appear quite otherwise to people possessed of a different order of apprehension. People of the same understanding see everything they come across in an identically ludicrous, beautiful or repellent light. To facilitate this common understanding the members of a

circle or a family often invent a language of their own with expressions peculiar to them, or even words which indicate shades of meaning non-existent for others. . . . Dubkov fitted into our circle fairly well and *understood*, but Dimitri Nekhlyudov, though far more intelligent, was obtuse in this respect.

In *Childhood, Boyhood and Youth* this understanding between the members of the family is also an understanding—intimate, sometimes almost incoherent—between Tolstoy and the reader. He depends on us to see the point of the private jokes that produce screams of happy, senseless, sometimes malicious laughter. "Katya, the *Russians*?"—cries Volodya, on a particular note of interrogation, meaningful only to himself and his brother the narrator; and the narrator goes crawling through the raspberry canes, repeating endlessly to himself "And by twenties and by sevens". This bid for *understanding* has often been imitated since by other writers. Its dangers are inconsequence, drift from one kind of intimate accuracy to another, and eventually to boredom. Moreover, there is a discrepancy between the intimate bid for understanding and the generalising, retrospective tone of the narrator: it is this that Tolstoy probably had in mind when he later spoke of the book as "insincerely written in a literary sense", and why he broke off without completing the whole work, to be called *Four Epochs of Growth*, which he had planned. In *War and Peace* the narration is unified, the incoherencies of family life organised and concentrated into the traditional patterns of idyll and epic. Instead of the appeal to understanding followed by the slightly pompous explanation of it, we have a plain descriptive transparency. We learn for instance that when the young Rostovs are talking, Sonya (like Lyuba and Katya) "did not quite keep pace with them though she shared the same reminiscences". But "she enjoyed their pleasure and tried to fit in with it".

There is an immense gain in clarity and purpose in the family life of *War and Peace*, but at the expense of that wonderful, maddening, inconclusive accuracy which reigns in *Childhood*. Since everything in the great book must be followed up, much must be left out. Its completeness is a magnificent illusion, and its steady pulse bears us onwards before the idylls can settle into poses that would reveal the artifice of their structure and what they omit. One of the most striking omissions is the kind of sexual awareness which permeates *Childhood*. We must remember, of course, that the version of *War and Peace* which we have was prepared for the press by the Countess Tolstoy, and that the early drafts are much more outspoken than the finished product was allowed to be. "Needs a husband, even two", Tolstoy wrote in his notes about Natasha, and Hélène is described as "a beautiful piece of meat in a skirt". These frank comments have no place in the book, where the sexuality even of Hélène is generalised and idealised on the epic scale. But with men Tolstoy is less successful in the idealisation process; male sexual desire is curiously furtive. The decorum of life so essential to the great work would be bothered by it; there seems no place for it in the great harmony of family and nation. The significance of this is considerable. Tolstoy only created a world that seems to embrace all reality by sealing off things that worried and disturbed him.

One might say that Tolstoy enjoyed contemplating female sexuality (with all that 'enjoyment' implies in such a creative intelligence) but he detested contemplating his own or that of other men. His marvellous marriage sequences are seen entirely in terms of the sexuality of the woman, to whom the man is merely a passive instrument. Both Pierre and Levin in *Anna Karenina* are surprised by the total subordination to family needs which their wives require of them, but their vanity is gratified by it and they submit. It is part of the nature of things. And not only in the marriage sequences.

He half rose, meaning to go round, but the aunt handed him the snuff-box, passing it across Hélène's back. Hélène stooped forward to make room, and looked round with a smile. She was, as always at evening parties, wearing a dress such as was then fashionable, cut very low at front and back. Her bust, which had always seemed like marble to Pierre, was so close to him that his short-sighted eyes could not but perceive the living charm of her neck and shoulders, so near to his lips that he need only have bent his head a little to have touched them. He was conscious of the warmth of her body, the scent of perfume, and the creaking of her corset as she moved. He did not see her marble beauty forming a complete whole with her dress, but all the charm of her body only covered by her garments. And having once seen this he could not help being aware of it, just as we cannot renew an illusion we have once seen through.

"So you have never before noticed how beautiful I am?" Hélène seemed to say. "You had not noticed that I am a woman? Yes, I am a woman who may belong to any one—to you too," said her glance. And at that moment Pierre felt that Hélène not only could, but must, be his wife, and that it could not be otherwise.

Like a composer Tolstoy converts even the angularity of real life—like the touch of Hélène stooping forward while the snuff-box is passed behind her—into the flowing rhythm of the passage. It was bound to happen; it was as right as a tune, and the gathering is caught up, as by a tune, into "the attraction of a healthy and handsome young man and woman for one another". "The human feeling dominated everything else and soared above all their affected chatter." As in the troika drive in which "a voice told Sonya that now or never her fate would be decided", the dominant note in the harmony is female, and Prince Vasili presides as an epic host on one level and as an epicene procurer on the other. His face, generally full of benevolence and goodwill, is apt on occasion "to assume the coarse unpleasant expression peculiar to him". Although his daughter resembles him, his attitude is hardly parental. He addresses her "with the careless tone of habitual tenderness natural to parents who have petted their children from babyhood, but which Prince Vasili had only acquired from imitating other parents". So, after all, have most parents! But the whole scene, which in *Ivan Ilyich* would be a nightmare of hypocrisy and ugliness, is here harmonious and full of delight. The Trollopian expedient by which Prince Vasili compels Pierre to accept his fate acquires in Tolstoy's hands a Mozartian brio, as if the prince were a conductor executing the final flourish. And Hélène manages the absurdity of sexual urgency as gracefully as when she stooped forward to allow the snuff-box to be passed behind her back.

"Oh, take those off . . . those . . ." she said, pointing to his spectacles.

Pierre took them off, and his eyes besides the strange look eyes have from which spectacles have just been removed, had also a frightened and inquiring look. He was about to stoop over her hand and kiss it, but with a rapid, almost brutal movement of her head she intercepted his lips and met them with her own. Her face struck Pierre by its altered, unpleasantly excited expression.

"It is too late now, it's done; besides I love her," thought Pierre.

"*Je vous aime!*" he said, remembering what has to be said at such moments.

Well, perhaps not quite so gracefully! She is her father's daughter. And Tolstoy ends the scene on a note that suggests he is about to revert to his ironic technique, the technique that the Russian critic Shklovsky called "making it strange".

This suggestive phrase refers to Tolstoy's use of an eighteenth-century satiric device much favoured by his admired Voltaire, who describes soldiers playing on a drum as "murderers six foot high, clothed in scarlet and beating a distended asses skin". The intention is to reveal what reason or "unclouded common sense" show to be true about a subject wrapped in romantic nonsense or ancient prejudice. It is highly important in *War and Peace* and we shall often have cause to notice it again. Obvious instances of its extended use are Natasha's visit to the opera, and Pierre's induction into the Masonic rites. It is common in battle scenes, where it merges with what Tolstoy learnt from Stendhal's factual style and lack of emphasis, as in the scene when Nicholas's horse is killed under him at Schön Grabern, or when at Ostrovna he hits the French dragoon with his sabre and captures him. Tolstoy not only uses it in many variations but interspersed with other methods of narrative to provide shades of contrast. At Schön Grabern, for example, Nicholas is enchanted to find just before the fall of his horse begins to "make it strange" that war is just like what he had hoped and imagined; that he is charging forward waving his sword—just as in the battle pictures—shouting 'Hurrah' and full of the intoxicating hope of killing somebody.

Voltaire and Swift use the method of 'making it strange' as satire: Tolstoy uses it dramatically. For the satirist it shows the object as it really is, but for Tolstoy it shows one way of seeing it. His other methods of narration put it on record that other ways of seeing the thing exist. At the end of the engagement scene Pierre says to Hélène " 'Je vous aime', remembering what has to be said at such moments". The implication is that such scenes are utterly insincere and fatuous, and that Tolstoy is recalling us to a sense of this. We certainly need to be recalled, for our impression of the scene, with all its comedy and harmony, was very different. The ludicrous and the beautiful appeared, as in *The Rape of the Lock*, as the substance of art and life. At such moments Tolstoy shows himself as very much a complete man of the eighteenth century: Mozart and Voltaire counterpoint one another, and the music of the narrative depends on their alliance even more than it does on epic association.

The next scene, though, shows old Prince Bolkonsky on his estate, awaiting the arrival of Prince Vasili, and now the poised glitter of the ballet gives way to a sober epic domination. No doubt this patriarchal country life was for Tolstoy the real thing, and the frivolous social life of the capital a mere excrescence, but the change does not mark a deliberate moral contrast. The old Prince is monarch of all he surveys; he refuses to play the social game, and when his steward incautiously reveals that he has had the avenue swept because a 'minister' is coming, he flies into a rage and gives orders for the snow to be shovelled back again. It is a gesture worthy of the epic man, as Prince Vasili's device to make Pierre declare himself was worthy of the Mozartian social one; and as Pierre's shame for himself, when he says "Je vous aime" because it has to be said at such moments is worthy of the rational and Voltairean man. The three methods, the three modes of living, are given the stature of originals, and contribute together to the greater harmony of the novel.

6. Sex

How does Tolstoy persuade them into this harmony, and how does he reconcile it with the demands of "reason, that is, good" on the one hand, and the mere intrusions of reality on the other? As I have suggested, one of his ways round the second, and perhaps the first as well, is to abolish the more inconvenient aspects of the male sex. *War and Peace* is dominated by the female principle; it is a profoundly feminine view of life. None of the three male originals I have been speaking of are as important as the women. To the rational and 'strange-making' view the party at Prince Vasili's is stupid, frivolous, insincere. But such things have a deep underlying necessity. They make fates, and fate in this world is both suffered and imposed by women. Pierre knows that he cannot escape, just as in his subsequent courtship of Natasha he knows that cannot escape. "Pierre felt that his freedom had completely gone." So we are told on the later occasion, and the moment is essentially the same as on the earlier one when "he knew that it would happen", and that "it could not be otherwise". Certainly on the second occasion he is happy and fearful and feels he is doing right, and on the first he is happy and fearful and feels he is doing wrong, but what matters is that fate is at work on both occasions. As in Schopenhauer, whom Tolstoy so much admired, the individual will goes for very little. Men are as helpless at parties as generals are on the battlefield. Pierre may continue to seek, to look for meanings and to find them, but he is really pre-empted by the fatalism of the plot, which controls the actions of individuals and nations, and determines that everything happens as it has to happen, and that everything turns out well. The salvation of Russia and the salvation of Pierre are alike the result of passivity, and although one is a historical fact and the other an invention of Tolstoy's, both have the quality of inevitability which Tolstoy's achievement confers.

Which came first, history or *War and Peace*?, is the question we ask ourselves after being in the grip of Tolstoyan invention. Are we to submit to fate because Hélène dies, because Russia is saved, Napoleon defeated, and Natasha gets a husband? Or is it that the novel requires these things to happen, so that Tolstoy's theories of history and human life—in which the individuals who think they lead and control are merely the bellwethers of the flock—become wish-fulfilment on a gigantic scale? Certainly Tolstoy is able to create his giant idyll by handing all things over to the female and fated principle, and by denying and suppressing male authority and initiative and the guilt and anguish about sex and death that troubled him as a male (and that troubled him, we should note, long before the crisis of *A Confession*). By handing the work over to fate and the female he in fact obtained for himself—and in a sense for us too—the last perquisite of the male—freedom—the freedom that Pierre feels in captivity and in his final submission to Natasha, the freedom that comes from the recognition of necessity. "Only what was really good in him was reflected in his wife, all that was not quite good was rejected." This might be one epigraph on the philosophy of *War and Peace*.

In *Some Words about 'War and Peace'* Tolstoy wrote:

> Why did millions of people kill one another when it has been known since the world began that it is physically and morally bad to do so? Because it was such an inevitable necessity that in doing it men fulfilled the elementary zoological law which bees fulfil when they kill one another in autumn, and which causes male animals to destroy one another. One can give no other reply to that terrible question.

We remember the other "terrible question" which confronted Natasha. "What am I to do if I love him and the other one too?" she asked herself, unable to find an answer to these terrible questions. Both are resolved by Pierre's discovery on the retreat.

> And now during these last three weeks of the march he had learned still another new, consolatory truth—that there is nothing in the world that is terrible. He had learned that, as there is no condition in which man can be happy and entirely free, so there is no condition in which he need be unhappy and not free.

The "terrible question" (the same word *strashny* is used in all three instances) turns out to be not terrible at all, nor a question. It is dissolved for Natasha because in Pierre she can have both Kuragin and Prince Andrew. Having played their part in the harmony Hélène and Kuragin die, like Macbeth, offstage, Kuragin having lost his leg (a terrible emasculation) at Borodino, and Hélène as the result of an abortion in Petersburg. Did they find there was nothing terrible in the world? They are not allowed to say, because anything they did say could only disturb the swelling unanimity. But in the mode which I have called the Mozartian they received all Tolstoy's creative intentness and care. The drawing-room ballet in which Pierre is entrapped by Hélène and her father is echoed at the operatic ballet (a real one) at which Natasha is first admired by Kuragin. This is of course "made strange" by Tolstoy in his most determined way.

> The cymbals and horns in the orchestra struck up more loudly, and this man with bare legs jumped very high and waved his feet about very rapidly. (He was Duport, who received sixty thousand roubles a year for this art.)

After meeting Kuragin, "who was much more sensible and simple with women than among men", Natasha is herself in the mood of opera and ballet, filling it with her own vitality and her pleasure in being admired. So far from being formidable and alarming, Kuragin seems so cheerful and good-natured, and this delights her as Duport now delights her. It is right that the fate of Hélène and Kuragin, who are such natural denizens of this artificial world, should not be the fate of Natasha, but an operatic fate, like that of Don Juan in Pushkin's *The Stone Guest*. Kuragin's pleasure in seduction is childlike, but it is seduction. "I'm as happy as a child," says Pushkin's Don Juan, clutching Leporello's hands, and this open Russian enthusiasm upon which Pushkin with poetic economy confers its proper dramatic fate, is very like that of Kuragin.

Yet there is no blinking the fact that Kuragin, for all his parade of the rake's part, never quite convinces us that he is one, any more than Nicholas and Pierre, for all their visits to "certain houses" ever really seem to us other than sexually innocent. Pushkin's Don Juan is one without need of words—for all his boyish enthusiasm we feel his devouring will and his zeal in intrigue—but Tolstoy seems to go out of his way to emphasise Kuragin's lack of any real sexual initiative.

> He was not a gambler, at any rate he did not care about winning. He was not vain. He did not mind what people thought of him. Still less could he be accused of ambition. More than once he had vexed his father by spoiling his own career, and he laughed at distinctions of all kinds. He was not mean, and did not refuse any one who asked of him. All he cared about was gaiety and women, and as according to his ideas there was nothing dishonourable in these tastes, and he was incapable of considering what the gratification of his tastes entailed for others, he honestly considered himself irreproachable, sincerely despised rogues and bad people, and with a tranquil conscience carried his head high.

Rakes, those male Magdalenes, have a secret feeling of innocence similar to that which female Magdalenes have, based on the same hope of forgiveness. "All will be forgiven her, for she loved much; and all will be forgiven him, for he enjoyed much."

In an early story *The Two Hussars*, as well as in a late obsessional tale like *The Devil*, Tolstoy is concerned with the sense in which "no passion is as serious as lust". But lust has no place here. It is passed off lightly in the three major modes—in the Voltairean irony of this passage, with the glitter and charm of ballet, and in the not wholly serious presentation of the rake as epic hero. When Anatole is surprised by Princess Mary as he is embracing Mlle Bourrienne he bows to her with a gay smile, "as if inviting her to join in a laugh at this strange incident". We join in the laugh too—it is a stage embrace. In the same scene Tolstoy exquisitely combines epic simile with this comedy lightness.

> The little princess, like an old war-horse that hears the trumpet, unconsciously and quite forgetting her condition, prepared for the familiar gallop of coquetry, without any ulterior motive and any struggle, but with naïve and light-hearted gaiety.

It is difficult seriously to believe in the reality of the seduction preparations, but we are ourselves seduced by the sight of Anatole looking in the mirror as he puts on "a fur coat girt with a silver belt, and a sable cap jauntily set on one side", and takes Dolokhov's hand to show him how his heart beats. "What? Feel how it beats! *Ah, quel pied, mon cher! Quel regard! Une Déesse!* Eh?"[1] As much as Petya in the Cossack camp just before his death "he was in a fairy kingdom where nothing resembled reality", and where all things are possible.

Balaga, their driver, supplies the heroic element.

> Balaga was a famous troika driver who had known Dolokhov and Anatole some six years and had given them good service with his troikas. More than once when Anatole's regiment was stationed at

---

[1] I have retained the French of the original. There is so much French in *War and Peace* that much of it is usually Englished in translation and the point is lost that persons like Anatole are continually lapsing into French while the Rostovs, for example, hardly ever use it.

Tver he had taken him from Tver in the evening, brought him to Moscow by daybreak, and driven him back again the next night. More than once he had enabled Dolokhov to escape when pursued. More than once he had driven them through the town with gipsies and 'ladykins' as he called the *cocottes*. More than once in their service he had run over pedestrians and upset vehicles in the streets of Moscow, and had always been protected from the consequences by 'my gentlemen' as he called them. He had ruined more than one horse in their service. More than once they had beaten him, and more than once they had made him drunk on champagne and madeira which he loved; and he knew more than one thing about each of them which would long ago have sent an ordinary man to Siberia. They often called Balaga into their orgies and made him drink and dance at the gipsies', and more than one thousand rubles of their money had passed through his hands. In their service he risked his skin and his life twenty times a year, and in their service had lost more horses than the money he had from them would buy. But he liked them; liked that mad driving at twelve miles an hour, liked upsetting a driver, or running down a pedestrian, and flying at full gallop through the Moscow streets. He liked to hear those wild, tipsy shouts behind him: "Get on! Get on!" when it was impossible to go any faster. He liked giving a painful lash on the neck to some peasant who, more dead than alive, was already hurrying out of his way. 'Real gentlemen!' he considered them.

7. *Dolokhov and the Family*

Dolokhov manages Anatole and supplies the will to intrigue, but he is not permitted by Tolstoy to supply the sexual element.[1] He more than anybody had to be prevented from doing the things that cannot be done in *War and Peace*, and there are times when we feel aware of this restraint, for he is an extreme character, who would be at home in Dostoevsky, but who cannot be relied on to fit into the Voltairean irony and the Mozartian measure, the opera and the epic. Dolokhov is unsurpassably *there* at the moments which he loves—the moment when he drinks the bottle of rum on the window ledge; when—on the last time we meet him—he switches his boots with his whip and says to the French

---

[1] The character of Dolokhov may have been suggested by a noted rake of the 1812 epoch named Dorokhov.

prisoners *"Filez, filez . . ."*; when he smiles at the infuriated Pierre "that smile of his which seemed to say 'This is what I like' ".

But how do we respond when we learn that he lives with an old mother and a hunchback sister, to whom he is "the most affectionate of sons and brothers"? This is one of the very few moments in the book when Tolstoy seems to step outside his bounds and his creative stride falters. Of course Dolokhov *might* have had such a home, but not here—there is no place for it among the myriad created "peepshows" (to use Tolstoy's term) that make up the book. This, at least, is surely our first reaction to "the unexpectedly rapturous and tender expression" on his face when he speaks of his old mother. Well really, we feel, Tolstoy is too much of an eighteenth-century rationalist to do this kind of thing successfully. He seems to be creating to order the sort of romantic Russian hero whom he elsewhere despises—the Byronic hero of Marlinsky's novels and of Lermontov—the hero whose sensibility is suddenly revealed through his armour of disdain. We remember the doctrinaire confidence of the author of *Childhood*. "I repeat once more that inconsistency in matters of feeling is the surest sign of their genuineness." Is Tolstoy merely making Dolokhov convincing according to this formula?

Far from it. This is one of the most striking examples, not only of the immense superiority in technique in *War and Peace* compared to Tolstoy's earlier works, but of how its flow can carry us along for a time in a puzzled and dissatisfied state, and how this leads to kinds of realisation which seem to come not from Tolstoy but from our own experience of life. He has widened our receptivity without our knowing it. It must have been difficult for the Tolstoy of *Childhood* to renounce his penetrating analyses, and to give up the credit of doing everything for himself—and be seen doing it. Of course, he still analyses in the first person in *War and Peace*, but his comments are the surface of the groundswell in which one character rubs up and down against another. It is young Rostov who sees that "rapturous and tender expression" on Dolokhov's face, and is melted accordingly. It is young Rostov who gets so friendly with him during his convalescence after the duel with Pierre, and who listens to his mother talking. It is in the unconscious humour of what the old lady says that we begin to perceive what is going on.

"Yes, Count," she would say, "he is too noble and pure-souled for our present, depraved world. No one now loves virtue, it seems like a reproach to every one. Now tell me, Count, was it right, was it honourable, of Bezukhov? And Fedya, with his noble spirit, loved him and even now never says a word against him. . . . And now— this duel! Have these people no feeling, or honour? Knowing him to be an only son, to challenge him and shoot so straight! It's well God had mercy on us. And what was it for? Who doesn't have intrigues nowadays? Why, if he was so jealous, as I see things he should have shown it sooner, but he lets it go on for months. And then to call him out, reckoning on Fedya not fighting because he owed him money! What baseness! What meanness! I know you understand Fedya, my dear Count, that, believe me, is why I am so fond of you. Few people do understand him. His is such a lofty, heavenly soul!"

Old Mrs Dolokhov is indeed the archetypal mother! We, who were present at the duel, and at the banquet which led to it, received a rather different impression. With the complacency which is a part of his generous nature, Nicholas Rostov is pleased to think he understands Dolokhov. "You must understand what a soul there is in Dolokhov," he tells his family, "you should see him with his mother! What a heart!"

Only Natasha disagrees. "Well, I don't know about that," she replies, "but I am uncomfortable with him." As good a comment as any on the Russian 'soul', which we remember Conrad describing in *Under Western Eyes* as a bottomless well of cynicism. So indeed it can appear. There are souls and souls, and Tolstoy can see them both under Western and under Russian eyes. Gasha, the maid in *Childhood* who prompted the original doctrine of genuineness through inconsistency, detested her old mistress but was the only one to weep passionately and sincerely at her death. This manifestation of soul is completely convincing, but Dolokhov's inconsistency is of a different kind. He combines unpredictability and calculation in a senseless void, out of which humanity and order cannot grow. He almost alone in the book is outside the shaping and moulding influences of nature and society. The phrase of Necker that Pushkin took as an epigraph for *Eugene Onegin*—"La morale est dans la nature des choses"—is equally appropriate to *War and Peace*, indeed more so. The great book might almost have been written to naturalise this piece of profoundly secular and European wisdom in the Russian soul.

Nicholas can see through ordinary calculators like Boris and Berg, but he is as enchanted by Dolokhov as his young brother Petya will be. Yet for Natasha, who adores Denisov and Nicholas's other comrades, "with this one, all is calculated".

> "I don't care a straw about anyone but those I love; but those I love I love so that I would give my life for them, and the others I'd throttle if they stood in my way. I have an adored, a priceless mother, and two or three friends—you among them . . . I have not yet met that divine purity and devotion I look for in woman. And believe me, if I still value my life it is because I still hope to meet such a divine creature, who will regenerate, purify me, and elevate me. But you don't understand it."
>
> "Oh yes, I quite understand," answered Rostov, who was under his new friend's influence.

Nicholas does not understand—does Tolstoy? If nothing Dolokhov says rings quite right, is this because he is 'insincere' or because his nature is genuinely incomprehensible to Tolstoy? What Dolokhov says to Nicholas certainly sounds repellent, a little like Iago's bluff double-bluff—"though in the trade of war I have slain men. . . ." He professes to "care for" Nicholas, yet Nicholas, no less than Kuragin, is his natural victim. Nicholas represents the settled interests with whom Dolokhov is naturally at war, even though he claims he would do anything for his friends. Like Iago, Dolokhov asserts a self-knowledge which he does not possess, and that is why his speech rings false. Yet when he asks Pierre, before the battle of Borodino, to forgive him—like so many enigmatic moments in Tolstoy it is a very unemphatic one—Pierre does not know what to say, nor do we. Pierre was brought up in Switzerland (Necker's country, and the scene of *Under Western Eyes*) and the Russian 'soul' is beyond him. Nothing in the book shows more subtly the remarkable combination in it of European and Russian reactions. These ideas of love and forgiveness—what do they mean? If this is not calculation, then what is it? Ultimately we know Dolokhov only by his actions. He makes nonsense of all Pierre's (and Tolstoy's) attempts to get the world and its denizens neatly sorted out, and this indeed is perhaps his biggest function in the book.

There can be no doubt that Tolstoy detests and fears people who aren't *there*. Not to be *there* is the ultimate form of calculation, the last intrigue, which steals from life while standing out against it, for only by putting our necks under the yoke of necessity do we show ourselves helplessly in our true role and as we really are. Strange as it may seem, Sonya is a kind of feminine parallel to Dolokhov, a white spirit to his dark one. Like him she is sterile, "a sterile flower". All through the book we are aware of the curious repugnance—and sometimes an active animosity—that Natasha and her mother feel for Sonya, especially when she is being particularly sweet, virtuous and self-sacrificing, and this often strikes us as unfair—her position, after all, is that of a dependant. But Tolstoy does not think it unfair. He gives Sonya the alienation treatment. Like Dolokhov, she is never allowed to *be* herself, but is always seen from outside. We have much more physical apprehension both of her and Dolokhov than we have of Nicholas and Natasha. We see her as the little kitten, with melting black eyes and enormous plaits, and we hear (a marvellous acoustic touch) her "painstaking high-pitched voice" as she reads the Tsar's proclamation. We see Dolokhov's broad-boned red hands, very hairy at the wrists, as he deals cards. These are real facts. The stoutness of Pierre and the slightness of Prince Andrew are by contrast simply signs to identify them and give them substance. The famous short upper lip of the Little Princess, with the dark down on it, is little more. It is an identification rather than an absolute manifestation. Brilliant as Tolstoy is at bringing out these manifestations of people, they generally imply his hostility. He hardly seems to notice what he gives us about the appearance of the Rostovs, and nor do we. He has *understood* them so completely by other means, as in *Childhood* this understanding is complete between some members of the family. It is those who do not *understand* who have to be described.

It is an effective shock when Tolstoy switches on this alienation, which has affinities with the "making it strange" process.

He does it when Princess Mary meets the Rostovs at Yaroslavl for the last days of Prince Andrew.

> On the left there was water—a great river—and on the right a porch. There were people at the entrance: servants, and a rosy girl with a large plait of black hair, smiling as it seemed to Princess Mary in an unpleasantly affected way. (This was Sonya.) Princess Mary ran up the steps. "This way, this way!" said the girl, with the same artificial smile, and the princess found herself in the hall facing an elderly woman of oriental type, who came rapidly to meet her with a look of emotion. This was the countess. She embraced Princess Mary and kissed her.
>
> "*Mon enfant!*" she muttered, "*je vous aime et vous connais depuis longtemps.*"

Tolstoy has made us into Princess Mary seeing the Rostovs for the first time (it never occurred to us she did not know them—she has only met Natasha and her father) and she sees the Countess in the same way that she sees Sonya. The shock consists in the fact that we know Sonya in this way but not the countess, who used to have those nightly chats in bed with her daughter and go off into "a deep unexpected laugh" at the nonsense they talked. So to an outsider she is "an elderly woman of oriental type"—how extraordinary! And we realise that thanks to Tolstoy we have never been outsiders in this family. But now the onward movement of time and change has turned us into them, as it does in life, and we shall be even more outsiders in the last family scenes. One cannot be on the inside of more than one family, and the death of Petya and of the old count has, as Tolstoy says, broken up ours.

Tolstoy knew that the family is a ruthless affair. There is nothing sentimental about our contact with the Rostovs. We are offered our 'insideness' at the expense of Sonya and Vera, and if we take it we connive in the way those two are treated. The suggestion is that on the inside of a family there are no moral decisions and 'good' acts—such things are left to outsiders like Sonya. If we compare the Rostovs with English nineteenth-century fictional families, in George Eliot, Thackeray, Mrs Gaskell, we see what inhibitions our novelists had about the family, and how they feed back their own mature moral preoccupations into descriptions of childhood and family life. Or perhaps most English Victorian families really lacked the spontaneity and the emotional atavism of family life in *War and Peace*? The Rostov family behave solely in accordance with their natures, and do exactly as they want and as they must. When the insiders are crying over the letter from Nicholas in which he tells them that all is well and that he has been made an officer, they look reproachfully at Vera when she remarks that they ought to be glad, not sorry, and the Countess wonders whom she can take after. Nothing shows the quality of this solidarity better or more humorously than when Tolstoy turns it inside out at the ball, and shows us Natasha's exasperation with it in that context. "The family gathering seemed humiliating to her —as if there were nowhere else for the family to talk but here at the ball."

Une mère de famille est capable de tout. The countess does not ask herself whether it is right to make Sonya give up Nicholas. She simply asks Sonya to write to him, and as she looks at her "Sonya read all that the countess meant to convey by these words. Those eyes expressed entreaty, shame at having to ask, fear of a refusal, and readiness for relentless hatred in case of such refusal." It is typical that Sonya, the outsider, thinks she is making a moral choice, and she writes—as no Rostov would— "my love has no aim but the happiness of those I love". She has accustomed herself voluntarily to self-sacrifice. And where Rostovs, simply and passively by being Rostovs, get what they want and should have, Sonya—like Dolokhov—must scheme for it. She thinks that she is making a moral choice, but it is only when she thinks Andrew will live that she writes to Nicholas. If Andrew survives and marries Natasha, then Nicholas will not be able to marry a sister-in-law, Princess Mary, because of the ecclesiastical prohibition. Having worked that one out, "Sonya was joyfully conscious of a return of that self-sacrificing spirit in which she was accustomed to live and loved to live", and she writes to release Nicholas. He is overjoyed—he had just prayed for this. It has come about so rapidly, though, "that it could not have come from God to whom he had prayed, but by some extraordinary coincidence".

The humour of this is alarming, and all the more so if unintentional. It reminds us of Gorky's comment that God and

Tolstoy were like "two bears in one den". Nicholas has prayed in a sense to the whole principle of the novel, and his prayer has been answered: God could not have fixed it so quick. As the Rostov heir and the incarnation of the Rostov spirit Nicholas must of course get what he wants. It is essential not only to the psychological movement of the work but to its social foundation. We are up against the bedrock of Tolstoy's familial self. In the tentative and laborious early drafts Tolstoy had tried all sorts of arbitrary ways of resolving the situation. Andrew was to recover; to renounce Natasha to Pierre because he feels he loves her more; and by this noble gesture to persuade Sonya to renounce Nicholas to Mary. Alternatively, Andrew was to marry Natasha, and Nicholas to part from Mary and return to Sonya. All these expedients not only cut across the deeper social and psychological necessities, but also allot arbitrary powers of choice and decision to the main characters. By the final arrangement these are removed. To borrow Tolstoy's phrase, the characters do what it is in their spiritual natures to do. Natasha and Nicholas get what they should get; Sonya, what she comes to feel she should get. Her expectations are more adaptable than theirs, and her desire to please so great that she comes to think she has pleased herself as well as pleasing others. Tolstoy refuses to give her any credit—perhaps, coming from him, it is a kind of compliment that he does not—and neither does Natasha, who ends by thinking that Sonya did not really want to get married but is attached, like a cat, not to one person but to the family and the house. It is a principle of growth and survival that we think what has happened must and ought to have happened, and Tolstoy lends it the whole weight of his artistic authority.

Tolstoy does not victimise Sonya; her role in life, indeed, is based on that of his own Aunt Tatiana, whom he adored. But he does connect her desire to please with the sincerity for which he always had such an eagle eye. She strikes Mary as "smiling in an unpleasantly artificial way"; she lacks the absolute confidence and spontaneity which is an essential part of *understanding*. When she and Natasha look for their fates in the glass Natasha of course sees nothing and says so—she could not do otherwise—but Sonya does not want to disappoint them. She pretends to have seen Prince Andrew and really begins to feel she has. After he is wounded she recalls the moment and remembers 'seeing' the pink quilt he has on his bed.[1] And Tolstoy demonstrates her ignorance of her true motives when she writes the renunciatory letter to Nicholas. This lack of self-knowledge relates her again, perhaps, to Dolokhov: what she says, like what he says, never quite rings true. It lacks naturalness, the utter unconscious confidence in themselves that the Rostovs have, and that Tolstoy thinks peasants like Karataev have. And it is this confidence he values above everything. It is for him both the ground of, and a guarantee of, self-knowledge. Lacking it, Sonya cannot put down roots into life, and Natasha quotes about her (though Princess Mary says she is misinterpreting it) the text "Unto him that hath shall be given, and from him that hath not shall be taken away". It might be our third epigraph for *War and Peace*.

Both Dolokhov and Sonya can of course be seen as characters with whom Tolstoy fails. Why not? For this kind of failure would not only indicate where and how he succeeds, but would tell us much about the moral scheme of the book. Dostoevsky would have given them both a vivid dramatic life, but Tolstoy either fails or abstains. They remain an open pair, a dangerous pair, who may—especially Sonya—enlist the reader's support against the good and settled heroes and heroines of fate and nature. Why does Dolokhov fall in love with Sonya? Tolstoy, who explains everything, does not attempt to explain this.[2] And, rather significantly, it is dismissed in what must be one of the flattest sentences of the book, almost a novelettish sentence.

---

[1] Oddly enough she said at the time she had seen "something blue and red", the colours that Natasha, in a discussion about what colour people are, allotted to Pierre. It looks as if there is room even for the supernatural in the harmony of *War and Peace*, or at least as if coincidence could become an almost inadvertent part of its design.

[2] The draft versions include scenes between Sonya and Dolokhov, all finally omitted, and a love letter beginning "Adored Sophie, I love you as no man ever loved a woman" (see R. F. Christian, *op. cit.*). Our Dolokhov could hardly have survived *that*, and it must have become clear to Tolstoy that he was *inventing* a character in the interests of plot instead of letting him develop. In general the requirements of plot interest in *War and Peace*, though they are so superbly justified by the results, gave Tolstoy great trouble for this reason.

It was evident that this strange, strong man was under the irresistible influence of the dark graceful girl who loved another.

It is clear why Sonya refuses him, as it is clear why she never marries, and why Dolokhov revenges himself on Nicholas at cards, but what was Dolokhov's motive—calculation or impulse? We never know. And in so transparent, so explained a work, this is in itself effective, whatever the reasons for it. Insiders as we are in the Rostov family, we are left to work it out for ourselves. The relative mode here reminds us of Proust; but when does Proust ever leave us in genuine uncertainty?—he has not the temperament for it. And Tolstoy, despite his firm convictions and intolerant views, and his wish to get things sorted out, can and does leave us this freedom.

However calculating Dolokhov may be, Tolstoy is careful not to let him become a true sexual intriguer, like Lovelace in *Clarissa* or De Valmont in *Les Liasons Dangereuses*. Whatever his part in Anatole's attempted seduction of Natasha, we know there is not the slightest chance of this seduction coming off. It is treated (even by Dolokhov) almost in the mock-heroic vein, and foiled by that sensible and forthright old battleaxe, Marya Dimitrievna. And yet it cost Tolstoy a great deal of bother, and was regarded by him as a pivotal episode. Part of the bother may have been due to his discomfort in having to handle such an obviously *novelish* episode, part to his need to make it appear an aspect of the 'good old times', when such matters were more dashing and spontaneous than they are now. There is a certain prejudice here, which is schematised and appears clearly in that rather irritating story *The Two Hussars*. The father in the tale, a Colonel of Hussars at the time of *War and Peace*, does everything spontaneously, duelling, gambling and womanising with great panache. His son, the second Hussar, is a calculating rake-borrowing money from an admiring comrade which he has no intention of repaying, and setting out in cold blood to seduce the daughter of his father's old friend. The object lesson is crude, but it has its bearing on *War and Peace*. Our fathers' amours were idyllic—their brothel-going cheery and innocent: with us these things have become ugly, planned and full of disgust. Anatole and Nicholas belong to the world of the Hussar father:

Levin in Anna Karenina and Nekhlyudov in *Resurrection* (with
its haunting picture of a shameful and fumbling seduction) to
the world of the son.

In re-creating the past Tolstoy is re-creating—in a sense for
his own relief—a world in which sexual guilt is minimised or
unknown. Like other dark and uneasy matters it is kept in the
wings and never allowed on the stage. It is at the conclusion of
War and Peace that we feel the pressure of all these uneasy
things most strongly, but Tolstoy—with his whole giant creation at his back—holds them off without effort. The concluding
scenes, as Shestov has pointed out, are shot through and through
with equivocations. Have we any right to be happy at the
expense of others? Should we loyally support a government which
flogs and oppresses the peasants, in order that our children should
live happily and securely as we have done? Are wives jealous
because society permits sexual licence to men but not to
women? As with characters, so with such questions. We can
puzzle over them if we want to: Tolstoy does not propose to
do so—not here, not now. He suspends his remorseless analysis,
holding it over our heads as he holds it over the heads of his
dramatis personae. Nothing is more striking about the conclusion
than Tolstoy's restraint; it contrasts immensely effectively with
the earlier copiousness of proclaimed fact and detailed analysis.

War and Peace, we finally see, is an 'open' novel in a carefully
limited sense. Rigorously it excludes all real and tormenting
problems which might be solved by actions and events other
than those of growing up, growing old, marrying and dying.
Or rather it does not exclude them so much as change their
nature. Soluble problems can be allowed in, but on the same
footing as insoluble ones. Arakcheev's military settlements,
with all their oppression and injustice, are contained by the
novel's vision on the same terms as dying in childbirth or in war,
or growing old like Bolkonsky and Countess Rostov. Such
things must not only be put up with: they are the point of living.

8. *Pierre*

" 'In our days,' continued Vera—mentioning 'our days' as
people of limited intelligence are fond of doing, imagining they

have discovered and appraised the peculiarities of 'our days' and that human characteristics change with the times . . .' " Vera Rostov (or Vera Berg as she has just become), that lady of limited intelligence, is dismissed for expressing this view, but as we have seen, Tolstoy was not at all above making use of it. As usual, he has things both ways. In asserting that "In those days also people loved, envied, sought truth and virtue, and were carried away by passion"—he is also saying that in the past everything is achieved and completed. They *did* the things which we are in the process of doing, or planning to do, and hence everything they did has the appearance of spontaneity, of something inevitable but unwilled. This is the sense in which the old times were better than the new. Our fathers gambled and womanised spontaneously because we can only see that they *did* it, whereas in ourselves we feel the motives, the scruples and the hesitations. And as with their loves, so with their battles. We can see that those battles took place, not as they were intended by this or that individual, but in accordance with the laws of power, of inertia, and of necessity.

Characters are indeed the same in the past as today, but the problems of willing and acting which distract us have vanished from the past, so that in contemplating it we can keep what Schopenhauer called "the sabbath of the penal servitude of willing". But at the end of *War and Peace* the past very nearly becomes the present. Its conclusion is moving and unique, because we feel as if the problems that Tolstoy was to wrestle with for the rest of his life are just about to break in. Tolstoy and ourselves are like conductor and orchestra at a sublime concert, for whom urgent messages and queries are being held over until the final movement reaches its close.

All's well that ends well, and the period culminating in 1812 is the perfect period for Tolstoy, because it both happened as it had to happen and turned out as it should. His first idea was a book about the Decembrists, but the logic of his own psychological and artistic needs forced him back into the period which—as he says, perhaps a little disingenuously—he felt he must first be master of in order to understand them. The Decembrists were a society of intellectual officers and gentlemen, many of them in the Guards, who had brought back from

Russia's victorious campaign in Europe the new ideal of political and social enlightenment. Pushkin was one of their friends, and always said he would have taken part in their attempted *coup d'état* had he been in Petersburg at the time. As it was, they failed in their bid to secure the accession of Alexander I's brother, Constantine, together with a constitution for Russia (the soldiers whom they ordered to cheer for 'Constantine and Constitution' supposed they were cheering the new Tsar and his wife— a touch that might come out of a Shakespeare history play) and most of them were executed by Nicholas I or exiled to Siberia.

Pierre was to have joined them, and then to have returned to Russia after prolonged Siberian exile about the time that Tolstoy was writing. In order to realise such a version of Pierre, Tolstoy tells us, "I had to carry myself back to his youth, and his youth coincided with Russia's glorious period of 1812". The point of this version of Pierre seems to have been that he was a *survival*, a grand old man from the days when liberal views in an aristocrat really meant something, and were not just a fashionable conjunction, and Tolstoy may have intended, according to his Russian biographer and critic Eykhenbaum, to use this Pierre as a stick to beat the materialists and political theorists of his own time. To call in a piece of living history to discredit the contemporary scene is a peculiarly Tolstoyan notion, which would go with his dislike of change and his patriarchal conservatism. But having gone back to Pierre's youth, Tolstoy ended up with the kind of man whom it is hard to imagine becoming a Decembrist. By appealing so compellingly to history Tolstoy destroyed his own scheme for the future old Decembrist, for he created a historical world too complete, and too well insulated for one of its denizens to survive into his own day.

Once back to 1812 his purpose may have changed, and required a removal further back still, to the débâcle of 1805.

> I felt ashamed to write about our triumph in the struggle with Bonapartist France without having described our failures and our shame. Who has not experienced that secret but unpleasant feeling of shamefacedness and mistrust when reading about the war of 1812? . . .
>
> And so having gone back from 1856 to 1805, I now intend to lead not one but many heroes and heroines of mine through the historical

events of 1805, 1807, 1812, 1825 [the Decembrist plot] and 1856
[end of the Crimean War]. I do not foresee in any one of these
periods a *dénouement* in the relations between these people. However
much I tried to think up a novel-like plot and *dénouement* I was convinced that it was not within my means, and I decided in describing
these people to bow to my own practices and my own powers.

This extract from a cancelled preface raises some fascinating
speculations. First, it shows how much more of a novel *War and
Peace* turned out to be than Tolstoy originally intended, for the
final version has a *dénouement*, and the relations between its
characters *are* resolved. In finally deciding to seal off for himself
a period of history, Tolstoy also sealed off—whether he wanted
and intended to or not—a framework for a novel. If he had
carried out his intention of continuing the work to his own time
we should have lost that remarkable and ambiguous resolution
that makes the end of *War and Peace* so memorable, and we
should inevitably have lost its unique impression of achievement,
which depends on ending before history becomes politics and
the timeless the contemporary.[1]

Tolstoy's altered purpose may have been to rewrite the
history of the past, rather than to use it to satirise the trends of
the present. He would rewrite the popular version of 1812 and
displace the official patriotic story with his own. In the process
it became a definitive vision of what *all* wars and upheavals are
really like, and as they are never seen to be like afterwards when
they are transformed to suit patriotic wish-fulfilment. Had
Tolstoy continued to give his own account of the Crimean
struggle—instead of using his personal experience of it to
generalise about the nature of *all* wars—this generalising
power would have been inevitably lost. Even Tolstoy could not
have 'made up' one war, and then gone on to give an eye-witness
account of another: the hiatus between two modes of composition could never have been joined. As it was, he returned to
1805, no doubt, in order to create a historical parallel in the
Austerlitz fiasco for the Crimean one. 'How Russian Soldiers

[1] This *achieved* aspect of *War and Peace*, to which Tolstoy finally committed
himself, fascinated the Russian formalist critic Eykhenbaum, for whom the
greatest art was "linked with death, not life". Compare in England the not
dissimilar theories of T. E. Hulme and Wyndham Lewis.

Die' (the title of one of his Sevastopol documentaries) when there is neither planning nor leadership, would be the same in both cases, and equally heroic. There would also be the same opportunities for xenophobia and satire on military theorists and armchair patriots who think that our side always wins. ("We gave Napoleon I a beating in 1812 and Napoleon III gave us a beating in 1856," observes Tolstoy sarcastically in one of the three abortive chapters of the Decembrist novel.)

We can only be grateful that the 'non-novel' was not allowed to take the extreme course it would have done had Tolstoy persisted in his plan of *The Decembrists* instead of isolating his subject in the past and "thinking up a novel-like plot and dénouement". *The Decembrists* would have been totally different in *kind* from *War and Peace*: it would have belonged to the same order of composition as *Childhood*, *The Cossacks*, and the *Sevastopol Sketches*. What those works have in common is precisely the inability to generalise: they are indifferent to universality. Of course we recognise in them the wonderful authenticity of what Tolstoy says and feels, and our response is often "how amazing that he knows that—now he's said it, I see that I feel just the same". But this is a very different thing from the generalising power—almost deliberately the opposite in fact. To take one example—that of war—the force and point of the Sevastopol accounts, and of the action in *The Raid* and *The Cossacks*, lies in their happening to a particular individual in a particular battle. Though we see Austerlitz, and the terrible Breughel-like panorama of the Augesd dam, partly through Prince Andrew's eyes, and the Cossack raid on the French rearguard through those of Petya, these eye-witnesses are not arbiters and owners of the scene—it has become universalised and depersonalised.

The significant thing is that Tolstoy only achieves this universalisation when he comes to terms with and makes use of the artifice of plot. The generalising power goes hand in hand with the need to *invent*. However laborious and unnatural he may have found it, when Tolstoy brings himself to invent all things are added to him. Artificiality is the key to real size: without it, he might always have remained a writer on a small scale. As he begins to invent a whole giant pattern of correspondences begins to declare itself, and the work to achieve unity. When he has invented the family of the Rostovs, with their involuntary 'inside' life and their *understanding*, this family begins insensibly to correspond to the Russians in their confrontation with the French, the non-family, the outsiders who do not understand. Nations are like families; ours is a good one and theirs—because it is not ours—a bad one. This is a crude way of describing the correspondence process, but it certainly takes place, linking national and family destiny together. Vera and Berg are virtually foreigners, on the other side, and Berg's boastfulness and his talk about the "holy struggle of Russia", etc., shows this, much as Sonya's conscious readiness for "love and self-sacrifice" shows that she is not really one of the family. Patriotism, like family affection, is not an affair of statements and intentions. Those who understand don't talk about it.

This national and family line-up made it more than ever unlikely that Tolstoy could succeed in writing about the Decembrists, or in making Pierre one of them. For the Decembrists not only "talked about it", and put their ideas and ideals in abstract form, but most of those ideas and ideals came from revolutionary France. Our Pierre capitulates as completely as Nicholas to the Russian pattern of fate and fulfilment, and to the benevolent matriarchal rule which permits a man his freedom in the world of intellect and ideas provided these do not upset the social and family life.[1] Nicholas is in Paris with the Russian army of occupation when the news of the old count's death arrives, and although he is next in line for the colonelcy he gives up his commission and returns home at once. First things first. Yet Tolstoy knew well that the officers who went to France, two of whom, Pestel and Küchelbecker, were to become leading Decembrist spirits, could hardly help comparing on their return the free European peasant with his Russian brother. The Russian

[1] The Soviet critic V. Ermilov takes for granted that Natasha would have accompanied Pierre to Siberia in *The Decembrists* as his devoted help-mate. So indeed she might, if she ever allowed the situation to get so out of hand, but it is as hard to imagine her letting Pierre bring such a fate upon the family as it is to imagine the Countess Tolstoy allowing her husband to join an actively subversive movement. Natasha might have made Pierre's life in Siberia a hell! Tolstoy at the end of *War and Peace* did not know what Natasha was capable of, any more than he knew what his own wife was capable of.

had helped to free Europe yet was in chains at home, and it was Europe who showed him this and showed him, too, the kind of institutions that should replace his own. How can the great celebrant of the Russian family and nation admit all this? And he would have to admit if it he had gone on to include the Decembrists in the book. In a tentative draft written with this in mind, he saved Andrew, and sent him with Nicholas—*after* their marriages—off to the army in Paris together. But in the final version Andrew is dead and Pierre married, so all risk is over, and France and French influence is finally separated from the tranquillity of the Russian family.

Tolstoy would have heartily agreed with what Küchelbecker had written about the Russian people.

> When I look at the brilliant qualities with which God has gifted the Russian people, first in the world for glory and power; for its strong melodious language which has not its like in Europe; for the cordiality, kind-heartedness and quickness of mind that are peculiar to it above all others, it grieves me to think that all this is crushed, withering, and perhaps dying out without bearing any fruit in the moral world.[1]

But *War and Peace* might almost have been written to show that it was not crushed or withering, that the moral fruit was already there without any need for the tree to be fertilised from abroad, ripening tranquilly on the estates of the good Russian nobility, who were right because they were happy, and in the hearts of peasants like Karataev, who were happy because they were good. If Russia required general ideas they were not those of militant republicanism but those of Voltaire and the eighteenth-century rationalists, of "reason, that is, good", ideas that were compatible with the benevolent patriarchalism of Nicholas Rostov and of old Bolkonsky, whose life on his estate is strangely reminiscent of that of Voltaire at Ferney.

In spite of Pierre's European past and liberal, questioning outlook, Tolstoy binds him to the Russian family by one vitally important characteristic—his absurdity and his capacity for self-derision. Only those who *understand* have a real sense of humour (Sonya obviously has none). The Masons had close contacts

[1] Quoted in Bernard Pares, *A History of Russia.*

with the Decembrists, and we remember how at the Masonic induction "a childlike smile of embarrassment, doubt, and self-derision appeared on Pierre's face against his will". It is not the quality of a zealous reformer or political fanatic. We cannot imagine any self-derision in Speransky, nor for that matter in Prince Andrew, who fears ridicule "more than anything else in the world". He and Pierre are in some ways like Don Quixote and Sancho Panza, and taken together they can no more 'do anything' about Russia than could the famous pair about Spain. Prince Andrew, moreover, is created for death and Pierre for life, and the only issue of Prince Andrew is his son, little Nicholas, who so much admires Pierre, and who is left at the end of the book as the one lifeline to the reforming future.

Dessalles slept propped up on four pillows, and his Roman nose emitted sounds of rhythmic snoring. Little Nicholas, who had just waked up in a cold perspiration, sat up in bed and gazed before him with wide-open eyes. He had awoken from a terrible dream. He had dreamt that he and Uncle Pierre, wearing helmets such as were depicted in his Plutarch, were leading a huge army. The army was made up of white slanting lines that filled the air like the cobwebs that float about in autumn, and which Dessalles called *les fils de la Vierge*. In front was Glory, which was similar to those threads but rather thicker. He and Pierre were borne along lightly and joyously, nearer and nearer to their goal. Suddenly the threads that moved them began to slacken and become entangled and it became difficult to move. And Uncle Nicholas stood before them in a stern and threatening attitude.

"Have you done this?" he said, pointing to some broken sealing-wax and pens. "I loved you, but I have orders from Arakcheev and will kill the first of you who moves forward." Little Nicholas turned to look at Pierre, but Pierre was no longer there. In his place was his father—Prince Andrew—and his father had neither shape nor form, but he existed, and when little Nicholas perceived him he grew faint with love: he felt himself powerless, limp, and formless. His father caressed and pitied him. But Uncle Nicholas came nearer and nearer to them. Terror seized young Nicholas, and he awoke.

"My father!" he thought. (Though there were two good portraits of Prince Andrew in the house, Nicholas never imagined him in human form.) "My father has been with me and caressed me. He approved of me and of Uncle Pierre. Whatever he may tell me, I will do it. Mucius Scaevola burnt his hand. Why should not the same sort of thing happen to me? I know they want me to learn. And I will learn. But some day I shall have finished learning, and then I will do something. I only pray God that something may happen to me such as happened to Plutarch's men, and I will act as they did. I will do better. Every one shall know me, love me, and be delighted with me." And suddenly his bosom heaved with sobs and he began to cry.

"Are you ill?" he heard Dessalles's voice asking.

"No," answered Nicholas, and lay back on his pillow.

"He is good and kind and I am fond of him!" he thought of Dessalles. "But Uncle Pierre! Oh, what a wonderful man he is! And my father? Oh, father, father! Yes, I will do something with which even *he* would be satisfied. . . ."

The marvellous concluding passage, shot through with humour and with Tolstoy's peculiar apprehension of childhood, is worth quoting in full to show how Pierre's image in the young mind is essentially childish, familial, absurd, but true and individual, whereas Andrew, though in the dream he replaces him, is not imagined by little Nicholas in human form. The implications of the passage are many, but its humour underlies them all, and with its humour its acceptance of abstractions—God, aspiration, glory—only through the security and atmosphere of the family, which is protected, even when he seems menacing, by Uncle Nicholas.

"Fearless self-derision" is for Tolstoy the great familial Russian quality, which gives them a kind of helpless superiority over all foreigners. It is quite compatible with—is indeed a part of—*samodovolnost*, self-assurance. Foreigners like Berg and Captain Ramballe of course do not have it and are ludicrous or touching in their self-importance and complacency. They are merely *borné*. But even minor characters like the frivolous Bilibin possess it, as does the envoy Balashev. When the French ask him about the roads to Moscow he tells them that there is "the one by Poltava, which Charles XII took", and is congratulating himself on the aptness of this *mot* when he becomes aware that it has fallen flat—the French (being French) do not get the point of the reference. Tolstoy must have been the first writer to exploit the notion—since grown dear to us—that the best way of establishing a moral superiority over an enemy is to deny him a sense of humour, and one of the subtlest ways of suggesting this is to show a member of your own side 'flushed with pleasure' at the aptness of a jest, and then crestfallen at its non-reception.

Pierre's 'dynamic absurdity', if we can call it that to distinguish it from the merely passive absurdity of foreigners and outsiders, has an important bearing on his role as a questioner, a seeker of reality. Tolstoy clearly wanted him to be more of a Russian Candide than one of Goethe's *Bildungsroman* heroes, but his absurdity has not had a universal appeal (D. H. Lawrence, whose heroes notably lack any touch of intended absurdity though they are sometimes unintentionally comic, referred to him disparagingly as "that porpoise of a Pierre"). Though he has had no childhood of his own in the book he acquires his vitality in relation to childhood. The young Rostovs, and especially Natasha, accept him at once as one of themselves. He is incapable of adult hypocrisy and has the child's power of penetrating adult falsity (Masonry is a kind of false adult game which first appeals to his aspirations towards goodness but which he cannot avoid seeing through). But his most significant connection with childhood is his capacity for living partly in a make-believe world.

> "England is done for," said he, scowling and pointing his finger at some one unseen. "Mr Pitt, as a traitor to the nation and to the rights of man, is sentenced to . . ." But before Pierre—who at that moment imagined himself to be Napoleon in person and to have just effected the dangerous crossing of the Straits of Dover and captured London—could pronounce Pitt's sentence, he saw a well-built and handsome young officer entering his room.

Equally delightful is his laborious fudging of the cryptogram to obtain the solution that 'L'Russe Besuhof' is the destined assassin of Napoleon, and his Walter Mitty style pantomime of how he will perform it.

> "It is not I but the hand of providence that punishes thee! Well then, take me, execute me," he went on, speaking to himself and bowing his head with a sad but firm expression.

Not only the charm but the goodness of Pierre—his stature

in the book as a part of the Tolstoyan consciousness—comes from the fact that this world of make-believe is *not* the world of adult obsession, the world in which Raskolnikov commits murder, and in which real political assassins (Pierre is so clearly not one) seek out their victims. Pierre is partly a scapegoat for the book's solipsism, which is the solipsism of childhood, and an ironic comment on it. It may also be that Tolstoy here intends an ironic comment on the individual who thinks he can change the course of history, but in that case he was on weaker ground, for assassinations can do this: during the writing of *War and Peace* Alexander II was assassinated and his liberalising measures suspended, and four years after Tolstoy's death another assassination began the Great War.

Had Pierre found Napoleon, who in fact was sitting safely in the Kremlin, would he have tried to kill him? No, says Tolstoy.

> ... He was tortured—as those are who obstinately undertake a task that is impossible for them not because of its difficulty but because of its incompatibility with their natures—by the fear of weakening at the decisive moment and so losing his self-esteem.

Pierre is unable to shut out the external world as a man with one idea has to do. It comes crowding in on him in all its Tolstoyan detail—Captain Ramballe; the servants and the French laughing at their mutual incomprehensibility; the fire "like golden fish-scales creeping along the walls"; the French soldier with the spot on his cheek saying "we must be human, you know"; the child Pierre rescues, "unattractively like its mother", which he sees alternately as "pathetically innocent" and as "a nasty little animal". All this pressure of life forces itself upon Pierre, and the vividness of his apprehension of it is, as with children, of the same order as his own vivid powers of make-believe. It is hard to imagine anyone but Tolstoy naturalising so effectively what seems such a crude little moral sequence: Pierre goes out to kill Napoleon and instead saves a child. The self-esteem that would not have been sufficient to have carried him through a task incompatible with his nature makes him want to save the child, and joins with the physical excitement ("he felt bright, adroit, and resolute") produced by the fire and the confusion.

This state of physical satisfaction remains with Pierre

throughout his experiences as a prisoner, and makes that time seem so memorable to him ever after.

> Every time he looked at his bare feet a smile of animated self-satisfaction flitted across his face. The sight of them reminded him of all he had experienced and learned during these weeks, and this recollection was pleasant to him.[1]

Everything—even the lice—pleases him, as it pleases the cheerful dog who has attached itself to them, whose furry tail "stands up round and firm as a plume". The appearance and conversation of Karataev himself are an aspect of this pleasure, the summation of those "irrecoverable, strong, joyful sensations". Separated from Hélène and the adult demoralisation of sex and society, Pierre is given back his childhood again, as the happy Nicholas can always re-enter "that world of home and childhood which had no meaning for anyone else but which gave him some of his best moments". And this rebirth is for Pierre a preparation for that happy married life which is a repetition of childhood by other means.

Yet Tolstoy is rather too determined, throughout Pierre's captivity, to persuade us of its meaning—its meaning for all of us as well as Pierre. In spite of, or perhaps because of, Tolstoy's extreme honesty there is something not quite right about the episode. This comes out if we compare it with Petya's idyll and death among the partisans, which follows it and is perfect. It is not Karataev's fault. Tolstoy is careful to emphasise that Karataev means little to Pierre at the time, except as an extension of his physical well-being: it is only afterwards that Pierre remembers him as someone saintly and symbolic. Afterwards Pierre begins to attribute a spiritual significance to something which at the time was purely physical. It is in Pierre's self-satisfaction and self-preoccupation at the time that Tolstoy's honesty becomes almost disconcerting. After all, many of the prisoners, including Karataev, die on the march, but these sad

---

[1] Pierre's feet become almost a symbol of the way in which he succeeds during these weeks in absorbing his surroundings and his body into the same harmony. On the march "he glanced occasionally at the familiar crowd around him, and then again at his feet. *The former and the latter were alike familiar and his own*" [my italics].

events join with the hardships in making Pierre feel better than ever. This is extremely human and convincing; what is not so convincing is the spiritual significance that Pierre, and Tolstoy, appear to extract from it. It is strange that Pierre's spiritual regeneration, through suffering and contact with his fellow men, should be the most satisfied and solipsistic episode in the entire book.

In general, of course, Tolstoy is inclined to take physical contentment as a sign of spiritual advancement—it is the same with Levin after his day with the mowers. And perhaps it is such a sign? But while the physical side is undoubted, and superbly conveyed, the spiritual claim is arbitrary and unproven —unproven by art. There is a definite discrepancy between what Tolstoy's art demonstrates to be true, and what he himself asserts to be true. Yet while the mowing sequence suffers both from Tolstoy's assertiveness and from his own presence as Levin, Pierre's time as a prisoner does not. For it is told by the 'peepshow' method, alternating with the illness of Andrew and accounts of the military situation, and culminating in the dramatic collision of two sequences—those of Petya and Pierre —and it shows how immensely successful that method is in *War and Peace*. It bears a remarkable resemblance to the historical technique which Shakespeare perfected in the later English histories and the Roman plays, and it is tempting to wonder whether this resemblance is coincidental. There is no evidence for direct influence, but Pushkin copied the Shakespearean technique closely in *Boris Godunov*, and though he thought as little of that play as he did of Shakespeare, Tolstoy might well have learned from it.

Thanks very largely to this method Pierre does remain a dramatic figure—that is the important thing. He never becomes a mere vehicle for Tolstoyan pronouncement. This appears from his famous meditation in the night bivouac.

> High up in the light sky hung the full moon. Forests and fields beyond the camp, unseen before, were now visible in the distance. And farther still, beyond those forests and fields, the bright, oscillating, limitless distance lured one to itself. Pierre glanced up at the sky and the twinkling stars in its far-away depths. "And all that is me, all that is within me, and it is all I!" thought Pierre.

"And they caught all that and put it into a shed boarded up with planks!" He smiled, and went and lay down to sleep beside his companions.

The second sentence, with its steady but unobtrusive human significance, shows Tolstoy's descriptive art at its best. But the distance between Tolstoy and Pierre, their enduring though precarious dramatic relation, comes in the contrast between this description and Pierre's self-gratified and very human comment —borrowed, incidentally, from Schopenhauer. All the shocks Pierre has received are tonic and self-confirming—his remark is that of a thoroughly satisfied man. Since satisfaction in *War and Peace* rests on physical equilibrium and contentment it is bound to be so. The physically contented Pierre is acting the part of the mentally tranquil philosopher, and Tolstoy is watching him do so: Pierre's reflection is not Tolstoy's.

Tolstoy is profoundly aware how the acting of a role, or finding ourselves—as Pierre does—in a stimulating and strange new role, both confirm us in our *samodovolnost*. Being ourselves is our best response to crisis. When her labour pains begin the Little Princess "wrings her hands with some affectation". What seems affectation to the observer has become her instinctive response. Even in his own state of fear and exhaustion, it seems to Nicholas on the field of Austerlitz that the groans of the wounded have a *feigned* sound (Tolstoy first noted the point in his *Sevastopol Sketches*). Even Prince Vasili, after acting the appropriate feelings at the death-bed of old Count Bezukhov ("if you do not understand these sentiments," he seemed to be saying, "so much the worse for you") finds, as he reflects that he is an old man and will soon die too, that he has them in fact. Anna Scherer overacts her own defect because she has found that it satisfies other people's expectation of her.

To be an enthusiast had become her social vocation and, sometimes even when she did not feel like it, she became enthusiastic in order not to disappoint the expectations of those who knew her. The subdued smile which, though it did not suit her faded features, always played round her lips, expressed, as in a spoilt child, a continual consciousness of her charming defect, which she neither wished, nor could, nor considered it necessary, to correct.

Prince Andrew can never be at home in the world of *War and Peace* because he has no appreciation of this equivocal harmony of life. When his wife faints at their leave-taking he does not see as we do (or think we do, for Tolstoy makes no comment) that it is not so much a pantomime of grief as a way of escaping from him at this trying moment. Both her faint and his reaction to it—"now go through your performance"—reveal their total lack of intimacy, and their different ways of showing their awareness of this lack.

Tolstoy is unrivalled in perceiving how people, without ceasing to be themselves, act a new part in a new situation; how they find, or reveal to others, that it is always a change to be oneself. This goes with his sense of how family resemblances, long unapparent, suddenly declare themselves in altered and unexpected forms. It is clear that Hélène will resemble her father, and even that the emotional life of Natasha repeats in its deeper and more vigorously female way the spontaneous and endearing emotionalism of hers: he and she *understand* that it is impossible to remove all their belongings from Moscow when there are wounded who might go in the carts. Vera takes after her mother—as appears all the more clearly from the fact that her mother wonders indignantly where her daughter's nature comes from—one does not recognise one's own traits exaggerated and simplified in one's offspring. We never know old Prince Bezukhov, but we apprehend him and his relation to Pierre in the strange, self-deprecating smile he gives him on his death-bed, and his legendary temper in Pierre's sudden delight in violence. Old Prince Bolkonsky we know very well indeed, and the relation between him and his son Andrew is as rich in illumination as that between the more famous 'fathers and sons' of Russian fiction, Turgenev's Bazarovs and the pair of Verkhovenskys in Dostoevsky's *Devils*. Turgenev and Dostoevsky see the relation, and the alienation, as a phenomenon of contemporary society: Tolstoy's seems true to its time but is also a timeless affair, and more profoundly familial. Little in the relation of the Bazarovs or the Verkhovenskys indicates they are physically fathers and sons—it is the *zeitgeist* of two epochs that separates them. But though Andrew's outlook is so different from his father's, the pair are held by the affection and exasperation which comes from recognising themselves in each other. They cannot escape that bond. Andrew is "both pleased and displeased" that his father has understood the nature of his marriage to the Little Princess; we sense that the father's marriage may have gone much the same way, and for the same reasons.

The Bolkonskys are as subtly characterised in the metaphors and properties of their lives as in their relationship to each other. It is Andrew who sees an image of himself in the oak-tree's spring renewal—Pierre has too much self-derision to apply to himself so poetic a metaphor, and it would certainly never have occurred to Nicholas to do so. The life of all the Bolkonskys is filled with images of search. Princess Mary wishes to go on a pilgrimage with "God's Folk"; Andrew's quest is typically double—the rational part of him seeks goodness and truth, the irrational longs for that confrontation with Kuragin in which his honour shall be avenged. But the most haunting image of search is their father's restlessness in the enchanted arrest of life at Bald Hills, where every night he has his camp-bed set up in a different room.

Other ties beside those of blood suggest themselves as the book goes on, and the most significant of these muted affinities is that between Pierre and Petya. The rescue of the one and the death of the other coincide, and if a work like *War and Peace* can be said to have a climax it comes here. We never have a feeling of more assured imaginative power, as if Tolstoy's obstinate awareness of plurality had at last been reconciled with his struggle for the One. And this climax is repeated in the next chapter—a feat in itself of great virtuosity—which ends at the same moment of Pierre's liberation.

Tolstoy alternates the heightened and totally subjective vision of the pair with an extreme objectivity of statement, perhaps even consciously modelling the whole passage on a fugue.

> Petya was as musical as Natasha and more so than Nicholas, but had never learnt music or thought about it, and so the melody that came unexpectedly to his mind seemed to him particularly fresh and attractive. . . . And what was played was a fugue—though Petya had not the least conception of what a fugue is.

In ecstasy Petya listens to and controls the orchestra which seems to be playing in his dream, and in which the horses neighing and the sound of his sabre being sharpened seem to mingle in the harmony without disturbing it. At the same moment Pierre is also dreaming.

Suddenly he saw vividly before him a long-forgotten, kindly old man who had given him geography lessons in Switzerland. "Wait a bit," said the old man, and showed Pierre a globe. This globe was alive—a vibrating ball without fixed dimensions. Its whole surface consisted of drops closely pressed together, and all these drops moved and changed places, sometimes several of them merging into one, sometimes one dividing into many. Each drop tried to spread out and occupy as much space as possible, but others, striving to do the same, compressed it, sometimes destroyed it, and sometimes merged with it.

"That is life," said the old teacher.

"How simple and clear it is," thought Pierre. "How is it I did not know it before?"

"God is in the midst, and each drop tries to expand so as to reflect Him to the greatest extent. And it grows, merges, disappears from the surface, sinks to the depths and again emerges. There now, Karataev has spread out and disappeared. Do you understand, my child?" said the teacher.

"Do you understand, damn you?" shouted a voice, and Pierre woke up.

He lifted himself and sat up. A Frenchman who had just pushed a Russian soldier away was squatting by the fire engaged in roasting a piece of meat stuck on a ramrod. His sleeves were rolled up and his sinewy, hairy, red hands with their short fingers deftly turned the ramrod.

Half-asleep, he sees Karataev's dog, and is on the point of realising that Karataev has been shot—

—but just at that instant, he knew not why, the recollection came to his mind of a summer evening he had spent with a beautiful Polish lady on the veranda of his house in Kiev. And without linking up the events of the day or drawing a conclusion from them, Pierre closed his eyes, seeing a vision of the country in summertime mingled with memories of bathing and of the liquid, vibrating globe, and he sank into water so that it closed over his head.

If anything could convince us that "there is nothing terrible" it would be the imagination and art of these two chapters. The enduring human wish to make sense, to create harmony, to see life as "simple and clear", and to absorb it entire into one's consciousness,—the wish that inspires Pierre's and Petya's dream visions and Karataev's tale of the merchant—seems in total accord here with mere biology, reflex, meaningless incident and random process; the animal instinct that makes the healthy Pierre avoid and "not think about" the dying Karataev "when he smelt the smell coming from him"; that animates the cheerful dog who grows sleek on "the flesh of different animals, men and horses" and who "ran merrily along the road, sometimes in proof of its agility and self-satisfaction lifting one hind leg and hopping along on three"; that makes the Cossacks realise what has happened when at Petya's death they saw that "his legs and arms jerked rapidly though his head was quite motionless". There is neither relish nor emphasis in all these facts and visions, as there might be in a story or slighter work, even one of Tolstoy's. They merge into the Homeric narrative without any trace of selection or presentation, and as a climax to the great sustained flight of the book they can do no wrong. They are War and Peace, *Voina i Mir*, the opposing and yet harmonising principles on which the book is founded. As well as peace, *Mir* in Russian means both universe and community. The association of the two words has wider and more metaphysical implications than can be rendered in English, and in these two chapters their association is revealed in its most intimate and most far-reaching form.

9. Family and System

We return to a more mundane confrontation. What are the elements in the antagonism, as Tolstoy sees it, between French and Russians? We have already seen that the Russians constitute a *family*: the French, by contrast, represent a system—the terrible *it* which Pierre becomes aware of when the Frenchmen whom he thinks he has got to know during his captivity are suddenly revealed as automata, controlled by some impersonal force which is pressing him towards destruction, a force which overrides humanity. When Pierre is taken before Davout his fantasy of killing Napoleon and his excitement at being *incognito* in occupied Moscow have evaporated: he is very frightened.

> They were now leading him somewhere with unhesitating assurance on their faces that he and all the other prisoners were exactly the ones they wanted and that they were being taken to the proper place. Pierre felt himself to be an insignificant chip fallen among the wheels of a machine whose action he did not understand but which was working well.

Davout accuses Pierre of being a Russian spy, and as he turns away Pierre breaks down completely.

> "No. Monseigneur," he said, suddenly remembering that Davout was a Duke. "No, Monseigneur, you cannot have known me. I am a militia officer and have not quitted Moscow."
>
> "Your name?" asked Davout.
>
> "Bezukhov."
>
> "What proof have I that you are not lying?"
>
> "Monseigneur!" exclaimed Pierre not in an offended but in a pleading voice.
>
> Davout looked up and gazed intently at him. For some seconds they looked at one another, and that look saved Pierre. Apart from conditions of war and law, that look established human relations between the two men. At that moment an immense number of things passed dimly through both their minds, and they realized that they were both children of humanity and were brothers.

It sounds well, in fact it sounds French, but can Tolstoy really believe it? Surely the pair do not discover in that look that they are brothers and children of humanity, but that they belong to the same class? By remembering that Davout is a duke, and by giving his own real name, Pierre is able to establish a *human* relation with him. This is only in effect ironic. We endorse the ideal of humanity when we feel physically akin to the person we are dealing with. And in terms of history the class kinship is strictly accurate, not only in general but also in particular, for a Russian gentleman called Perovsky recorded in his memoirs, which were known to Tolstoy, his actual interrogation by Davout.

Pierre is doubly fortunate. He is physically preserved by meeting a member of his own class, and restored spiritually by his encounter with a peasant. Karataev's difference from Pierre, which is so comforting and rehabilitating, might in a different context and epoch—say that of a novel about the revolution—have had just the opposite effect. The peasant as interrogator would be then the appalling figure, because there could be no communicating with him. Similarly, it would then be a consolation to meet in prison a member of one's own class. It is not in fact the humanity in Davout and in Karataev that saves and comforts Pierre: it is the reflexes and attributes of their class and station.

There is nothing devious and incoherent, it seems to me, in these instances of what Shestov would call the *mensonge* of the work. Tolstoy does not conceal the fact that the confrontation between the human and the non-human can also be seen in terms of class against the system. To be human is to be a representative of one's class; to be non-human is to be an instrument of the system. This deeply conservative point of view both underlies and strengthens the Rousseauism of the imprisonment sequence. The idea of brotherhood can be simply and easily stated by Tolstoy; the conservatism that goes with it is more imponderably conveyed. In the cancelled Preface to *1805* he had anticipated the objection that "in my work the only people who act are princes speaking and writing French, counts and so on—as if the whole of the Russian life of the time centred on these people".

> I agree that this is untrue and illiberal, and I can give only one answer—an irrefutable one. The lives of officials, merchants, theological students and peasants do not interest me and are only half comprehensible to me; the lives of the aristocrats of that time, thanks to the documents of that time, and other reasons, are comprehensible, interesting, and dear to me.

In the final version of *War and Peace* the emphasis has of course changed. Honest and defiant conservatism has given place to a much less open and ingenuous approach. Peasants and soldiers, as well as aristocrats, are deeply interesting to Tolstoy, though how far they are understood is another matter. The intermediate classes are still almost unrepresented, but the peasant is as necessary to victory and salvation as the aristocrat and military leader. These classes, which are natural and human, destroyed the Napoleonic military system, which was not. And, being natural, the Russian classes achieved this not through any conscious or concerted action but simply by being what they were.

Their communal action comes under the heading of what Tolstoy calls "swarm life". Though it is ordered by the Governor, Rostopchin, the killing of the alleged traitor Vereschagin is not, like the French executions, the system at work but the swarm at work—the victim is killed as bees ball one of their number to death. At the meeting of notables which Pierre attends, communication and agreement is achieved not by argument and command but by the mass emotion typified by old Count Rostov "who agreed with whatever speech he had just heard" and "understood everything in his own way". Pierre forgoes his own attempts at reason and distinction in the general enthusiasm (one cannot call it the general will) and, like Petya and Nicholas when they see the Tsar, is carried away, is "ready to go to all lengths and to sacrifice everything". Tarutino, the unnecessary battle, with its mass of unnecessary orders, is 'won' by some Cossacks who see it as a chance of plundering horses and horse-gear, the properties of their way of life. Kutuzov's great strength is to understand this Russian swarm life and to use it to get the French out of Russia with the minimum of military action and loss.

Class, then, is insensibly associated by Tolstoy with swarm life, and in contrast with *the system* both receive praise. Tolstoy implies a further contrast between ancient, mellowed class— the way of life of the Rostovs and Bolkonskys—and the jumped-up aristocracy of Petersburg—Scherers, Kuragins, etc. Though this may be a desideratum for Tolstoy it was hardly a fact. Few indeed of the old Russian boyar families had survived Ivan the Terrible and his successors. The new aristocracy created by Peter the Great had become *the* aristocracy, as Pushkin ironically notes in one of his poems, and Tolstoy had little cause to be proud of his ancestor the diplomat who had served Peter. Peter's class system, with its artificial fourteen divisions, was as unnatural as anything could be, and could hardly sustain Tolstoy's idealistic approval. But this brings us back to our starting-point, that only the year 1812 will serve for the ideal historic vision. In that year all paradoxes can be resolved and all uncomfortable facts transcended.

What transcends them above all is the grand inconsistency which is a part of the conservative outlook. The conservative (or so Tolstoy implies) is capable of 'self-derision' in a way that the reformers and new men are not. And Tolstoy himself certainly combines his deep affection for everything that is natural, incoherent, instinctive and *absurd*, with his piercing penetration, his Gallic love of distinction and irony, his ability to remain outside. At the meeting of the notables, he is at one with them in the flesh while at the same time observing ironically how amazed and disconcerted they are, when it is over, at their own emotion and what it has led them to promise. All forms of inconsistency, whether in men or institutions, make a deep appeal to him. Pierre's sense of incongruity makes him never at ease among the Masons. Speransky's laughter, and the party tricks of his coterie, are unpleasant because they are merely a continuation of his solemn official life, not a true renunciation of it.

When the Rostovs, with characteristic tardiness and ineffi-ciency, are evacuating their Moscow house, their son-in-law Berg shows a comic consistency that is almost sublime—all he can think about is the wonderful chance of buying for a song the chiffonier that he and his wife Vera have always wanted for their Petersburg flat. And yet the contrast between him and the Rostovs is not such a simple one. When the Rostovs give up some of their carts for the wounded it is not so much 'human feeling' that triumphs as the behaviour ideally to be expected of a certain class, and even that is equivocally presented. "The club is closed and the police are leaving!"—the count's cry echoes down the century and might have been uttered by his descendants in 1917. Yet the count and his daughter have a deep sense of what becomes them—"Are we Germans or something?" cries Natasha—and the Countess sees that for once she cannot prevail. Her "Oh, do as you like—am I hindering anyone?" expresses perfectly her irritated sense that she must yield to a kind of generosity which she cannot feel herself, and which she knows will be a last blow for the family finances. When the wounded are put in the carts it seems natural to everyone that this must be done, "just as a quarter of an hour before it had not seemed strange to anyone that the wounded should be left behind and the goods carted away, but had seemed the only thing to do". The equivocation in this marvellous scene is completed by the fact that most of the goods *do* get taken because Sonya—quietly working while Natasha supplies the inspiration and *joie de vivre*—sees that they are.

It is an irony of swarm life, which Tolstoy fully appreciates, that the merely accomplished at once takes on an appearance of the inevitable: when the bees have swarmed and settled it at once becomes clear that it could have happened at no other time and in no other place. We see how this applies to the decision about the wounded and the carts—Tolstoy is quite capable, in such contexts, of a little self-mockery of his own principle of historic inevitability. Another instance is Prince Vasili's contempt for the lazy and oldfashioned Kutuzov, which changes, as soon as Kutuzov has been appointed Generalissimo, to a genuine and sincere conviction that he is the only man for the job. Kutuzov himself is the prime instance of a character whose whole mode of being would at once have been established as the cause of failure had failure occurred[1]: after success it became the explanation of success. Kutuzov himself is well aware of this, and aware how little difference he makes to the situation. The French advance is "like the velocity of a falling body", and the Russian retreat is equally gravitational. By merely repeating Bennigsen's protest about "defending Russia's sacred and ancient capital" Kutuzov shows how meaningless it is in the scale of such natural facts, and it is no use getting in the way of nature.

This swarm life, the mysterious rightness of whose instincts and operations is exemplified in the events of 1812, is Tolstoy's ally against the kind of criticism which Chaadayev, who had been a friend of the Decembrists, levelled against Russian society in his famous *Letter* of 1836. Russia, he wrote, was neither of the West nor the East, and had the traditions of neither. There is "no regular movement of the spirit, no good habit, no rule for anything . . . each of us has to take up for

[1] So would that of Churchill in the last war.

himself the thread broken in the family". *War and Peace* is in some sense an answer to these pessimistic remarks. It denies that the thread need be broken in the family, if it is the kind of family where its strength is felt rather than understood and lived with rather than formulated into a rule. Pierre is singularly unconvincing when in the last chapter he tries to give expression to the best instincts of conservatism rather than (like Nicholas) simply embodying them. "We want a society of true conservatives, a society of gentlemen in the full meaning of that word . . . we join hands only for the public welfare and the general safety". Though the views of the Decembrists varied enormously, *that* kind of ideal was hardly what they aimed at. True, they were gentlemen, and with them, as Professor Pares observes, "ceased for ever the dominant role of the Russian gentry", but they were political revolutionaries as well. Tolstoy celebrates and idealises the last years of that "dominant role", but he could not have gone on to describe with sympathy the means by which the Decembrist leaders aspired to dominate. One of their number, Pestel, was an able staff-officer, somewhat in the position of Prince Andrew; another was the poet Ryleyev. Had they succeeded in overthrowing Tsardom, their ensuing rivalry might almost have anticipated that between Kerensky and Lenin. "Paul Pestel," says Professor Pares, "will always be an interesting study."

> At the point which he reached in his rapid political evolution, he stood for a Jacobin conspiracy to overthrow the autocracy, with the murder of the sovereign and reigning family. But this was to be only the preface to a gigantic social reform. The peasants were to be freed, all class distinctions abolished, a central government established with all the instruments of power, including spies and censorship to prevent a counter-revolution. . . . Ryleyev religiously left all final settlements to an elected constituent assembly: Pestel wanted to settle everything himself.

He could hardly have been an interesting study for Tolstoy. He and the movement would have had to be treated as negatively as Speransky and the Masons.

Moreover the Decembrists exhibited in defeat a characteristic which must—from its frequent recurrence in Russian history—

be called distinctively Russian, but which one feels Tolstoy
could not have borne to mention. They abased themselves totally
before authority, admitting their errors and (at least in the case
of Pestel) betraying all they knew about their friends. Even
Chaadayev, as Professor Pares points out, shares in this abase-
ment, as if it were a relief to prostrate oneself before a government whose triumph demonstrated its inevitability. "Now they
are right and we are wrong", as was observed by a thwarted
palace conspirator of Catherine's time, whose career Tolstoy
once thought of treating historically. The same pattern was to
repeat itself under Communism in the Moscow treason trials.

It is impossible to imagine Pierre or Prince Andrew in this
situation, as it is impossible to imagine Tolstoy himself. It
underlies *War and Peace* only in the dignified form of the wise
submission to nature and necessity. Passivity, in military as in
personal matters, is the law of life, but to kiss the rod is another
matter. Tolstoy ignores much here—no wonder a Russian critic
observed that as we read *War and Peace* we wonder where
Gogol's Russia came from, the Russia of trickery, evasion and
incompetence, monumental hypocrisy and abject superstition,
shoulder-kissing and every sort of creepy-crawliness. These
were as much the characteristics of old Russia as anything in
War and Peace. But Tolstoy rejects out of hand the notion of
such characteristics. Human nature does not change, and while
there are rogues, hypocrites and time-servers in any age, the
basic human pattern of goodness, dignity and simplicity remains
unaltered.

I know what "the characteristics of the period" are that people do
not find in my novel—the horrors of serfdom, the immuring of wives,
the flogging of grown-up sons, Saltykova [a notorious landed
proprietress who murdered many of her serfs] and so on; but I do
not think these characteristics of the period as they exist in our
imagination are correct, and I did not wish to reproduce them.
On studying letters, diaries and traditions I did not find the horrors
of such savagery to a greater extent than I find them now or at any
other period. . . . If we have come to believe in the perversity and
coarse violence of that period, that is only because the traditions,
memoirs, stories and novels that have been handed to us record
for the most part exceptional cases of violence and brutality. To

suppose that the predominant characteristic of that period was turbulence is unjust as it would be for a man, seeing nothing but the tops of trees beyond a hill, to conclude that there was nothing to be found in that locality but trees.

As they exist in our imagination is the key phrase here. Tolstoy distrusted the imagination. His letters often refer scornfully to something in a novel being all imagined, all "thought up". He would have regarded with distrust Wordsworth's purpose to "throw a certain colouring of the imagination" over scenes and episodes of common life.

For the imagination returns us to the author himself, and never more so than in a historical novel. By using only what he knew on his own account, and facts from historians and memoir writers which rang true to his own experience, Tolstoy avoided creating his own imaginary picture of the past. His imagination is never secretly in league with something it finds in the past and not in the present. Of authors who emphasise a certain aspect of a period we are inclined to think: yes, perhaps this is so, but why did he want to put it in? We have the feeling that Dickens may have set a novel in the time of the French Revolution because he was fascinated (like many imaginative writers) by dreams of terror and liberty, blood, executions, guillotines. *A Tale of Two Cities* is thus open to the sort of criticism which Tolstoy makes of our pictures of the past—that Saltykova was always flogging and torturing her serfs; Kutuzov always on a white horse and pointing a telescope; Rostopchin always setting fire with a torch to Moscow, etc. Tolstoy forbids his imagination, and ours, to indulge in the otherness of the past, to use it for our own daydreams and suppressed desires.

We find in the past what we want to find, and Tolstoy is no exception to this rule. But he has the advantage of only wanting to find in the past what seems to him most important and most enduring in the present. And in terms of accuracy of historical tone this can have unexpected advantages. When deploring the brutish conditions of old Russia, Dostoevsky describes how government couriers beat their drivers on the back of the neck, savagely but absentmindedly, as if they were merely going through the motions of some prescribed ritual, and how the drivers received the blows in the same spirit. This gives a clue

to Tolstoy's method, for it is the *writer* who is supplying the
indignation and the excitement in Dostoevsky's account: he is
distancing himself from courier and driver by his own feelings
at their lack of feeling. It is not too much to say that Dostoevsky's creative imagination absorbs the incident, that he identifies himself with the pair in turn and finds pleasure in the role
of each. An actual situation disappears into his mind, in much
the same way that the situation of Pierre and his fellow-
prisoners disappeared into Pierre's body. Now if Tolstoy
describes anything comparably brutal, like the flogging of the
suspected French spy in Moscow, the frequent floggings of
Lavrushka, Nicholas's orderly, or Nicholas's own habit as a
landowner of beating up his serfs when they irritate him, he does
it without comment. Lavrushka and the others took it for granted, so Tolstoy does too. If he insisted on it he would have to
dissociate himself from it, and create an alienation effect of the
sort he attributes to Pierre at the Masonic ritual or Natasha at
the ballet.

Tolstoy clearly felt at times the historical novelist's desire to
re-create a period, but these considerations prevented him from
succeeding with any other time than the one he chose in *War and
Peace*. Like all Russian writers he was fascinated by Peter the
Great, and in the surviving fragment of the novel he projected
about Peter and his times he ran head-on, as if with deliberate
perversity, into the kinds of falsification he had analysed so
clearly in *Some Words about 'War and Peace'*.

The fragment reveals the accumulation process beginning, as
we see it in the first drafts of *War and Peace*. One character, that
of Prince Boris Golitsyn, Peter's adviser, seems promising, and
it is possible that Tolstoy might have worked him up (as he did
with the more famous historical character, Kutuzov) into a *War
and Peace*-like being whose nature would be open and comprehensible to us. But that in a sense is just the trouble. Kutuzov
gave Tolstoy great difficulty, and had to be altered to suit the
Tolstoyan version of 1812. He retains his historic appearance
and manner, his scarred eye-socket, his fondness for pretty girls
(though his lechery is much toned down) and for dull society
novels. But he derives most of his reality not from these properties but from his association with the *unhistoric* characters of

Pierre, Andrew and his father, and the Rostovs. It does not matter in the least that Pierre and Prince Andrew are modern men who have obviously read Kant, Schopenhauer, etc., because we do not feel they have been inserted into the past by Tolstoy either to represent him or to represent young men of their age. With Boris Golitsyn, on the other hand, we feel that Tolstoy is projecting a study of what he himself might have been like if (like his great-great-grandfather who was first made a count) he had lived at that time and under those conditions. And to bridge the gap between himself and Peter's age he would have had to invent not only plot, which he does so well in *War and Peace*, but personality.

Moreover, with the air of a man deciding to get the worst over at once, Tolstoy starts by describing the interrogation under torture of the leader of the *Streltsy*, the royal bodyguard, who had been conspiring against Peter. The scene is painful as nothing is in *War and Peace*, not, however, from its subject but from its air of embarrassed conscientiousness. In most episodes of this kind authors remind us of their presence by taking too much interest in what they are describing: Tolstoy reminds us of his by taking too little. As we read we cannot avoid seeing what the author's problems were, and this is the nemesis of the historical novel. As we read *War and Peace* it does not occur to us that there could be any problems—we only discover about them afterwards when we begin to investigate and enquire.

Curiously enough, one of Pushkin's poems, also a fragment of what was evidently intended as a historical narrative, breaks off in much the same way as Tolstoy's Peter the Great, and perhaps for much the same reasons. Pushkin describes an *oprichnik*, one of the special police of Ivan the Terrible, galloping at night across the Red Square, which is still covered with the grisly apparatus of the day's executions. We can see that Pushkin, like Tolstoy, is trapped by the crudity of this local colour, which nevertheless appears necessary for the prosecution of the theme, and so abandons it. In *The Bronze Horseman* it is significant that Pushkin, instead of going back to the time of Peter the Great, brings Peter, in the person of his statue, *forward* into the present. The flood, and the statue towering above the waves, combine like a terrible revisitation from the past and a reminder of how much the past is still alive. In thus creating the past through the present Pushkin was doing essentially the same thing, with high poetic intensity, that Tolstoy slowly and meticulously pieced together from memoirs and recollections, from memories and experiences of aunts, grandparents and in-laws. The secret is to bring back the past into the present so that it retains its character without recourse to historical pastoral.

10. *Pastoral*

By 'Pastoral'—not the ideal term but I cannot think of another which suggests the same range of literary effect—I understand the process of making everything in a work of literature *characteristic*. There may be many motives for doing this, straightforward and deliberate or undeclared and almost unconscious. In his book, *Some Versions Of Pastoral*,[1] William Empson used the term to cover a wide range of effect in which the unifying factor is 'putting the complex into the simple', so that a readily accepted convention exerts social, political, or emotional influence on the reader in ways to which he is partly conditioned, but to which the skilled or inspired pastoralist will give an unexpected turn.

Almost all literature is pastoral to the extent in which it accepts conventions, characters and situations without attempting to see them—at some stage of the creative process—in the uncharacteristic, unframed, and unproffered way in which they appear to the seeing eye of quotidian experience. Documentaries, biographies, detective stories, historical novels, all make use of pastoral for seeing their subjects in a given frame from which they cannot be allowed to escape except at the pastoralist's pondered behest. A detective story may have a mad detective, a blind detective, a religious detective, or an elderly female one— it will always have a detective. The individual must be determined by his setting and be a part of it, however eccentric or unexpected a part. A coalminer, or a retired colonel in Camberley, are seen by pastoral in their functions and their characters— the fact that they may not feel like or be aware of themselves as a coalminer and a colonel cannot be considered.

[1] Chatto & Windus, London.

Conrad's *Nostromo* is a *tour de force* and a remarkable novel, but it is a pastoral novel. The politico-romantic framework of the imaginary South American state of Costaguana holds and determines the characters in a way in which the ship-board setting of *The Shadow Line* or *The Nigger of the Narcissus* does not; for the sea for Conrad is not a pastoral setting but the natural and instinctive setting of felt and experienced life.

Many of Tolstoy's most enthusiastic critics and supporters have seen *War and Peace* as the most sublime and complete of all pastorals. It says (they imply): "this is what human life should be like and shall be like". They confuse the involuntary ideality of the work with a conscious pastoral ideal. Considered pastorally, the characters of *War and Peace* at once become lifeless and almost repellent. We must return to this, but let us first notice an important difference between the two main uses of pastoral ideology today. In the east it is used as an image of what human life shall be like in the good or Socialist State: in the west it is the image of what human life eases itself of the perpetual burden of humanity by seeing itself *as*. Soviet man (or woman) is an ideal: 'Mrs (or Mr) 1970' is an opiate. Only superficially does the Western pastoral image call: come and be like me! Deeper down, its function as art is sedative; it calls us, as sleep does, towards passivity and non-existence. Our need for this kind of pastoral expresses our deep hunger for something apparently the same as ourselves but in fact quite different —our desire for a mirror world in which every activity, every gesture, every garment, exists beatifically in and for itself.

At the level of art what we may call the Eastern and the Western pastoral join hands: the Communist ideological image and the capitalist advertising image function through much the same techniques. The Western critic and consumer is less likely than his Eastern counterpart to see art (and even the greatest) as serving, in some sort, the social functions of pastoral. Our conception of those functions is defeated, knowing, stopped off. Our pleasure in everyday pastoral images assumes that they are incapable of high artistic achievement. But the deeply learned and perceptive Marxist critic, Lukacs, is predisposed by his faith to see not only Tolstoy but the whole tradition of European realism in the novel as disposed towards pastoral and capable—

by reason of their very excellence—of serving its ideological ends.

The tradition of realism in the novel can be so understood by Lukacs precisely because its realism can be interpreted according to the highest pastoral standards. It is as far as possible from being escape art, in the sense that popular novels are escape art. *The Quiet Don,*[1] Sholokhov's post-Tolstoyan novel, is totally a pastoral, but it is also a fine novel in the highest traditions of realism. It is conceived out of a complete love and understanding. But this process of affection is also a process of enclosure, of caging. Its mode of *possession* reminds us not of Tolstoy but of Balzac.

The *Comédie Humaine* is the most gigantic pastoral enterprise ever undertaken by a novelist. Balzac intended it to do for modern society what Scott in the *Waverley Novels* had done for the past. Both Scott and Balzac love to contemplate human beings in their habits as they lived, or are living. But Scott was a poet in a sense that Balzac was not; and his greatest creations, though seen and loved because they are *characteristic*, are also coloured by the subjective dream of his historical imagination. Balzac's enthusiasm for the characteristic is more earthy, more lovingly factual. Pastoral realism does not put the complex into the simple. Its purpose is to enfold a total complexity in terms of itself, so that it does not merge with the uncharacteristic and transparent being of our own lives

Pastoral experiences continually occur to us in life of course. We have one when we acquire a new name or a new suit,[2] move into a newly done-up flat or are promoted to a new status. For a while the whole of our experience is seen by ourselves in terms of this new circumstance, which determines what we do and how we feel—we do not behave in our normal transparent and open way in terms of our own consciousness, but see ourselves behaving in a novel and limiting character. Very soon the new

---

[1] The English translation is for some reason *And Quiet Flows the Don*.

[2] When Natasha decided to put on her dress "which had the property of producing cheerfulness in the mornings", she was courting a pastoral experience, and we are seeing the act and the wish from the inside. The heroine of a pastoral novel would be wearing an appropriate garment as a part of her *character*, and we should be invited to contemplate the tableau from the outside.

circumstance becomes submerged in the general flow of life and ceases to dictate a consciousness suited to itself. But in pastoral art the authority of the circumstance remains constant, fixed: we continue, as it were, to see ourselves within the definition of circumstance: there is no play between the fixity of character and the freedom of consciousness.

The morale of a revolutionary state depends upon conditioning its members to see themselves in a pastoral character—indeed the desire to bring about a pastoral state in which everyone can be seen to be playing an appropriate part is an aspect of revolutionary mythology. In practice this state of affairs can hardly endure for long, but the function of revolutionary literature is to assume that it does, and to continue to present a total pastoral image. Hence the gap between the image of living in Soviet literature and the reality of doing it day by day. Hence, too, our tendency to see Russians and Chinese in a pastoral light, as we see people set in a historical novel, set in the past or the future. Socialist realism is pure pastoral, for the reality exists as a means towards a given end, and the whole tradition of realism can be absorbed and seen as stages in the process. Even epic can be seen in this way. Lukacs comments on the fact (first noticed by Lessing in the *Laokoon*) that it is the manufacture rather than the appearance of Achilles' armour which Homer describes, the dynamic process rather than the static detail. This is the clue to Lukacs's distinction between *realism*, in which the 'totality of objects' is integrated in the processes of living, and *naturalism*, in which objects and people are seen in great detail but as dead matter. Not only Balzac and Tolstoy, but Homer and Shakespeare, are for Lukacs examples of the first: Flaubert and Zola of the second.

This is a just distinction, but unfortunately it ignores the issue of pastoral. There is an immense difference between the world of *War and Peace* and the world of epic pastoral, whether in Homer or in Balzac. Tolstoy's characters are never contemplated; they are never seen doing what characters of their sort do. Balzac and Homer would know, cherishingly, what Andromache or Eugénie Grandet were doing at any moment of the day, and it would always be the right thing. But we can no more say what Natasha or Pierre or even Kutuzov would be doing than we can say what we ourselves would be doing—they seem a part of Tolstoy's and our own indistinguishable activity. Eugénie Grandet, by contrast, seems a kind of relief from Balzac's human activity; she joins the vast capital of his repose, despite the fact that we see the making of money in this and in Balzac's other novels as we see the making of arms in Homer. Eugénie and her father are magnificent examples of pastoral creation, and the theme of money is perfectly suited to creation of this type. Balzac's leisurely, loving, long-distance account of how old Grandet continued to make money during successive regimes—revolution, empire and restoration—persuades us without apparent intention that nothing but money is real. It is as completely in control of society as the Grandets are controlled by Balzac's pastoral.

Tolstoy can use pastoral, but he never allows it to dominate his creative imagination because he neither accepts the heroic world as Homer does, nor sets out as Balzac does to accomplish what Lukacs sees as the task of the great realist—"to depict man as a whole in the whole of society". General Bagration, for example, is seen almost entirely in terms of heroic pastoral, as natural and inevitable a fighter as Achilles.

> His face wore the look of concentrated and happy determination seen on the face of a man who on a hot day takes a final run before plunging into the water. . . . The round hard eagle eyes looked ecstatically and rather disdainfully before him, obviously not resting on anything, though there was still the same deliberation in his measured movements.

But Tolstoyan reality interposes at the moment when he enters the English club for the dinner given in his honour, "wearing a sort of naïvely festive air, which, in conjunction with his determined and manly features, gave an expression positively rather comic to his face". Even Bagration is not always permitted, as he would be in total pastoral, to do *the right thing*.

The most remarkable use of pastoral by Tolstoy for his own purposes takes place at the end of *War and Peace*, and the change it makes in our conception of the characters shows how different they were before. Natasha, in particular, becomes fixed in Tolstoy's contemplation of marriage—she becomes a figure of repose. All the details about her, the nappies, the preoccupations, the disregard for her own appearance, become the *right* details, not for the individual she has been but for Tolstoy's conception of the ideal married woman: she is now fixed in her fated social and historical background. The partial alienation we feel from her at the end is extraordinarily right in terms of the whole natural scope of the work, but it is not, I think, intended by Tolstoy. It is the consequence of his use of her as a conclusion in terms of pastoral, in which his own vision of what is right and characteristic dominates over all earlier individualities and episodes. We must return to this when we consider the ending of *War and Peace*.

"To depict man as a whole in the whole of society"—it is an intensely literary ideal. When Rastignac at the end of *Le Père Goriot* gazes out over Paris, the town he has promised himself to conquer and exploit, we feel that Balzac too is standing there, and promising himself that conquest. Neither Balzac nor Henry James could possibly have said, as Tolstoy did, that they were "not interested" in many of the pursuits and classes of Society. Because they remain in their lives *outside* the world they take possession of it in their books, they must necessarily be interested in everything *inside* it. Those who are inside anyway— like Tolstoy and, in her different way, Jane Austen—have no need to feel this compulsive interest. In the Preface to *1805* Tolstoy had admitted his lack of interest in "merchants, peasants, and theological students". He had no interest in society for its own sake.

Lukacs's conception of realism exactly fits the French authors who set out "to depict man as a whole in the whole of society", but it suggests a degree of masterfulness[1] and manipulation quite alien to the Russian writers of the nineteenth century.

---

[1] Stendhal is the prime example of this sort of masterful sophistication. Could anything be more literary than the comment which Stendhal wrote in the margin of his own copy of *La Chartreuse de Parme* opposite the sentence: "Fabrice went for a walk, listening to the silence". Addressing "the reader of 1880" Stendhal comments: "In order that an author should find readers in 1838 he had to write such things as 'listening to the silence'." Fabrice, in fact, is not to be allowed a sensibility that accords with his age in case we might think his creator shared it.

Lukacs chose to ignore the immense difference in tone between Tolstoy and the European realists. As a critic he is far more *literary* than was Tolstoy as a writer. He has an admirable sense of tradition and of the historical continuity of literature. "Those who do not know Marxism," he points out, "may be surprised at the respect for the classical heritage of mankind which one finds in the really great representatives of that doctrine."[1] It is this sense of traditional values, rather than a reliance on the dialectic, which makes most of his judgments so sound.[2] He condemns the literary naturalist "who makes a speciality of describing the social life of the present", and who confines himself in a theory from which there is no way back to life, such a theory as Zola's scientific naturalism or Flaubert's *impassibilité* which turns life into art.

> This alienation has for its inevitable consequence that the writer disposes of a much narrower and more restricted life material than the old school of realism . . . if the new realist wants to describe some phenomenon of life he has to go out of his way specially to observe it.

This is a judgment on Kipling as well as on Flaubert, and brings out what Tolstoy had himself implied in *What is Art?*

The theory of the dialectic does indeed account convincingly for the 'open-ended' nature of great realistic novels, their assumption of a continually changing and self-transforming social process of which the writer himself need not be fully aware. "No writer is a true realist," observes Lukacs, "if he can direct the evolution of his own characters at will." A true realist narrates (*erzählt*): the bad realist or naturalist only describes (*beschreibt*) the unmeaning detail of life around him, with a precision which is the artistic equivalent of political despair. But

---

[1] These and most of the quotations from Lukacs come from *Studies in European Realism*.

[2] This instinctive understanding of how great literature works and how it reveals its truth to us, so evident in *Studies in European Realism*, was to get Lukacs into trouble later on, when his enemies accused him of recommending to the factory workers not Zola but Balzac, not Priestley and Pirandello but Shakespeare and Molière. See Jozsef Revai *Lukacs and Socialist Realism: A Hungarian Literary Controversy*, introduced by Eric Hobsbawm (Fore Publications, 1950).

it is also true, and less conveniently, though it does not seem to worry Lukacs, that Balzac *owns* his world as Hegel owns his system, and in the same way ("Balzac's world," says Lukacs, "is, like Hegel's, a circle consisting entirely of circles"). Balzac does not only narrate, but sets out to dominate his material, like his character Rastignac.

There is nothing for us here which relates to Tolstoy. Quite apart from Tolstoy's lack of its systematic artistic intention, the actual technique of *War and Peace* is as different as possible from that of the *Comédie Humaine*. As we have seen, Tolstoy does not for one moment stand back from the series of episodes he is relating. The distaste for detail—for what Lukacs calls *Beschreibung*—which he was to express in *What is Art?* is already implied in the episodic method. None of the million details in the book are allowed to group themselves in the pattern of a set piece. To take one instance, we are never allowed to contemplate a house, though the great houses have an enormous importance in *War and Peace*. Balzac goes to all lengths to solicit our attention to every detail of the Maison Vauquer in *Le Père Goriot*; unless we have seen a Russian country-house of the period, or a picture of one, we have not the faintest idea what Bald Hills or Otradnoe looked like. More important, we are never allowed to contemplate the detailed dossier of a life. Epic figures like Bagration are given no life outside what we can see in them for ourselves. Balzac would have spent pages on his early career and probably given us a graphic flashback of him trudging over the snowy Alps on one of the epic marches he undertook with Suvorov.

War and Peace is ideally suited to this unique episodic method, with its steady fidelity to the facts of its narration, not to those owned by its narrator; and this appears all the more significant when we see Tolstoy attempting, with less success, to retain it in *Anna Karenina*, whose situation and story are strictly comparable with a novel of Western realism. We cannot help but think of Anna in the context of such a novel, and so our ignorance about her upbringing and background are not an unmixed advantage.

Marxist critics do not object to an element of pastoral contemplation—the success of *The Quiet Don* shows that—and many of them, though not Lukacs, are apt to discover it in *War and Peace* in order to emphasise 'types' and examples of what if not exactly socialist reality is at least the soil from which it sprang. Natasha in particular is singled out for praise as the type of Russian womanhood, close to the *narod* and instinctively at one with all that is best and most characteristic in Russian life, the life which has now become identified with socialist reality. It is curiously bothering to listen to a Soviet critic in ecstatic contemplation of Natasha, even though it is difficult in a sense not to admit that his admiration for her is not only 'correct' but largely justified. But we are embarrassed by the way in which such eulogies (sometimes indulged in by Western admirers too) ignore and cut across the tendency of Tolstoy's whole method. That method requires that she be totally subdued into the texture of *War and Peace*, an aspect of the world in which Tolstoy and ourselves are involved. She is in no sense a close female 'study', like Eugénie Grandet, Emma Bovary or Isabel Archer. She is, significantly, closer to the English tradition of Emma Woodhouse and Becky Sharp (Tolstoy greatly appreciated Thackeray).

We *study* the character whose situation is presented as interesting—Isabel Archer or Dorothea Brooke—as we *contemplate* the character—Eugénie Grandet—who fits exactly in to a pastoral world. The intelligence of George Eliot or Henry James leads us on to speculate about their heroines, as the lack of intelligence in Emma Bovary leads us to speculate about Flaubert himself. None of these attitudes means a thing where Natasha is concerned—with her we merely participate. If, from whatever motives, we abstract her and *see* her as the incarnation of Russian spontaneity and natural goodness—a forerunner of the Soviet girl, with a golden corn-shock in her arms and a sunburned *traktorist* near at hand—we shall end by disliking her, and rightly so. She *is* dislikable in some ways, but when we are one of the *War and Peace* family we can accept this without its affecting our family solidarity with her.

Soviet critics have abstracted Captain Tushin in the same way and presented him as the first plebeian officer, unaffected, unimpressive, but modestly brave and first-rate at his job. The same objections apply. Tushin is not a type, and his characteristics do not permit us to make up a theory of our own about him. In fact he started life in Tolstoy's first drafts as an aristocrat, not unlike the final version of Prince Andrew. This laborious process of trial and error shows us why we cannot take out and use Tolstoy's characters when they have finally settled into the book. It may also show, curiously enough, why there is such a sharp contrast between Shakespeare's characters, even the minor ones, and Tolstoy's. Shakespeare's minor characters often appear to possess a reality so greatly in excess of their dramatic function that every sort of hypothesis can be entertained about them—their vivacity calls up a corresponding vivacity of speculation. Figures like Dogberry, Enobarbus and Paulina strike us as having been immediately and decisively created, shot into the drama wrapped in their own comprehensive but unopened dossiers. We feel that as well as participating in the play we can, if we wish, abstract each man's nature and history from it. Shakespeare avoids pastoral by this extraordinary impression his characters give of latent individuality—they are never types. Tolstoy avoids it by making us one of the family, so that it hardly occurs to us to wish to know more or to make up more about the other members or to extrapolate them into a different world.

In fact we do not need to consider *War and Peace* as 'reality' or its method as 'realism'. Like Count Rostov at the meeting, once we are in it "we understand everything in our own way". It is this that makes Lukacs's discussion of the book in terms of realism seem—for all its interest and acumen—a little beside the point. And yet we must admit that reality has never been a negative notion in Russian literature; it never settled down into Western pastoral contemplativeness. And *pravda* is a semantically committed word—it means what is right and authoritative as well as what is true—so that realism to a Russian is a method of getting at what should be as well as what is: the two are not distinguishable. Nor are the ideal and the real separated—*War and Peace* may truly be seen as making the two into one, as embodying a magnificent disregard for their separateness, yet it is this same disregard for the difference between the actual and the ideal which becomes ludicrous, if not odious, in later novels of socialist realism. It becomes the lie against which Pasternak's Dr Zhivago registers his protest.

The nemesis of realism as a theory is that it has decided what is real before the imagination has proved it; before truth, in Wordsworth's phrase, has been carried alive into the heart. Lukacs's censor, Jozsef Revai, passes judgment on works "in which it is the writer who speaks through the character, and not reality". This is the final clamping down of a theological tenet which Lukacs never invokes with total devotion, though he makes use of it. "Tolstoy," he says, "never identifies capitalist reality with reality as such. He always saw capitalist society as a world of distortion, and he therefore always contrasted it with another natural, and hence human, reality." Tolstoy's men and women of any spiritual value must inevitably be disappointed by life, because their hopes of solving its problems are frustrated by "the meaninglessness of life in a capitalist society".

This raises an echo in an unexpected quarter. The theorist of fiction can beg the question of reality in the same way as the Marxist critic, though for different reasons. In his essay *Le Roman Comme Recherche*, Michel Butor describes the conventional novelist as "the accomplice of that profound malaise, the night in which we are all struggling". Though the exact nature of this sad state does not become quite clear, it obviously bears a close resemblance to Lukacs's "meaninglessness of life in a capitalist society". True reality, then, is something the novelist can help us towards, for Lukacs by having a 'correct' view of society, for M. Butor, by inventing new forms of seeing reality. Both reject the concept of reality as "everything that is the case", and consider it as something to be made sense of in the interests of our morale. Experimenters in form are the true realists of today, claims M. Butor, because they have the confidence to make reality what they wish it to be. So far from being opposed to it, formal experiment "is the *sine qua non* of a more far-reaching realism". The formalist is both explorer and denouncer, because he will not let us remain in the swamp of our cherished literary habits, the malaise of our inherited sense of meaninglessness, but will urge us on to see things in a new and therefore meaningful way.

This may be a crude summing-up of M. Butor's thesis but I do not think it misrepresents it. Any theory of the novel must be crude which starts from the premise that we are all struggling in the night of a profound malaise. Both socialist realism, and the new realism for which M. Butor argues, propose the novelist as the arbiter and ally of true reality; and the comparison shows that the attitudes behind socialist realism have been more fully accepted by Western theorists of the novel than they themselves may be aware.

Now the gulf between these theories and the actuality of *War and Peace* consists in this: that Tolstoy takes for granted and conveys with overwhelming assurance the authenticity of the individual vision. *All* his characters see reality as it really is. The assurance of his solipsism is so great that it can create a comparable solipsism in his characters; he does not reach them so much by intuition and sympathy as by endowing them with the same power of absolute and primaeval being that he has himself. We have to look to Shakespeare for anything like it, but Shakespeare as a person is absent from his creation. Tolstoy is overwhelmingly there, but his characters are overwhelmingly there too. His vision is wider, more comprehensive, but no more *authentic* than theirs.

It is this which explains the absence of *tone* in *War and Peace*. The impression of reality in a novel will nearly always be found to be conveyed by tone: the novelist produces a tone and holds it as a singer holds a note. To hold the tone successfully is to hold the audience, and it is this skill that Tolstoy does not need in *War and Peace*.[1] There we are dominated by a more primitive compulsion.

Enclosed by the tone of a novel, we think of changing the style, changing the viewpoint—devices which novelists like Joyce have practised with craft and success. The novelist takes pains to withdraw himself from the order of his creation; another aspect of things is given. But neither in Proust, Joyce, Faulkner nor any other novelist do we really get the impression that the world changes and is different, from person to person and from thing to thing. Tolstoy is master of the primitive world of isolation, which existed before men saw it, and before they came to see themselves in each other. Gorky perceived this

[1] Criticising *War and Peace*, the novelist Brigid Brophy once remarked to me that she could not "get its tone", whereas she could get that of *Anna Karenina*.

primitivism when he compared him to a Russian God "who sits on a maple throne under a golden lime tree, not very majestic, but perhaps more cunning than all the other Gods".

It is not for nothing that Pierre, trying to make himself as small as possible in his father's sick-room, "placed his huge hands symmetrically on his knees in the naïve attitude of an Egyptian statue". The image of those crouching dog-headed statues gives us the thick, three-dimensional presence of Pierre, trying unsuccessfully not to be there, but succeeding completely in not belonging to the tone of the surrounding novel. Beside the novelish personalities of Anna Mihailovna and the Princesses Bezukhova, and their struggle for the inlaid portfolio, he is an uncouth separated being. They are keeping a novel going: he is not. He is different from them in a more absolute sense than that in which one character in a novel is different from another. So it is with old Prince Bolkonsky's servant, Alpatych, whose imitation of his master surrounds him with the same sort of solitude. When he drives to besieged Smolensk he seems alone in the world—indeed he *is* alone in the world, so powerful is the illusion of external events being kept at bay by his single-minded pursuit of his master's instructions. Yet events proceed inexorably outside him. Smolensk is bombarded; the cook at the inn has her thigh broken by a shell splinter; fire breaks out in a nearby building. And at this moment we read with a shock of incredulity the calm sentence: "The crowd was evidently watching for the roof to fall in, and Alpatych watched for it too". His identification in the mass response brings home to us not only the extraordinary nature of the events, but the fact that Alpatych too is a human being, with the same curiosities, fears and desires. Yet how oblivious of this we were, when we knew him in the isolation of his individuality.

In order "to depict man as a whole in the whole of society", socialist realism allows for the individual as well as the type. But it postulates a rigid and schematic relation between the two. In *The Canterbury Tales*, which share the same primitive vitality and joy as *War and Peace*, the relation is achieved by art and in the interests of art, not in conformity with social theory. Chaucer starts out by describing his characters in his Prologue in terms of pastoral. Typification is complete. But when they speak and tell their tales we receive a different impression of them, as if the speaker could not—very naturally—see himself in terms of Chaucer's pastoral sketch. The type he represents is not disowned by the speaker, but isolated by him and left elsewhere. Having contemplated the type, we hear the man, and the two are far from joining to represent "man as a whole in society". Rather they reveal how theoretical that idea is. The gap between objective description and self-expression is shown by this genial yet sophisticated art to be unbridgeable. No more than in *War and Peace* can we be certain in Chaucer of the *tone*, though in his contemporary, Langland, it is unmistakable. What, for instance, are we to feel about Chaucer's *Parson's Tale*? Is it some kind of joke, or is it Chaucer's way of separating his character absolutely from his fellow-pilgrims? These sorts of separation could be effected more formally and more drastically in mediaeval and renaissance art than in the era of the novel, and their presence in *War and Peace* reminds us again how misleading a judgment of it in terms of the novel may be. To English readers, *The Canterbury Tales* can give a surer indication of these aspects of Tolstoy's work than do Thackeray or Jane Austen.

It is significant, too, that Chaucer, like Tolstoy, is a profound and delighted connoisseur of self-satisfaction—indeed he can be even more consistent than Tolstoy in allowing his characters the full freedom of it. Tolstoy is apt to jeopardise his god-like art of bestowing individuality by intervening in his own person as a man. The success of Alpatych, or of Andrew's vision of the oak-tree, and of the little girls stealing the plums, must be set against Natasha's visit to the opera. Here Tolstoy is determined to "make it strange", and this he has to do himself—he never succeeds in making one of his characters do it convincingly for him. In the opera scene he tries to make Natasha do it. "She knew what [the scene] was all intended to represent, but it was so pretentiously false and unnatural that she felt first ashamed for the actors and then amused at them." The whole process by which Natasha's feelings and those of the other spectators are made first to contrast with one another, and then coincide, is vigorous and effective, but by Tolstoy's highest standards it is strikingly crude. It reminds us of how Flaubert might have manipulated Madame Bovary in such a setting.

The nearly naked Hélène sat near her, smiling at everyone with the same smile, and just such a smile Natasha bestowed on Boris.

Was it really, by Tolstoy's standards of discernment, *just* such a smile? Wouldn't it rather have been, in its blend of attempted convention and touching revelation, more like the face with which Natasha confronted Princess Mary on that unfortunate occasion of their first meeting? But when he is surrounded by bare shoulders Tolstoy's vision is apt to become a little blurred. He is determined that the corrupting ambience of opera shall make Natasha accept her situation as exciting and delightful, when it is in fact frivolous and obscene. It is the most dangerous and sterile type of Tolstoyan manœuvre, remarkably rare in *War and Peace*, and very different from the contrasting Mozartian and Voltairean modes which we noticed in the scenes with Hélène and Prince Vasili at Pierre's engagement. There the point played itself like music: here it is made with the crudity of a Flaubert or Maupassant, and with a glint of triumph not unlike theirs.

In fact one detail shows that it would have been actually impossible for Natasha to have watched the third act quite in the way imputed to her.

In the middle stood a man and woman, probably meant to be a king and queen. The king waved his right hand, and, obviously nervous, sang something very badly and sat down on a crimson throne. The actress, who had been in white at first and then in blue, was now in nothing but a smock, and had let her hair down. . . . One of the actresses, with thick bare legs and thin arms, went to the wings to adjust her bodice, then walked into the middle of the stage and began skipping into the air and kicking one leg rapidly against another.

Natasha could not have seen her go into the wings (*kulisi*—the corridors adjoining the stage)—only Tolstoy did. And having scored his point he rubs it in at the end of the chapter with a neat flourish. The audience are screaming for Duport, the star performer.

Natasha did not now feel this strange. She looked about her with pleasure, smiling joyfully.

"Isn't Duport wonderful?" said Hélène, turning to her.

"Oh yes!" answered Natasha.

In the Russian text the point is made even clearer, for Hélène's query and Natasha's reply are in French. It is one of the comparatively few occasions in the book when the equation French = pointless artificiality, Russian = natural reality, is so crude and explicit. It is also one of the few occasions when a contrast is indeed being made between two kinds of life, a real and an unreal, almost between what Lukacs would call "capitalist reality and reality as such".

A much more subtle contrast exists between Tolstoy's presentation of different kinds of self-satisfaction. There is a difference between the natural *samodovolnost* of Natasha and the ludicrous and infectious mass satisfactions of society. The first springs from its own authentic sense of being: the second is bogus, and induced by the social assumption that what is fashionable must be marvellous. Natasha's true gaiety is self-regulating, like a physical process. "She was gay because she had been sad too long and because she was feeling well." When, before her engagement, she is disappointed that Prince Andrew has not turned up she returns to "her favourite mood, love of—and delight in—herself". Her internal soliloquy is like everybody's: "What a charming creature that Natasha is! Pretty, a voice, young, and she's in no one's way—only leave her in peace". But she feels immediately she can't be at peace. True *samodovolnost* is hurried inevitably by the processes of living from self-delight to agitation and despair and back again. Only those who are patronised by Tolstoy and ourselves can achieve a settled complacency, like Vera and Berg. In the world of *War and Peace* solipsism calls to solipsism; conceit recognises and falls in love with its own form of conceit. Thus Berg sees his own in Vera and thinks *"Das soll mein Weib werden"*, and thus Andrew recognises Natasha. Both Andrew and Natasha are seekers, making of themselves a channel for the flow of experience, he on the conscious mental level, and she on the unconscious physical one. Only in Tolstoy is self-satisfaction compatible with quest, and indeed a part of it. In *Sevastopol* the young Tolstoy made a characteristic observation on *samodovolnost* which contrasts with the deep organic role it plays in *War and Peace*.

> Vanity! vanity! vanity! everywhere, even on the brink of the grave and among men ready to die for a noble cause. Vanity! It seems to

be the characteristic feature and special malady of our time. How is it that among our predecessors no mention was made of this passion, as of small-pox and cholera? How is it that in our time there are only three kinds of people: those who, considering vanity an inevitably existing fact and therefore justifiable, freely submit to it; those who regard it as a sad but unavoidable condition; and those who act unconsciously and slavishly under its influence? Why did the Homers and Shakespeares speak of love, glory, and suffering, while the literature of today is an endless story of snobbery and vanity?

It is remarkable how the perception which produced this crudely complacent denunciation (it shows both that Tolstoy had been reading Thackeray and had *not* read the *Iliad* or *King Lear* with much attention) buried itself in the principle of characterisation which underlies the whole novel.

11. *War*

In war *samodovolnost* is vitally important and very revealing.

He was obviously thinking of nothing at that moment except that he was marching before his commander in fine style. With the complacency of a man on parade he stepped lightly on his muscular legs, as if sailing along without the smallest effort, and this lightness contrasted with the heavy tread of the soldiers keeping step with him. He wore by his leg a slender unsheathed blade (a small curved sabre, more like a toy than a weapon) and looking about him, now at the commander, now to the rear, he turned his whole powerful frame without getting out of step.

"more like a toy than a weapon"—naturally! Fully armed in his sense of himself he does not need one. We are brave because our self-attachment cannot easily be ruptured by contact with the known dangers of war—it is never ourselves who are to be killed. (In fact the officer described in this passage is knocked over by a bullet on the next page.) There are many aspects of bravery, but most depend on the ability to create, as Petya does before his death, a complete world of our own in the midst of alien circumstance. Nicholas finds that one cannot get used to being shot at, but that the secret is to think about something else, and he is one of those fortunates who have no trouble in doing so. Neither has Tushin, who thinks of the enemy guns as men smoking pipes at him. "From the sight of all these things a fantastic world of his own had taken possession of his brain and afforded him pleasure". We remember the world Pierre discovers when a prisoner.

But even more than the quality of their bravery, the self-absorption of men in battle exhibits their pathetic isolation. The happy officer was genuinely unconscious of everything except himself, and when he fell no one was in the least conscious of him. The officer who tells Pierre about the disposition of the trenches before Borodino does so "with a smile of satisfaction" because he had helped to make them. And he goes on to say, as if he also took a personal pride in that fact, that "many a man will be missing tomorrow". He cannot separate this from his pride of ownership, and no one expects him to, but his sergeant interrupts at this point, "and the officer appeared abashed, as if he understood that one might think of how many men would be missing tomorrow, but ought not to speak of it". We remember the contented look—"as of a boy happily in love"—on Napoleon's face before Austerlitz, when he sees that "his predictions were being justified", and at such moments we see the horrifying connection between solipsism and power. The Russian officer realises, though too late, that one cannot speak of the fate of men as if it were a part of one's own satisfaction. Berg in his small way, and Napoleon in his large and terrible way, have no such realisation. For Berg the abandonment of Moscow means his gratification at the chance of getting the chiffonnier "dear Vera has long wanted". By conveying the varieties of self-absorption in touches like these, Tolstoy gives living reality to his theoretical attitude towards history's 'great men', who think they influence events when in reality they are in the grip of forces they cannot understand or control. Berg and Napoleon can no more help regarding everything as arranged for their benefit, or by their will, than Nicholas or Bagration can help their instinct for doing the right thing at the right moment, in the crises of war as of hunting.

The most moving moments in the military sequences of *War and Peace* are produced by the unexpected removal of the absurd or dreadful self-isolation which war reveals so clearly. At such moments human beings seem in natural communion with each other. One occurs in the camp the night before Petya's death.

> "What are you sharpening?" asked a man who came up to the cart.
> "Why, this gentleman's sabre".
> "That's right", said the man, who seemed to Petya to be a hussar. "Was the cup left here?"
> "Over there by the wheel". The hussar took the cup. "Soon be daylight", he remarked, yawning, as he went off.

Another occurs in the camp at dusk after Borodino, when Pierre is given food by some soldiers, and then returns to his own world when his coachman finds him.

> The soldiers halted.
> "Well, found your own folks then?" said one of them.
> "Well, goodbye to you—Pyotr Kirillovitch isn't it?"
> "Goodbye Pyotr Kirillovitch" said other voices.

Such moments have in Tolstoy no aggressive effect of 'together-ness'—he detested German emphasis on the comradely aspects of war—and in their simplicity there is no trace of the emphatic. They stand out in their queerly moving way in the narrative only by the release that they represent from individual self-absorption. Are they moving because they record the momentary let-up of our habitual alienation, perhaps even of that "alienation of the upper-class from the other classes" which Tolstoy had remarked on as a predominant characteristic of the period? Or because they emphasise it? Perhaps both. The soldiers in the darkness saying goodbye to Pierre; the hussar who comes for the cup and who, after a casual remark, has perhaps 'simply vanished', as Petya feels—they are both extraordinarily real and extraordinarily subjective, phantoms of Pierre's fatigue and of Petya's excitement.

Tolstoy's military narrative is remarkably flexible and capable of unexpected variations. Like Shakespeare, who now makes a straight use of Holinshed or Plutarch, now creates an incident entirely in his own way, Tolstoy can suddenly elect to follow a traditional historical account almost word for word, as when a captured Russian colonel is introduced after Austerlitz to Napoleon.

"Are you the commander of the Emperor Alexander's horse-guards?" demanded Napoleon.

"I was in command of a squadron," replied Repnin.

"Your regiment did its duty honourably," said Napoleon.

"The praise of a great general is the soldier's highest reward", said Repnin.

"I bestow it upon you with pleasure," said Napoleon. "Who is this young man beside you?" Prince Repnin gave his name—Lieutenant Sukhtelen.

Looking at him, Napoleon said with a smile, "He is very young to come and meddle with us."

"Youth is no hindrance to valour," said Sukhtelen in a breaking voice.

"A fine answer," said Napoleon. "Young man, you will go far."[1]

This was how all the participants saw themselves at that moment so that for once, Tolstoy implies, the absurdity of historical accounts is quite in accord with what happened naturally. The little historical tableau is observed by the unhistorical Prince Andrew, who is too dazed and stunned to play the same part, and who sees the whole charade, so engrossing to the others, as quite without meaning, "compared to the lofty, equitable, and kindly sky". When Napoleon addresses him he says nothing, but the Emperor is far too wrapped up in his own satisfaction to notice this lapse of cue.

On Empire battle canvases in the Louvre, and the same with their opposite numbers in the Hermitage, every face is turned towards the centre: the wounded soldier gazes soulfully at Napoleon or at Kutuzov; the adroit A.D.C. prompts; admiring officers complete the circle. Tolstoy paints the classic and endur-ing picture—the Uccello, Piero, or Velasquez—where the opposite is the case. His faces, like theirs, have a photographic horror or tranquillity, they are insulated in the preoccupation of individual being. But he knows, too, that there are moments in war when—to continue the pictorial analogue—even Gérard and David have a fleeting validity, that the compositions they imagine *can* occur. Stendhal, though his master, as he admits, in the art of describing war, perhaps did not know this? Stendhal

[1] Tolstoy copied this from *The War of* 1805, by Danilevsky, who had himself translated the episode from the French of Prince Repnin's memoirs

would have made some comment on this scene (like his note on Fabrice "listening to the silence") in order to show that he knew war never in the least resembled its reconstruction by painters and historians. Tolstoy seems to know that the actualities of war, as of life itself, can appear in every possible form.

An entertaining case of technique is what might be called 'the reversed pastoral', when Tolstoy sets the historical *cliché* against his own account of what really happened. The French have captured what they take to be a Cossack, an "enfant du Don", but we know that this Cossack is merely Lavrushka, the servant of Nicholas Rostov. Realising that he is in the presence of Napoleon, he at once enters in to the spirit of the thing, and puts on a suitable air of awe and astonishment when the god-like figure discloses his identity, gives the "enfant du Don" a suitable present, and (says the French historian Thiers) "had him set free like a bird restored to its native fields". Tolstoy thus implies that pastoral is good enough for the French, who see all life in terms of it (another instance is Captain Ramballe's continual references to "ma pauvre mère") but that we Russians prefer the simple truth. We hardly notice that in order to reveal "the simple truth" Tolstoy has recourse to the thumping coincidence of the 'Cossack' being our old friend Lavrushka. And what if Thiers was right, and the prisoner really had been impressed when told who Napoleon was?

In general, though, Tolstoy in *War and Peace* contrives to lay coincidence, oversimplification, and even his early mania for cataloguing types, at his characters' door: he does not have to bear their burden himself. When Nicholas rescues Princess Mary it is just as well that this should be so.

> When she saw his Russian face, and recognised him by his words and gait for a man of her own class, she looked at him with her deep, luminous gaze and began to speak in a voice trembling with emotion. It at once seemed to Rostov that there was something very romantic about this meeting. "A defenceless girl, crushed by sorrow, alone, abandoned to the mercy of coarse, rebellious peasants! And what strange destiny has brought me here?" thought Rostov, as he listened to her and looked at her.

Except for one sentence, this has almost the note of a historical pot-boiler, like Zagoskin's romance of 1812, *Roslavlev*, which

Tolstoy had read and enjoyed. But it is Rostov whom this meeting immediately strikes as a romantic event, not Tolstoy. And his simple response to it absolves Tolstoy from any further consideration of the strange and incomprehensible motives of the Bogucharovo peasantry, who have prevented Princess Mary from leaving. Their intransigence is reduced to meek submission by Rostov, who behaves as instinctively as he would in action or when hunting, swearing at them and knocking them about. Old Alpatych at once sees that "this unreasonable action might produce good results", for he knows that "the chief way to make them obey is to show no suspicion that they might possibly disobey" (like so much else in the book this is also an analogue of the writer's attitude towards his reader). Tolstoy implies that the men of 1812 made that epoch *right* in a social as well as in a military sense, by their instinctively confident behaviour; but it is Rostov himself, with his simple romanticism and his simple response, who bears the actual weight of any such implication.

In a very early story, *The Woodfelling*, Tolstoy gives us the results of his own analysis of military types.

These principle types, including many sub-divisions and combinations, are:
1. The submissive.
2. The domineering.
3. The reckless.
The submissive are divided into (*a*) the calmly submissive, and (*b*) the bustlingly submissive.
The domineering are divided into (*a*) the sternly domineering, and (*b*) the diplomatically domineering.
The reckless are divided into (*a*) the amusingly reckless, and (*b*) the viciously reckless.

In *War and Peace* it is not Tolstoy but the beady-eyed Boris who has made a comparable sort of analysis from his military experience, and concluded that beside the hierarchic subordination "prescribed in the military code", there was another kind of hierarchy in military circles which depended upon birth, confidence, and tone, upon being one of 'Les Nôtres' and 'the understanders'. He realises this most clearly when he sees Prince

Andrew patronising an obsequious purple-faced old general, and he becomes "more than ever resolved to serve in future not according to the written code but under this unwritten law". No doubt the young Tolstoy had made the same sort of resolution. But Boris's discovery receives an immediate and ludicrous check, for the old general, "evidently not sharing Boris's conception of the advantages of the unwritten code of subordination", stares at him so sternly that he soon hastens to become obsequious himself. In such ways does Tolstoy subdue himself and his methods to individual character and its consequences in the run of the book. His own perceptions and the fruit of his own analyses is given to his characters, and not necessarily to those with whom he feels most in sympathy.

Tolstoy's habit of cataloguing types was not uncommon in other Russian fiction of his time. Gogol had practised it in his own fantastic way, and in Pisemsky's long novel *A Thousand Souls*, published in 1858, there is a particularly lively catalogue of the various types of servility shown by officials, as well as a good deal of sententious and Thackerayan expatiation on the author's part. But Tolstoy is unique in handing over all such obvious flourishes in *War and Peace* to his characters and effacing himself behind their psychological discoveries, while retaining his own generalising powers for the larger kinds of assertion.

His presentation of war is singularly consistent in one respect: success in it can only be attained by passivity. As Kutuzov says, "tout vient à celui qui sait attendre". To justify oneself in war one must obey the larger law of life, and surrender one's individual will to fate. To be successful is to discern the momentum of the inevitable and to move with it. Before Austerlitz Kutuzov knows that everything is bound to go wrong because the generals are trying to work it out beforehand, but he knows there is nothing he can do to stop them and so at the council he simply goes to sleep, acquiescing in defeat before defeat has occurred. Napoleon is the arch-villain of war because he thinks he is its master: in fact he only wins because his enemies try to behave in the same way as he does, and because a Weyrother or a Dolgorukov—or Alexander himself—seek to impose their will on the battlefield.

I have already remarked on the curious parallel in Tolstoy between male sexual activity and the willed and wanton aggressions of war, and so faithfully does he follow out this parallel that it produces some curious inconsistencies. At the council before Austerlitz it is natural that Miloradovitch, who is later compared to Murat, the epitome of stupid military panache, should represent the absurdity of mere pugnacity for its own sake. His "impressive but meaningless gaze" is like the meaningless smile of Anatole Kuragin. But Tolstoy is faced with the fact that Kutuzov himself was a noted rake and womaniser, even in his old age. What was to be done? Instead of concealing the fact, Tolstoy does the next best thing: like Pierre's visits to the brothel, he leaves it in the dim world of alleged fact—he fails to make it imaginatively positively true. All we hear is the bald statement that at Vilna Kutuzov gave himself up to dissipation (a term which, like 'carnage' or 'debauchery', conveys no practical realisation to the reader). Once we see him chucking the pretty wife of a priest, his hostess, under the chin, and calling her "my beauty", but in this as in so much else he seems only like an old Russian gnome, *domovoi*, who presides over the ancient household routine that is threatened by the French invasion.

As well as removing actuality from Kutuzov's amours, Tolstoy omits to mention that he had been an aggressive and enterprising commander, trained in the tactics of Suvorov, and his partner in the Turkish wars. Here Tolstoy makes an epic detail —the seamed and empty eye-socket—suggest the general's ancient experience of war while at the same time distracting us from the actual nature of that experience. Suvorov himself, the most remarkable of all Russian commanders, has a strangely equivocal position in the book. He belonged to no Tolstoyan category; neither to the cold vain Don Juan-like war-lovers, like Napoleon, nor to the pathetic and dedicated purists, like Weyrother and Pfuel, nor to the boasters and strong men, like Murat and Miloradovitch. Regrettably for Tolstoy, he seems to have combined great personal charm, intelligence, candour and directness with a temperament devoted entirely to war as such. His letters from his various campaigns, which Tolstoy must have known, are some of the best in Russian literature

(Mirsky calls them second only to Pushkin's). He served
Catherine the Great against the rebel Pugachev, and the mad
Emperor Paul against the best of the French generals in Italy
and the Alps, where he came near to toppling the military power
of the young republic. When anxiously asked by his Austrian
colleagues what his objective was, he replied simply: "Paris".
It is clear why this formidable and astonishing figure, whose
little army, like Hannibal's, was devoted to and identified with
its leader, had to be kept out of *War and Peace*.

Yet he is not kept out entirely. His presence can be felt, and
it gives a clue to our acceptance of so much that is inconsistent,
slanted and downright perverse in Tolstoy's theory of war. We
accept him on the level of theory because the inevitable objections to theory are always registered on the level of art. Military
adventurism, whatever its motive, was disapproved of by Tolstoy: he is as much against the campaigns of 1813 and 1814,
which brought the Russian army to Paris, as he is against the
campaign of Austerlitz, and as he was to be against the Slav
liberation movement at the end of *Anna Karenina*. But in *War
and Peace* his disapproval is dissolved, as it were, in the continuity which flows into the book at both ends. The conclusion
that does not conclude, and the beginning that is not really a
beginning, mean—in effect—that Tolstoy's own dogma is
equally relative and equally subject to historical attrition. As
the book looks forward to, but does not treat of, the Decembrist
movement, so it looks back to the Europe of Voltaire and Fred-
erick the Great, the epoch in which both war and peace were in
the hands of individuals, not swayed by larger idealistic and
nationalistic forces. And as Pierre is the representative of the
future, so old Prince Bolkonsky is that of the past.

He is not only perhaps the most perfectly realised character in
the book, but the only one who is in some sense a true historical
reconstruction. Almost he is Suvorov himself. Like Suvorov he
has been both honoured and victimised by the Emperor Paul,
who exiled him to his country estates. Dry, witty, explosive,
Voltairean, he represents an attitude to war which is the reverse
of Tolstoy's own. For him it is a question of honour, profession-
alism, service, the devotion of a lifetime and—above all—the
occupation of a *man*. Significantly he likes talking to Pierre, who

171

is full of futuristic notions like the Abbé Morio's scheme for perpetual peace, and these he dismisses with the serene cynicism of the eighteenth century. "Drain the blood from men's veins and put in water instead—then there will be no more war!" He accepts the aggressive nature of man as he would accept his sexual nature. There is, too, something very deliberately impressive and resonant about the moment when old Bolkonsky takes leave of his son, and entrusts to him his memoirs and a special sum of money—"a premium for the man who writes a history of Suvorov's wars". At such a moment other wars enter the book, in the same way that other lives and other truths do.

Just before Borodino Napoleon receives a report about the battle of Salamanca, where Wellington had defeated Marmont in Spain. It is a slighter instance of a contradiction obtruding itself in the midst of Tolstoy's war thesis, for Salamanca was almost the perfect example of a battle fought in a style in which Tolstoy insists that battles can never be fought. But Wellington, like Suvorov, was in many ways an eighteenth-century general, manœuvring with an army of limited size. Napoleon himself had remarked that a hundred thousand men was as much as one general could command, and at Borodino he had almost twice as many. At Leipzig, an equally shapeless battle, the numbers on both sides were even bigger. Tolstoy's conception of generalship is hardly valid retrospectively, or even about the Napoleonic wars as a whole, but it contains an important element of truth, and above all it was prescient. Of the 1914 war, just four years after Tolstoy died, it was appallingly true.

It is not the only one of Tolstoy's perceptions about war which seems to have acquired a special and sinister relevance in our own time. The whole notion of responsibility for 'war crimes' emerges from the conversation between Denisov and Dolokhov about what should be done with the French prisoners.

> "I send them away and take a receipt for them!" shouted Denisov, suddenly flushing. "And I say boldly that I have not a single man's life on my conscience. Would it be difficult for you to send thirty or three hundred men to town under escort instead of staining—I speak bluntly—staining the honour of a soldier?"
> "That kind of amiable talk would be suitable for this young count of sixteen," said Dolokhov with cold irony, "but it's time for you

to drop it . . . Yes, for you and me, old fellow, it's time to drop these amenities," he went on, as if he found particular pleasure in speaking of this subject which irritated Denisov. "Don't we know those receipts of yours. You send a hundred men away and thirty get there. The rest either starve or get killed. So isn't it all the same not to send them?"

". . . That's not the point. I'm not going to discuss the matter. I do not wish to take it on my conscience. You say they'll die. All right. Only not by my doing."

Another participant is the Cossack captain, "with his narrow light eyes, and calm self-satisfaction in his face and bearing". He quite agrees with Dolokhov. For him, as for the soldier Tikhon, whose pockmarked face "beams with self-satisfied glee", the enemy are there to be killed in one way or another. For Petya the whole thing is an exciting game, and even when it is clear that Tikhon has killed in cold blood a French officer he was bringing back, thinking him "not suitable", Petya cannot quite believe it. Denisov knows what happens, but his own nature and his honour as a Russian officer won't let him do it himself; what happens elsewhere is no affair of his, as it was not with so many more recent commanders concerned to uphold 'the honour of the German fighting man'. Dolokhov is a different case. He enjoys it, and masks his enjoyment under the pretence of total honesty: that is the way things are, and only hypocrites try to compound the fact.

The whole episode of the partisan *coup* shows how faithfully Tolstoy confines the problems and realities of guerrilla warfare to what his five protagonists can make of them. There is no detachment. They are happily engrossed in their job. Petya's death means more to Denisov than the massacre of unarmed Frenchmen that presumably follows it, but the survivors would no more dwell on the one than they would on the other. In Isaac Babel's stories, by contrast, which clearly owe much to the Tolstoyan tradition, some point about the nature of such warfare is always being made. And the point of the story necessarily also expresses both the author's self and his artistic detachment. To be detached as an artist in such cases, oddly enough, is to be present as an author. He is asking us to understand what goes on as we might try to understand some savage tribe. When in *War and*

Peace the incendiarists are shot in Moscow there is the same presentation from a single viewpoint—that of Pierre, or Pierre-Tolstoy. The guerrilla episode is more finely done, and is moving on more than one level. The author is not requiring us to standardise our response towards the thing—how can we?—because we ourselves are probably like one or more of the characters involved—like Petya if we first read *War and Peace* at about his age, and at a later reading perhaps more like Denisov.

In Tolstoy's early military sketches he often presents to us a perfectly realised character—Velenchuk in *The Woodfelling* is one such—whom he can then do nothing more with. In *War and Peace* such portraits are not worked up in the fictional sense—the early tales are in this respect more like conventional fiction than the big plotted work—but they afford Tolstoy the basis for some further awareness about military life, an awareness that does not come over as a 'point'. Everyone with some experience of an organisation has known in it someone like the withdrawn and quietly conscientious Konovitsyn, and the *faux bonhomme* Ermolov, who tries to do the former down just because he is conscientious, and who does not care if his spite jeopardises the whole communal effort. Shakespeare also knew that one is far more absorbed with the manœuvring among those on one's own side than with that of the enemy. And, beginning with character again, it is in a sense Tolstoy's most damning comment on the nature of war that Dolokhov gets on so well at it. Nicholas enjoys the "irreproachable idleness" of the military life; a simple unregenerate soul like Tikhon enjoys the self-importance of an expert killer; but Dolokhov is the embodiment of military diabolism, the man for whom the essence of war seems to have been specifically created.

His last satanic appearance opens with an unexpected sartorial detail. He appears in the partisan camp, where everybody is dressed according to circumstance (though Petya is bothered about the state his trousers have got into) wearing an extremely smart and correct guardsman's uniform. This is just what Dolokhov would do. His clothes have always expressed in some way the difference between him and others. We remember how he discomforted the colonel who abused him before Austerlitz for wearing the wrong coloured greatcoat, and how he turned up at the Moscow ballet in Persian costume. It is a touch that should connect him with the homeliness of *War and Peace*—its grasp of the incongruity and absurdity of life—but in fact it detaches him from it. For Dolokhov takes no ordinary satisfaction in his appearance. His most demonic quality is his lack of *samodovolnost*, which unites other human beings in unexpected ways and holds them at a level of common good. However "dreadful but enjoyable" war may be for them, the good soldiers in the book would have been more useful and more at home in peace than in war. The military qualities which Tolstoy most admires are those which a peaceful society most relies on. Unobtrusive hard work, humanity, unpretentiousness are the virtues for peace as well as in war; and courage itself is not a virtue to be singled out for admiration, but to be made use of discreetly, as occasion requires.

Dolokhov's queer, discordant boastfulness is not agreeably absurd, like Berg's: instead of amusement it arouses discomfort in those who hear him. We laugh when Berg refers to the "truly antique valour of the Russian army, which they—which it (he corrected himself) has displayed". But we hardly know what to think when Dolokhov talks of "rendering a service to my country for which I am ready to die", and the phrase disconcerts Kutuzov and the others. Berg, after all, is conveying something which in some sense he feels, otherwise he would not be able to express it even in this pompous way—pomposity shows an inadequacy of sensibility rather than of deep feeling. But if patriotism cannot be silent it should at least be pompous: Dolokhov's impudent use of its platitudes is curiously shocking.

At the Augesd dam he ran on to the ice, a demonic bell-wether leading the flock, and shouted that it would bear. Was it an act of bold initiative? We only know that for those who followed him the consequences were as terrible as they were for the Frenchmen whom his final exploit rounded up. And at the end we have one swift and startling detail about him which surprises us more than anything that has gone before. In the last seconds of his life, Petya sees Dolokhov "with his face a pale greenish tint". Any soldier has the right to a green face in battle, but this last touch makes Dolokhov an even more enigmatic figure. Was he a coward after all, as Don Juan was really afraid of women? Will war always be with us in order that Dolokhov can show that he is brave, and so that he can be himself—the self that others can be in peace? Our experience of war ends on this query, and shows us how inadequate the description "epic" is to the total nature of that experience in *War and Peace*. Dolokhov lives in another world to that of such an epic warrior as General Bagration. Yet there seems no doubt that Dolokhov the Russian is the personal incarnation of war in the book, as Napoleon the Frenchman is its public and historic one.

IV

Endings

The good become the Pharisees—they have no choice.
                NIETZSCHE, *Also sprach Zarathustra*

Pierre felt that his way of life had now been settled once and for all till death, and that to change it was not in his power.
                        War and Peace, Epilogue I

I

I HAVE suggested that Tolstoy uses pastoral at the end of *War and Peace,* and this might mean that before the book ends we are no longer sharing in the lives of the characters but contemplating them; that the men and women who have been changing, developing and discovering with us have now become distant, representative and static. We could put it another way by saying that *War and Peace,* which up till now has been like nothing except itself, ends as a novel.

And a novel with a hero. It is not Pierre who seems to be assuming that function, but Nicholas. And together with the hero it also acquires a tone, which is naturally triumphant but which is also incipiently oppressive, as every achieved tone runs the risk of being. For the first time the note of perception becomes a note of definition, and the dogma hardens into an assertion of authority which is no longer to be questioned by the continuation of life—that is, of the book. In a sense the thing is inevitable: life can only be cut short by recourse to the artificiality of the novel. Fates are sealed, like Sonya's, and because sealed, open to no further appeal. Of course, it was Tolstoy all along who decided what was to happen to whom, but now we can see him doing it.

Tolstoy has to settle matters, and he does so with the air of a man who after an absorbing and delightful evening looks at his watch and realises with a sudden start how late it is. There is a distinct hiatus between the progress that Nicholas has made with Princess Mary before the epilogue and his behaviour at the beginning of it. We are told that his pride would not let him communicate further with her, after his father's death has left his affairs in so bad a state, but we do not quite see the inwardness of this—Nicholas has developed characteristics which there is no time to prove to us, as all his earlier characteristics have been proved in the earlier perspectives of the book. In some ways, of course, this cessation of full understanding is just like life. The death of old Count Rostov has changed not only the lives of the rest of the family but their community with each other and our community with them—like Natasha and Pierre in Petersburg we do not fully realise what is going on. The sense of an inevitable separation, brought about not by any estrangement but by preoccupation with the nucleus of new family groups is deeply moving. But to bring Princess Mary and Nicholas finally together, Tolstoy resorts unashamedly to the novel.

> She turned round. For a few seconds they gazed silently into one another's eyes—and what had seemed impossible and remote suddenly became possible, inevitable, and very near.

Accomplished as rapidly as this, the solution is inevitable not in terms of life but in terms of literature—it seems a Thackerayan necessity rather than a Tolstoyan one.

Curiously enough, by resorting to the winding-up processes of the novel Tolstoy exposes his own position much more openly than before. After getting Nicholas married, he proceeds to give a picture of him as the model landowner. And this is not cunningly and laboriously made out of histories and memoirs, stories and observations of relatives, and all the complex material of past and present life, but directly from his own experience at the time of writing. Individuality is lost: there seems no essential difference at this point between Nicholas, the Levin of *Anna Karenina*, and Tolstoy himself. Momentarily we lose contact with the most important part of individuality— Nicholas's *samodovolnost*. In a few more lines he is dead and sanctified—"the memory of his administration was devoutly preserved among the serfs". We remember that *War and Peace* appeared not long after the serfs' liberation, in the troubled years when every objection was being made to the scheme, and every crisis and confusion arising from it interpreted as a bad augury: and we have a moment's uneasy feeling that the whole dimension of the book has shrunk to a defence of the good landlord in what the reformers call the bad old days. But at this moment Tolstoy pulls himself up, and Nicholas is jerked back to life again, in both senses.

> In the winter he visited his other villages or spent his time reading. The books he read were chiefly historical, and on these he spent a certain sum every year. He was collecting, as he said, a serious library, and he made it a rule to read through all the books he bought. He would sit in his study with a grave air, reading—a task he first imposed on himself as a duty, but which became a habit affording him a special kind of pleasure and a consciousness of being occupied with serious matters.

Tolstoy had also collected such a library, and no doubt liked to think of himself occupied with serious matters, as do we all, but the point is that here is Nicholas himself again—and virtually for the last time. For in almost the next sentence we hear that strange note of equivocation which is the most remarkable and even the most impressive thing about the epilogue.

The source of this equivocation seems to be the loss of individuality which total marriage entails—the note of equivocation is the note of conjugal harmony. It is a further indication of how much the clarity and openness of what has gone before depends on the completely realised individuality of the main characters: now that they are to lose that individuality the whole outlook is changed. Tolstoy tells us that the harmony between Nicholas and his wife grew closer and closer, "and he daily discovered fresh spiritual treasures in her". What are these spiritual treasures? From the scenes that follow, culminating in their evening conversation in the bedroom, it might appear that they are the signs of Mary's readiness to be absorbed by Nicholas, and to subdue herself to his outlook and function.

> Had Nicholas been able to analyse his feelings he would have found that his steady, proud, tender love of his wife rested on his feeling of wonder at her spirituality, and at the lofty moral world, almost beyond his reach, in which she had her being.

Almost beyond his reach? In which she had her being? In the next paragraph we read that Nicholas "rejoiced all the more that she, with such a soul, not only belonged to him but was part of himself". He starts to tell her (though she knows already) how he lost his temper in the dispute with Pierre about politics, and how Natasha rules over Pierre.

> "And yet there need only be a discussion, and she has no words of her own but repeats his sayings," added Nicholas, yielding to that irresistible inclination which tempts us to judge those nearest and dearest to us. He forgot that what he was saying about Natasha could be applied word for word to himself in relation to his wife.

His wife agrees with him, and in these terms.

> "As I see it, you were right, and I told Natasha so. Pierre says that everyone is suffering, is tortured, and is being corrupted, and that it is our duty to help our neighbour. Of course he is right there," said Countess Mary, "but he forgets that we have other duties nearer to us, duties indicated to us by God himself, and that though we might expose ourselves to risks we must not risk our children."
>
> "Yes, that's it! That's just what I said to him," interrupted Nicholas, who fancied he really had said it. "But they insisted on their own view—love of one's neighbour and Christianity."

Nicholas is upset, as he was back in 1808 when he witnessed the treaty celebrations between Alexander and Napoleon, and when the sight of all the diplomatic hypocrisy gave him strange and disconcerting thoughts that no loyal officer should entertain. But then he had no Countess Mary to aid him in the process of dismissing such thoughts. He rejects them by appealing for her confirmation of the claim that what he does for her and the children is itself a sacrifice. "Is it for my own pleasure that I am at the farm or the office from morning to night?"

> Countess Mary wanted to tell him that man does not live by bread alone, and that he attached too much importance to those *businesses*. But she knew that she must not say this, and that it would be useless to do so. She only took his hand and kissed it. He took this as a sign of approval and a confirmation of his thoughts, and after a few moments reflection continued to think aloud.

"With an eager face" he goes on at once to speak of the chances of buying back Otradnoe (the Rostov family estate) before long.

Countess Mary listened to her husband and understood all that he told her. She knew that when he thought aloud in this way he would sometimes ask her what he had been saying, and be vexed if he noticed that she had been thinking about something else. . . . She looked at him and did not think, but felt, about something different. She felt a submissive tender love for this man who would never understand all that she understood.

Unlike her husband she is not disturbed by the implications of the argument with Pierre, but "she promises in her heart to do better and to accomplish the impossible, as Christ loved mankind". This thought gives her the spiritual look at which Nicholas gazes with awe, and which makes him go to the ikon to say his own prayers.

In other writers the tone of this passage would mean one of two things: a prodigious irony or a pious ignorance. Tolstoy's calm clarity gives no indication of either. Flaubert, enthusiastic over the rest of *War and Peace*, said that the end *dégringole affreusement*, and that in it we see the author and the gentleman —*Le monsieur*— where before we saw only nature and mankind. This is a cogent criticism, and does indeed apply to Tolstoy's account of Nicholas as a landowner, where he makes use both of the novel-ending convention and of his own image of his life at the time. But the masterly equivocator who takes over at the words—"As in every large household, there were at Bald Hills several perfectly distinct worlds which merged into one harmonious whole"—how can we call him "L'auteur et le monsieur"? Tolstoy has escaped again, and Flaubert's exasperation seems to be caused by this new shift in artistic diplomacy. How is he to take it? Since it is evidently not the placing irony which he himself knew well, and which is built into the whole method of objective realism, he lays it at the door of the author and the gentleman.

In fact Tolstoy has escaped by talking to us as if we were the other half of a marital whole. The clue to the amazing and marvellous method of the epilogue is the marital dialogue of which it gives two unsurpassed descriptions. And rather naturally Flaubert is hostile to this dialogue, as an author would be who had written: "*Un amour normal, regulier, nourri, et solide, me sortirait trop hors de moi . . . m'a été nuisible toutes les fois que j'ai voulu le tenter"*. The clarity, complexity, and omissive assurance of the epilogue resembles the mode of married converse which Nicholas and Mary have come to possess, and also Natasha and Pierre. It is "talk such as only a husband and wife can talk, that is, with extraordinary clearness and rapidity, understanding and expressing each other's thoughts in ways contrary to all rules of logic, without premises, deductions, or conclusions, and in a quite peculiar way". Without premises, deductions or conclusions . . . Tolstoy contrives to give us everything without giving us those. Misunderstandings and incomprehensions are, as it were, allowed for and regulated by the method. Princess Mary "knew that she must not say this", but she does not feel any omission or victimisation in not saying it. "Is it for my own pleasure that I am at the office or farm from morning to night?" demands Nicholas, and runs no risk of her pointing out that he is one of the fortunate for whom duty and inclination coincide. In these ideal family circumstances, doing what you want is the same as doing what you must. Each compounds for the other and ensures their mutual peace of mind. Though she hardly listens to him, Mary is absorbing in her turn the same sort of family reassurance as Nicholas. It is because of him and their communion together that she can retain untroubled her 'spirituality'—the equivalent of Nicholas's outlook as a landowner—that she can calmly put aside the duty of "helping our neighbour" which the quarrel with Pierre has brought up, and can tranquilly "promise herself in her heart to do better and to accomplish the impossible". "Her soul strove toward the infinite," says Tolstoy, "and could therefore never be at peace." But if it is not at peace that he has portrayed her, peace is not given to human beings. In their relation, Nicholas is reassured and released from guilt by the potentially dangerous, alien and unsatisfied element in her; and she in turn is reassured by her unjudging love of him and his self-limiting convictions.

Like all human relationships it is full of potential trouble: it will have to modify itself ceaselessly in order to last, and it may not last. But this is suggested by the art of the epilogue, not by what we know of Tolstoy's married life. Aylmer Maude observes that Tolstoy's own nature could never be at peace, and that through the figure of Princess Mary he is already anticipating his own spiritual pilgrimage. The backward deduction may be justified biographically, but in reading *War and Peace* we should do better to forget it. Tolstoy describes with Mozartian distinctness how "nature and mankind" may and do achieve happiness:

> *Mann und Weib, und Weib und Mann,*
> *Reichen an die Gottheit an—*

and he also suggests, by the same marital mode, how endlessly temporary is this happiness, whose confidence is won, not from security, but from the dialogue daily resumed.

In our later readings of *War and Peace* it is instructive to interrupt the dialogue and decline to meet Tolstoy as a marriage partner; to withhold the clear and rapid interchange of assumptions, and to supply the "premises, deductions and conclusions", which are taken for granted in the mode. "When one reads him young," says Shestov, "with what joy one contemplates that transparent and luminous depth." But the reward of re-reading him later (and how many readers never go back, thinking that transparency all they would ever re-discover there?) is to see how many things lurk in the depths, and how insidiously instructive is their relation to what is clear. *War and Peace* is one of the very few classics which become more and not less disconcertingly informative each time we read it. And this is because of the endless interest of Tolstoy's relation with his characters—a truly dramatic relation. He is almost at war with them; he seeks their alliance or submission, feints and withdraws with every resource of diplomacy except that last one. In creation he may have envisaged them as allies, but their reality has turned them into opponents and equals, just as we ourselves are —or can become—in relation to him.

In *The Philosophy of Tragedy* Shestov points out that in Dostoevsky and Nietzsche we cannot but find a moral—"some would recognise an old one, others discover a new"—and this despite the destructive message of those two *féroces*, and their war upon our notions of the Ideal and the Good. "It may be," he goes on, "that future generations will read these writers with as much calm as we read Goethe today." This is indeed the nemesis of literary Messianism. Not only have the conservatives and the good no choice but to become pharisees, as Nietzsche said: the same fate is reserved for the new, the startling, the terrible—for Nietzsche himself. Already today the tenets of existentialism, apparently so pitiless and so searching, have become the opiate of the sub-intelligentsia, the props on which the common reader interested in ideas can cheerfully recline. Every novelist who shocks us today will eventually be read calmly and securely, if he is read at all. In *War and Peace* we expect calm and security in any case, and we get them, but with each re-reading we become less aware of these desirable things and more aware of how fertilising to our moral intelligence, in its most quotidian functions, the book and its epilogue can be.

Our daily morality cannot but be equivocal in a sense, because it records the difference between how we find ourselves living and how we reflect on the way we live. *War and Peace* combines the serenity of reflection, the serenity of the past, with the second by second process of living at the latest moment of our own lives and of history. The epilogue seems to bring the book to an end at the moment we are reading it—it is perpetually modern. And this is the ultimate weakness of Shestov's position; penetrating as his analysis is, he approaches Tolstoy as a historian of attitudes and ideas. Like a sardonic curator, he shows us round an exquisitely arranged museum of moral dubieties, and of assumptions about the Good which seemed as certain as the hills but which he proves to be as fragile as porcelain. For Countess Mary he has the reverence of a connoisseur. How admirable is her "of course", he remarks, when she says that Pierre is "of course" right that it is our duty to help our neighbour!

Another step, and hypocrisy becomes a law, and, dreadful as it seems, a law of the moral conscience. Indeed the words of Countess Mary show that this step has already been taken. But the strangest thing is that Tolstoy behaves as if nothing had occurred, as if he did not see what an abyss he had cleared in one leap. . . . What 'psychology' Dostoevsky would have expended on it! But Tolstoy knows from experiment that when one approaches such an antinomy one must do so with a pure and pious face—goodbye otherwise to the *a priori* and the solid ground of principle. In this diplomatic craft he has no equal. One can see in it the long line of ancestors who, in

the service of the state, had learned how to preserve a parade-
ground imperturbability. . . . Until Tolstoy, idealism was ignorant
of these refined techniques. It had to use crude deceptions, fine feelings, eloquence and unreal colours.

To Shestov, whose continual thesis is that human beings must
accept death and anarchy instead of looking for a coherent
universe and a rule to live by, the spectacle is as essentially
pathetic as the structure created by every moral idealist must be.
To him it makes no difference that our duty to help our neighbour has become subtly metamorphosed into our duty to be
happy and to bring up our family in happiness—the thing is an
ideal just the same. But Shestov ignores the fact that Tolstoy,
unlike most idealistic novelists (George Eliot for example) is
profoundly aware of the difficulty that he is in. He wants certainty and peace in the conviction of doing the right thing, but
he knows he cannot have them. How much Tolstoy would like
to be Countess Mary; how much he admires her position, and
how painfully he reveals its weakness. His own, too, he reveals.
Pierre blames Alexander—"he seeks only for peace, and only
these people *sans foi ni loi* can give it to him . . .", Arakcheev
and the other tyrants. Tolstoy too seeks for peace and knows
that only people like Nicholas Rostov can give it to him—what
Arakcheev was to Alexander, Nicholas is to Tolstoy.

Yet before the book is over Tolstoy has surprised us again
(as Alexander, according to the legend which Tolstoy was to
follow, escaped from his detractors by his mysterious abdication). For Nicholas's hero status turns out not to mean so
much after all. And this is not because Pierre and Natasha are
contrasted with Nicholas and Mary, and presented as the
worthier pair, the pair of the future. On the contrary. Tolstoy's
authority in assuming and presenting difference appears nowhere more extraordinarily than in his account of the relation
of the two married couples. It is apparently almost identical, and
yet it is entirely different, for they are different people. Any
other writer, we feel, would almost involuntarily have made a
sharp distinction between the pattern and mode of the two
marriages. In terms of the novel the opportunity would seem
overwhelmingly tempting, and the reward great. But Tolstoy
does not do so. Nicholas's heroic status, on which Shestov—

dissecting the epilogue in terms of attitude and idea—rightly insists, is in fact dissipated not by the contrast between his position and that of Pierre, but by the resemblance.

They are two entirely different people in the same boat. And each justly perceives how the similarity of their position as happily married men is displayed by the *other*—they do not consider how their status affects their own selves. Nicholas sees that Pierre is under his wife's thumb; Pierre sees that the social ideas and discussion which he thinks so real and urgent to himself are for Nicholas "an amusement, almost a pastime"—that was why he got so angry when these ideas in Pierre's mouth seemed to be threatening the fabric of his life. Yet in practice both men are helpless, caught by life in the same conjugal understanding which both settles all issues and leaves them forever unsettled. The "several perfectly distinct worlds" have "merged into one harmonious whole". And again Tolstoy employs the dream analogy.

> Just as in a dream, when all is uncertain, unreasoning, and contradictory, except the feeling that guides the dream, so in this intercourse.

In his own room, young Nicholas is dreaming, leading his army of cobweb threads into the future, accompanied by his Uncle Pierre and thwarted by his Uncle Nicholas. Nicholas and Mary are having their bedtime discussion, and in another part of the house Pierre is talking to Natasha "with self-satisfaction and enthusiasm", while she listens with a quiet happy smile to "his complacent reflections on his success in St Petersburg".

II

Like *War and Peace*, *Anna Karenina* ends with an epilogue and an argument. Anna is dead, Vronsky is going off to fight for the Serbs. Why do people join such movements? Is it because they are expressing "the will of the people", or for other motives, more various and dubious? M. O. Katkov, in whose monthly magazine *Anna* was appearing, was an ardent Slavophil and refused to publish the epilogue. Tolstoy would not tone it down and finally withdrew it completely, breaking with Katkov. Another writer was commissioned to make a brief sketch, which appeared in the magazine under the title: "What happened after the death of Anna Karenina".

In spite of being an afterthought of Tolstoy's, prompted by a political question of the moment, the epilogue of *Anna* seems very much more a part of the novel—and in general part of a *novel*—than does that of *War and Peace*. The reason is in the tone. Not only is the tone self-consistent throughout the epilogue—·it is at one with the novel as a whole. Notwithstanding the criticism that Tolstoy spoilt the form of the novel by tacking on this appendage, what in fact strikes us is the way in which it echoes and dilates the same themes, preoccupations, even metaphors. It is as if Tolstoy could not avoid repeating these, almost obsessively, even when his attention had been drawn to an apparently quite different problem. This instinctive repetition and retexturing is artistically effective and coherent—it justifies the appendage. But it also means that we miss the seemingly guileless freedom and variety of the *War and Peace* epilogue, and its blithe alternations of tone. We might say that for all the evident intervention by the author the epilogue of *War and Peace* is dramatic, complex and multiform, even Shakespearean. That of *Anna* is economical, fictional, metaphorical.

The main 'point' made by *Anna* can be stated—this in itself separates it from *War and Peace*. It is the discovery that life will not stand still, and that to get what you want—so far from "settling life once for all till death"—leads to a disillusionment that must find relief in further search. To the supposition that life cannot remain fixed in one place, however admirable and agreeable, Tolstoy—as Shestov says—turned at the end of *War and Peace* a pure, naif, and pious face. Without denying it, he creates the married converse of the two couples, and in that converse it ceases to have meaning. The four of them deserve their happiness because it does not seem in their power to change it.

Now Anna is happy with Vronsky when she begins to live with him, outrageously, incredulously happy, and so is Kitty with Levin. But this happiness is very different from that of the two earlier couples. Even in her happiness Anna has no martial dialogue with Vronsky: we might expect that if Tolstoy's hand is against them, but we shall find it is also true of the lawfully wedded pair. And can we imagine Pierre deciding, as Levin does, that it is no use trying to tell Natasha what he is feeling and hoping? Nicholas takes particular pleasure in confessing to Mary when he has knocked his serfs about. She forgives and exonerates him. In the last paragraph of *Anna* Levin admits to himself that he will still get angry with the coachman, and that "even my wife I shall still blame for my own fears and shall repent of it". Guilt and repentance are solitary things now, not shared. After seven years of marriage Pierre and Natasha are fixed in their state of total communion. At the end of *Anna Karenina*, Vronsky and Anna are parted by death, and Kitty and Levin, already separated, are themselves being carried onward inexorably towards further disharmony and alienation.

We often assume that Tolstoy planned to show, parallel to one another, a disastrous liaison and a good marriage. And so far as the scheme of the novel goes this is indeed the case. But Tolstoy never relied on the ready-made artistry of such contrasts, as we see with the two marriages at the end of *War and Peace*. It is not a question of contrast but of two—and, counting Dolly and Stiva, three—couples who inhabit the book, and all such relations in the book seem to have a disquieting amount in common and to be heading the same way. An unobtrusive touch in the epilogue underlines the point. We hear from Stiva that the amiable Veslovsky, whom Levin had told to leave his house for trying to flirt with Kitty, is both going to the war and joining the doomed marital procession. "Veslovsky married recently. A fine fellow, isn't he?" Unobtrusive as it is, there is nothing "naif and pious" about this touch. It is very different from Mary's—"Of course it is our duty to help our neighbour"— which so enchanted Shestov. So Veslovsky married recently, and now he is off as a volunteer to the wars—well well! Everything points the same way, and every touch is directed with deadly effect. The railway station and the war themselves fill the atmosphere with failure and the desire to get away.

The Epilogue is indeed a kind of metaphor which compresses and reinforces the tight metaphorical life of the book. The good marriages of *War and Peace* have become bad marriages, and the result is that life has become less spacious, less widely differentiated. Happiness distinguishes, but disaster unites. Ironically enough, the movement and method of the novel contradicts its famous opening sentence—"All happy families resemble one another, but each unhappy family is unhappy in its own way". By the time we reach the Epilogue it is unhappiness which wears the same face and has the same flavour. The metaphor of the Epilogue is search, and a search that is bound to be futile. "Between Vronsky and myself," thinks Anna at the last, "what new feeling can I invent?"

Why do people go off to the wars? Because they grasp at the chance of feeling—like Levin, they have "a desire for desires". "Everything that the idle crowd once did to kill time, it now did for the benefit of the Slavs." They hope from it, as Koznyshev earnestly wishes for Vronsky, "outward success and inward peace"—the same success and peace that Karenin, after his desertion by Anna, strives to find in his work and in the cult of evangelism. Koznyshev throws himself into the Slavophil movement because his book on 'Forms of Government', from which he has hoped so much, has fallen flat. Now he has again an absorbing occupation with plenty of letters to write and important things to do. This summation of human activity casts a nightmare shadow backward over all the motives in the book.

To find one's true place in life, to realise oneself to the full, has become a dubious activity, as if the desires of Natasha and Pierre were on a par with those of Hélène and Kuragin. For a gambler like Yashvin the joy of life is to put one's last shirt on the cards; for Anna it is to escape from safety and frustration into her love for Vronsky. Vronsky rejoices because his love brings out the full power of his nature—a power unexercised, as he knows, in the social life of Petersburg. But later he will have to turn to painting, and then to estate management, as Anna to an interest in the hospital and in the little daughter of the English groom. What seems the deepest fulfilment leads only to triviality and getting through the time somehow. The happiest are those like Stiva, and Levin's friend Sviyazhsky, who have no notion of self-fulfilment and require only that tomorrow shall be like today.

Instead of releasing him from the predicament of Vronsky,

Anna and Koznyshev, Levin's marriage only brings him closer
to them.

> It was necessary to look after the comforts of his sister-in-law and
> her children, and of his wife and child, and it was impossible not to
> pass a small portion of each day with them. All this, with shooting,
> and his new hobby of bee-keeping, filled up the whole of that life of
> his, which seemed to him, when he thought about it, to have no
> meaning.

In this sinister and apparently inevitable merging of different
responses and activities even Levin's mowing with the peasants,
an anodyne that gives him a comfortable feeling of physical
exhaustion, seems not dissimilar to the earnest activities of
Vronsky; and the idea of self-destruction comes to haunt Levin,
who becomes afraid to carry a gun in case he should be tempted
to shoot himself, as it haunts Anna. Indeed, we even have the
strange feeling that Anna kills herself because Levin is tempted
to do so—that Tolstoy's iron distinction between individuals
has lapsed, and that Anna's act is not personal to herself but
rather the culmination of a generalised urge.

This ominous alignment into which the characters are brought
saps their status as individuals and subordinates them to the
metaphorical disquiet which comes to a head in the Epilogue.
We have seen how at the end of *War and Peace* Tolstoy takes
leave of his characters, distancing them in the process, and yet
though they are to some extent withdrawn from us they remain
separated from each other. At the end of *Anna* they seem drawn
together and back into their creator, and this despite the fact
that *Anna* is a novel in ways which *War and Peace* is not. I have
remarked that we seem to see Tolstoy himself when he employs
the winding-up devices of the novel at the end of *War and Peace*:
and he strikes us as more insistently *present*—by an odd paradox
—in the art of the novel, than when he comes openly before us
as commentator and historical partisan.

We might say that characters divide, but metaphors unite.
And as a novelist Tolstoy relies much more heavily upon
metaphor than he did when he disclaimed the title. We learn

that Levin, not unlike Pierre, had attempted to do something "for the good of everybody"; that when he married all his activities seem necessary, and therefore good; and that like a ploughshare he now involuntarily cut deeper and deeper, "and could not get out without turning the sod". The anxious and laborious metaphor does not convince us, just because it is intended to be so physically clinching. Levin is not a ploughshare: he is, or should be, Levin. By emphasising the virtue of necessity in this metaphorical way Tolstoy in fact brings it close to the haunted and terrible freedom of Anna and Vronsky—the freedom of railway stations and of waiting beside moving wagons for the right moment to jump; of horse-races where the skilful jockey makes an unforeseeable but unpardonable error at the last fence. The metaphor about Levin is intended to convey something quite different, a contrast, but it helplessly attracts the other metaphorical life of the book as iron filings come together in a magnetic field.

In *War and Peace* figures of speech are often forceful and simple—like that of the Russian as a duellist who throws down his rapier and picks up a club—sometimes clumsy, like the comparison of the old man at the deserted estate to a fly on the face of a dead beloved. But they are almost always innocent and immediate: they do not possess any extended and controlling life. Only the reiterated *roundness* of Karataev begins to oppress us, and it is this reiteration of metaphor, and its substitution for the actuality of a person, that we find in *Anna Karenina*. Indeed, from now on Tolstoy will use metaphor more and more, as if it was a way of making what he had to say more true and more obvious. His art of the amateur and the diplomat is replaced by an art that grows from now on more steadily professional, and more insistent on itself. It is a strange paradox that the more Tolstoy drew away from the expression of art in his beliefs, the more often he invoked the theory of it. At the time when he had come to consider his great novels without value he had become as emphatic in his ideas about art as a Flaubert or a Zola. Critics are right to insist that Tolstoy never ceased to be an artist— the trouble is that he becomes so insistently, so tyrannically, an artist.

His theory of art draws attention to art, for art with a specific purpose—that of reaching everyone and infecting them with the right emotions—can hardly help drawing attention to itself. Both *A Confession* and *Hadji Murad* are art as the aesthetes conceived it—chiselled, proportioned, not a word wasted. And the queer thing about *Hadji Murad*, Tolstoy's last and more carefully-wrought tale, is that it is like a parable without a point. It begins and ends with a metaphor, that of the red 'Tartar' thistle, which is so difficult to pick and which looks so out of place among other flowers. Even though a cartwheel passes over it, the thistle springs erect again. The qualities of this thistle resemble those of Hadji Murad—very well—but why this elaborate comparison at the beginning and end of the tale? No doubt a rustic audience would appreciate it and perhaps be moved by it, but this in a sense is just the trouble: the individuality of Hadji Murad is being passed through the dehumanising processes of a careful artistic theory, and for nothing—for the tale does not illustrate anything, but is about Hadji Murad *tout court*. But having become a worker in metaphors and significations Tolstoy cannot discard them. At the end of his life he wanted to tell a straight story, a story going back to his early days in the Caucasus. But his method had become ineradicably parabolic, and in achieving what he thought of as simplicity he had lost his own kind of naturalness.

We can say, then, that Tolstoy's conversion, the beginnings of which are foreshadowed in *Anna*, makes him more, not less, literary. There will be no more 'unique' works; there will be parables, essays, novels and stories. His many methods—his tentative plotting, his discursive variety—all give place to a single dedicated and selfconscious method. One of the byproducts of his theory of art is that what comes hardest and is most difficult to do must be better as art. The point is by no means self-evident—indeed it looks almost like a justification of the difficulty Tolstoy found in going against the grain. At the end of *What is Art?* he tells us that "to write a rhymed poem dealing with the times of Cleopatra . . . or compose . . . an opera like Wagner's, is far easier than to tell a story without any unnecessary details, so that it will be remembered by those who hear it". "The old man wrote it well." So Tolstoy (according to Gorky) was heard to murmur about his story *Father Sergius*. He did indeed, but we cannot imagine him feeling or saying the same thing about *War and Peace*. The fact was that he had come to take a perverse pride in the artificial construction of a simple story with wide appeal.

The popular metaphors and ways of speech that "unite men in art" and "draw them towards unity" (*What is Art?*) also remove individuality. Not that Tolstoy cared—indeed the individuality to which he had given such marvellous expression eventually became for him the enemy both of art and of the good life. *Samodovolnost* is characteristic only of those who have not seen the light. We can see the process beginning in *Anna*, but it does not harm the truth and variety of the characterisation—it throws it into a stronger relief and makes us see it from a different angle than that of *War and Peace*.

Tolstoy is still a magician at suggesting the individual—sometimes by turning the tables against himself. Levin in turn finds himself saying things which are not his own, and feels his own personality disappearing. When he remarks about some foreign malefactor who is being deported from Russia—"one might as well punish a pike by throwing it in the water"—he realises that not only has someone else in the party used this very phrase but that it is in fact a proverbial saying. Levin appears as an individual through the very fact of his discomfiture at finding he is saying the same things as everybody else. There is something in common between Levin's annoyance here and the sturdy refusal of Uncle Eroshka, in *The Cossacks*, to recognise his own phrase—"when you die the grass grows over you and that's all"—when it is repeated back to him by the admiring hero. Eroshka's phrase is meaningless to him in the mouth of another, not because he invented it but because in saying it he was himself.

Such phrases do depersonalise, and Tolstoy's own use of metaphor will put him in a position not unlike Levin's. He compares him to a man in the frost who has exchanged his thick fur coat for a muslin garment, and to a man seeking for food at a toyshop or a gunsmith's. This suggests he is a mechanical creation—an engine without steam, a hinge lacking oil—metaphors sprout other metaphors in the mind but none of them leads back to the individual. That, in a sense, may be Tolstoy's purpose. Levin's predicament was not personal, but universal. But who is to persuade us of this? If we are to believe in it, we want to see how it affected *him*, as we have got to know him. We feel the same, I think, about the candle which is grimly and movingly personal to Anna when it dies out as she lies waiting for Vronsky, and the shadows rush together on the ceiling and the idea of death seizes her. But her last moments are depersonalised by the candle repeated as a metaphor.

> The candle, by the light of which she had been reading that book filled with anxieties, deceptions, grief and evil, flared up with a brighter light than before, lit up for her all that had been dark, flickered, began to grow dim, and went out for ever.

Moving as the sentence is, it takes over Anna, as does the pat fulfilment of her nightmare—"a little peasant, muttering something, was working at the rails". There is a determination to solve, with metaphor as the means of solution. And we remember other deaths in Tolstoy, like the death of Petya, which evidently needed no solution. The Tolstoyan determination to conclude and control in his own way, as with the death of Ivan Ilyich, emerges too in that inconspicuous clause—"lit up for her all that had been dark".

Yet it is highly effective, this alternation at the end of *Anna* between the characters as they are in themselves, and as metaphors expressing what Tolstoy was beginning to see as general in the human predicament. Levin's predicament—like that of a man in the frost with only a muslin garment—is impersonal, but the moment of revelation which comes to him could have come only to *him*—it is as personal as Prince Andrew's apprehension of the oak-tree and of the clouds above the battlefield, or as Pierre's exclamation in the hut among the prisoners. Levin is talking to a peasant who mentions an old man "who lives for his soul and remembers God".

> "How does he remember God? How does he live for the soul?" Levin almost cried out.
> "You know how: rightly, in a godly way. You know, people differ."
> "Yes, yes, goodbye," uttered Levin, gasping with excitement.

It is the fact that he *does* know which excites Levin, and which he sees as the true and significant point. "He says we must live for truth and God, and at the first hint I understand him. . . . I have discovered nothing. I have only perceived what it is that I know." We feel with Levin at this moment and see why he is so excited. His outburst of joy is made real to us by the Tolstoyan reality of the things that are suddenly about him—"the juicy broad-bladed forest grass", the green insect crawling up a stalk and hindered in its ascent by a leaf. (So real is this insect in the context of Levin's joy that we hardly notice the probability that it is a metaphorical analogue of Levin's own progress and the sudden removal of the painful obstacle before him, the leaf.)

For the rest of the Epilogue metaphor alternates with reality in a highly effective, and even diverting, sequence. Levin's determination to hang on to the revelation, and be quite different from now on, takes a metaphorical form: but life continues to reassert itself with comic inflexibility. "The words the peasant had spoken produced in his soul the effect of an electric spark, suddenly transforming and welding into one. . . . 'There will be no disputes; with Kitty never any quarrels again. . . . I shall be amiable and kind . . . everything will be different.' " But immediately he gets into a quarrel with his coachman, and as he returns to the house he hears with sinking heart that visitors have arrived, and he realises how wrong had been his conclusion that "his spiritual condition could at once alter his manner when confronted with reality".

Again, however, Levin is able to take refuge in a metaphor, a particularly laborious one. Because of the guests, whom he has to show round his apiary, "reality had temporarily veiled the spiritual tranquillity he had found, but it remained with him". (Shestov might have savoured the relation between 'reality' and 'the spiritual' in this sentence.)

> Just as the bees, now circling round, threatening him and distracting his attention, deprived him of complete physical calm and forced him to shrink to avoid them, so the cares that had beset him from the moment he got into the trap had deprived him of spiritual freedom. . . . And as, in spite of the bees, his physical powers remained intact, so his newly realised spiritual powers were intact also.

There is a further strange parallel between Levin's stream of consciousness after his revelation and that of Anna in her ride through the streets on the way to her death at the station. Like Levin, Anna has a sudden revelation of what her situation really is. A bright light seems suddenly turned on herself, Vronsky, and Karenin, and the clarity with which she sees herself and them gives her pleasure. When she alights at the station this clarity goes, muddle and distraction returns, and she begins to think that all may be well and that life will go on somehow, but in the railway carriage the "piercing light" returns and again "reveals to her the meaning of human life and human relations". In the earlier drafts Tolstoy emphasises even more her joy at the revelation. It is a revelation which beckons her to death— ("There", she thinks, looking at the moving wheels, "the light will go out, and I shall be beautiful and pitiable"[1])—while Levin's beckons him to life, but we are more struck by the affinity of the two moods rather than by the contrast between them.

The argument which Levin and his guests get into at the picnic by the beehives appears not unlike that at the end of *War and Peace*, with Koznyshev taking the part of Pierre and Levin that of Nicholas Rostov. But it is less dramatic and more truly a discussion *à thèse*, less heavily weighted by our accumulated interest in the participants and their motives. Instead of the elemental difference between Nicholas and Pierre, and the dramatic play between the uneasiness of the one and the ingenuous complacency of the other, we see that Levin and Koznyshev are close together, united by the anxiety with which Tolstoy has impregnated the whole world of *Anna*, the need to feel we are going somewhere and that life is worth while. It is this that makes Koznyshev "as irritable as if we were defending the last

---

[1] Quoted from an early draft, which gives greater emphasis to the turning on and off of the "piercing light". It is noticeable that the light metaphor is merged with, and indeed confused with, that of the candle. Analysing the passage, one wonders what is the relation between the "piercing light" in which Anna sees her situation, and the candle whose final flare reveals "all that had been dark"? It is not surprising that so literal a writer as Tolstoy should have metaphor trouble—the transparency and syntactic exactitude of his style points it up. Equivocation and word-play are never a natural depth of his style and language, as in Shakespeare, or in Henry James.

of his possessions", and Levin determined not to get irritable in order that he should not threaten his new spiritual discovery.

None the less the discussion does clear the air, like the thunderstorm that follows it. Our oppressive sense that all human beings are haunted by the same problem—and have their lives squeezed together by Tolstoy's hand in consequence—begins to lift. Humour helps. Levin is less comic than Pierre, but he both sees and is seen with a sense of the absurd, and old Prince Shcherbatsky—one of Tolstoy's best unobtrusive portraits—helps the process. So, unintentionally, does old Mikhaylich, the bee-keeper, who gravely listens to and agrees with the gentlefolk, "clearly neither understanding them nor wishing to understand". When Levin and his father-in-law stoutly deny that "the people has spoken", because they themselves don't feel it, the presence of the old bee-keeper underlines their point, though not precisely in the sense they intend. Tolstoy's equivocation here is not 'naif and pious', but seems to be making deliberate use of the contradictions in his own position.

> "I come not to bring peace, but a sword, said Christ," rejoined Koznyshev . . . quoting quite simply, as if it were quite comprehensible, the very passage from the gospels that always perplexed Levin more than any other.
>
> "Yes, that is so," observed the old man, who was standing by, answering a glance that was accidentally thrown at him.

Old Mikhaylich gravely agrees with this sentiment, since Christ has uttered it and the gentleman quoted it. How therefore does the peasant infallibly know what the law of goodness requires? Even if it is grounded in goodness, his passivity will cheerfully lend itself to abuse. As so often it is the contradictions in Tolstoy which lead us to the sensitive and significant point, and in the Epilogue Tolstoy is not concerned to cover up the contradictions—as he will do later on—with the willed simplicity of parable art. Indeed, the final analogy which occurs to Levin in the discussion is a particularly live and disconcerting one, carrying us back as it does to the historical surveys of *War and Peace*, and making of old Mikhaylich a Kutuzov-like figure whose passivity is Russian and saves Russia.

> Levin said the same as Mikhaylich, and the people who expressed

their thought in the legend of the invitation to the Varyags [the Norse chiefs invited by the early Russian tribes to rule over them] "Come and rule over us! We joyfully promise complete obedience. All labours, all humiliations, all sacrifices we take upon ourselves; but we will not judge or decide."

Taken out of the Dark Ages (or out of 1812), and put in the context of 1875, Levin's idea of Russian passivity assumes an oddly prophetic form. Historically he is more justified than his brother Koznyshev—and Tolstoy than Dostoevsky, for whom it was "the people's will" that the Slavs should be liberated and Constantinople "ours". Instead, new Varyags were soon to reach Russia, by way of the Finland station, and under Lenin and Stalin the old obedience would again be promised, and the old "labours, humiliations and sacrifices" undergone anew.

This sense of Russian history and Russian destiny is not the only thing that links the Epilogue of *Anna* with *War and Peace*. Levin has perceived what it is he knows, and it is what Nicholas and Mary unconsciously take for granted at the end of *War and Peace*. All theories, convictions, movements, are equally futile: what matters is to recognise the truth that is under one's nose. The equivalent of the conjugal duet, which resolves all problems, is here the discovery made by the baby Mitya.

> Directly Levin approached the bath he was shown an experiment that succeeded perfectly. The cook, who had been called specially for the purpose, bent over him. He frowned and moved his head from side to side in a protesting way. Kitty bent over him and his face lit up with a smile; he pressed his hand into the sponge and bubbled with his lips, producing such a contented and peculiar sound that not only Kitty and the nurse, but Levin too, went into unexpected raptures.

Though nothing comes between us and this scene, though it is as openly and simply true as are all such family events in Tolstoy, there is yet a touch of defiance about it, something deliberative that gives it the pose of a tiny *scène à faire*. If we compare it to the happy confusion at the end of *War and Peace*, we cannot but notice the difference. And yet the significance is the same. "The point was that Mitya had that day obviously and undoubtedly begun to recognise his own people." For the last time it is the family which has the last word.

V

"This novel . . ." *Anna Karenina*

Les climats, les saisons, les sons, les couleurs, l'obscurité, la lumière,
les éléments, les aliments, le bruit, le silence, le mouvement, le repos,
tout agit sur notre machine, et sur notre âme; par conséquent tout nous
offre mille prises presque assurées, pour gouverner dans leur origine les
sentiments dont nous nous laissons dominer.

ROUSSEAU, *Les Confessions*

And so by the motions of muscles or nerves we enter shortly and
directly into the internal world of his characters, begin to live with
them, and in them.

MEREZHKOVSKY, *Tolstoy as Man and Artist*

"THIS novel, the first I have attempted, I'm taking very seriously", wrote Tolstoy to his friend Strakhov in May 1873. It had quite driven out the winter's elaborate preparations for a work of the *War and Peace* type about Peter the Great. The more he found out about that period, the more he disliked and disapproved of it, and the equivocal part that his own ancestor had played in the execution of the Tsar's son Alexis did not help matters. Yet it is possible to imagine him rewriting the time of Peter, as in a sense he had rewritten that of 1812, and setting himself against the whole tradition of awe and reverence for the great Tsar. Such an attempt at historical revaluation would have been a fascinating one, and the 'Seer of the Flesh', who could not withhold the powers of his physical sympathy even from Napoleon, would surely have entered imaginatively into the overwhelming physical being of Peter?

But there was too much antipathy. Sexually, Peter was gigantically and happily immoral. Tolstoy had become an agonised moralist, and—as we have seen—even in *War and Peace* dislikes male lust to the point of trying to get rid of it altogether. Peter adored foreigners, especially Germans (the dissolute Elector of Saxony was a boon companion of his) and did his best to Germanise Russian society. Tolstoy loathed Germans and everything connected with them. In one of the *Sevastopol*

Sketches he contrives to say of Captain Kraut, an apparently faultless Russian of German origin, that "as a man he seemed to lack something just because everything about him was so satisfactory". More fundamentally, Tolstoy had now turned against history itself, through his rejection of the history of his own time. In the first version of his attack on the pro-Slav movement, which was modified and dramatised into the Epilogue of *Anna*, he equates contemporary history, "otherwise called politics", with fashion, the mere restless desire for change, which is "deprived of any true goal".

He wanted a subject now, an external theme which would echo the growing drama inside him and resolve it, at least on the level of art. It is no longer a question of the subject that interests and appeals to him, but of one that obsesses him.

If his wife is right, the idea for it had been haunting him since 1870. He had told her of his notion of writing about a married lady of the *grand monde* who would ruin herself, and he felt that as soon as he got the clue for such a character all the other persons in her world would immediately become real. Nearly two years later, the mistress of a neighbouring landowner committed suicide at a station near Yasnaya Polyana by throwing herself under a train. Tolstoy saw the body, and the experience left a deep impression on him. A little later he happened to pick up a copy of Pushkin's *Tales* which his wife had been reading to their son Serge. In a letter, written to Strakhov but never sent, he spoke of his renewed enchantment by Pushkin's method. The opening of an untitled fragment: "the guests had assembled at the country house", seemed to act as a catalyst: the persons and events of a possible novel began to assemble in his head.

Novelists are notoriously misleading about the sources of their novels, or rather when the thing is clear in their minds they think they see, and may then tell us, how it came into existence. We need not necessarily believe all these details about the genesis of *Anna*, but what remains significant is the conjunction of an obsessional idea with the vision of a form—it is almost a classic case of how a novel which conforms to a strict convention of the *genre* comes into being. The *Notebooks* of Henry James supply us with many instances of the same process: an event or anecdote touching off a long-brooded idea, and the corresponding treatment or approach. Levin, we should note, was an afterthought, almost a diversion to cover Tolstoy's tracks. It is Anna who matters initially, and it is Anna who has the classic relation to her creator—the relation of Isabel Archer to James and of Emma Bovary to Flaubert. In such a relation it does not matter how apparently dissimilar is the creator from his creation: it is not a kinship of externals and ideas but of a deeper psychological identification. In breadth and vitality of conception Anna infinitely exceeds any personal case. And yet, like Flaubert with his heroine, Tolstoy—had he been given to such comments—could have said: "Madame Karenine, c'est moi".

For Tolstoy had begun to see himself in Anna's position, separated from his own kind by his growing sense of personal crisis, and already aware of the possibility of a further and more fundamental separation. What happens when you cut yourself off from society, or are cut off by it? Both in the first drafts of *Anna* and in the finished work this is the most insistent question. In some of the earlier plans Vronsky and Anna get married; their problem is apparently solved, and yet the result is always the same. Why? Because they were unaware of the extent to which they were created by the society they lived in, and of how much they needed it. Once they have gone against it they can never be in the same easy and unconscious relation to it again. Lacking society, lacking the family, they are destroyed by a conflict of wills that arises with appalling inevitability. Without the freedom of society their passion becomes a prison. Tolstoy puts it in a characteristic metaphor: we can sit motionless for hours if we know we can stretch our legs at any time; but we develop agonising cramp if we feel we cannot.

Tolstoy's whole outlook and upbringing led him to rely upon society, and on his family's high position in it, in just this spacious and unconscious way. But the spiritual crisis which had been brewing in him for years now made him see the possibility of solitude and of an insurmountable barrier between him and his own kind. He was prophetic. After the notoriety which his fame was to bring him he could never take a place in his hereditary *milieu* on the old footing. Chertkov, the ex-Guards officer who was to become his most masterful and in some ways most sinister disciple, had all the more influence on Tolstoy because he came from that *milieu*. They spoke the same language (as Yashvin and Vronsky speak the same language) although their views had become so different from that of the society in which they had learnt it. It is significant that Levin can enter this society whenever he wants, and though he shuns and despises it, when he does enter it he thoroughly enjoys himself, as at the great supper-party in Part Seven when he drinks too much champagne.

> "Let me have your hat, sir," said the porter to Levin, who had forgotten the club rule that hats must be left at the entrance. "It's a long time since you were here. . . ." This hall-porter not only knew Levin but knew all his connections and relatives as well, and at once mentioned some of his intimate friends. . . . There was not one angry or anxious face among them. All seemed to have left their cares and anxieties behind them in the hall with their hats . . . .

It is as idyllic as Count Rostov's banquet in *War and Peace*, though in its "tranquillity, decorum, and pleasure" there is an air of valediction.

But there is also the old marvel of transparency and of liberation. The fact is that Levin is of a different order of creation from Anna, and though he is often taken to be a walking argument, an autobiographical excrescence, he liberates the book so that it can grow to Tolstoyan size; he saves it from the classic—and diminished—novel pattern of Flaubert and James. Compared with *War and Peace*, the creative process in *Anna* is reversed. It begins in fiction and invention, whereas *War and Peace* only makes use of them after its wide perspective has been unrolled by history and by memory. *War and Peace*, we might say, is brought to its full scope by invention; *Anna* by recourse to autobiography and polemic. The two great vessels move on opposing courses.

Because she begins in a novel, Anna herself has to end in one. Only after many false starts and trial runs did Tolstoy decide what was to happen in *War and Peace*, where the characters seem to take hold and decide for themselves what their fate is to be, but the fate of Anna is the fact of the novel. In the first drafts there is uncertainty about the relations and the personalities of

Anna, Vronsky and Karenin; whether there will be a divorce; whether Anna and Vronsky will marry; but there is never any doubt what the end will be. Tolstoy himself was not wholly disingenuous about this. Quoting Pushkin's comment on Tatiana in *Eugene Onegin*—"my Tatiana has gone and got married, I should not have thought it of her!"—he implies that Anna has similarly taken matters into her own hands. True, Tolstoy's characterisation makes it seem inevitable—there is nothing unlikely about the suicide, as some English critics have felt—yet it is as predetermined as that of Emma Bovary.

It was, no doubt, to escape from the fact of the novel that Tolstoy added Levin. With his instinctive dislike of the elements of subterfuge in a fiction—the author's concealing of himself and disguising of his own relation to the work—he expanded Levin into a quite open figure, with whose career he could identify himself without pretence, as he had done with Olenin in *The Cossacks* and with Irtenyev in *Childhood, Boyhood and Youth*. It is Levin who liberates the novel from itself. Through him we escape from the novel back into life. For a tale from which there is no escape, and in which Tolstoy's relation with the hero is as obvious yet undeclared as it is with Anna, we must look to the later period and to *Father Sergius*.

What may be Tolstoy's first draft begins quite differently from the finished novel, and may well have been intended as its opening scene. Its first sentence recalls the phrase of Pushkin. "After the opera, the guests gathered at the house of young Princess Vrasski." The party is like that given by Princess Betsy in Chapter Seven of *Anna*, except that the host and hostess are young instead of middle-aged. Kitty is mentioned, and the hostess wonders aloud if something hasn't occurred between her and Anna. Vronsky (also referred to as Gagin) is known to be in love with Kitty, and the suggestion is that Anna may be trying to take him away from her. Conversation is barbed and allusive. "Naturally they talked of persons known to them all, and, equally naturally, they talked scandal about them: there would have been nothing to say otherwise, since happy people have no history." The hostess says that Anna is certainly not attractive, but that she would fall for her if she were a man. A diplomat remarks that now or never is her moment to become the heroine of a novel.

Stiva enters, already recognisable, but his opening dialogue is crudely handled. Accused of being a bad husband, he bursts out laughing and says he doesn't like being bored. "We men are all the same, Countess. And she's always up to her neck in domesticity you know—children, school, and so forth. She doesn't complain." Then Vronsky appears. We are told at once of his chin, dark blue though freshly shaved; his strong teeth; his head nearly bald but beautifully shaped, with dark curls on the nape. He and Stiva arrange to dine the next day. He keeps looking towards the door. . . .

> They were certainly an odd pair. He was pallid, wrinkled, dried up. She had a low forehead, a short, almost retroussé nose, and was far too plump—a little more and she would have seemed monstrous. Indeed, without the great black eyelashes which made her grey eyes wonderful, the black curls on her forehead, a vigorous grace of movement like her brother's, and small feet and hands, she would have been downright ugly.

So these are the Karenins! If Tolstoy had retained the passage, even in a modified form, could we ever have got over the shock? We should have seen this little Renoir figure, this plump kitten, for the rest of the novel. She, Vronsky and Karenin would have been like the other fascinating but rather grotesque denizens of the high social jungle. It is a remarkable instance of the crudity of Tolstoy's initial externalisations. It has the vitality of Thackeray or Pisemsky but is certainly no better.

And in spite of the Pushkinian opening sentence Tolstoy has already ruptured the spell of Pushkinian narrative. That depends on a remarkable blend of simplicity and economy *without* externalisation. Unlike Mérimée and eighteenth-century prose narrative, which it in some ways resembles, it is both bare and warm. Pushkin's complete, but as it were wordless, sympathy makes us intimate with his characters without his describing them. Tolstoy must describe: he positively itches to; but this early draft shows how important it is that he should first let us inside his main characters. It is all very well for these inhabitants

of the *haut monde*, for a Kuragin, even for a Karenin, to be for us
what they first look like; but for the vital persons it is different.
Tolstoy expresses this difference in a comment in the completed
novel about Anna. "Her charm lay precisely in the fact that her
personality always stood out from her dress, that her dress was
never conspicuous on her." If for 'dress' here we read 'outward
appearance' we see that Tolstoy knows very well what has to
be done. But of course a total personality can be treated by a
novelist as Tolstoy in the first draft treats externals. Flaubert
may not have known the colour of Emma's eyes, but he leaves us
in no doubt that he knows everything about her personality. He
shows us round it much as Tolstoy shows us round the salon in
this first sketch. So does Proust with his characters. We do not
forget that we are being shown something, and that this is the
point of the exercise, and hence our growing gloom as the demonstration of Emma goes meticulously on. But with Tolstoy,
personality has to stand out from description and dissection as
Anna's stood out from her dress.

How is this to be done? In the first sketch Tolstoy made Anna
a *jolie laide*, attractive to men in spite of being too plump and
not pretty. In a second he tries another tack. Tatiana Sergeyevna
(as she is now called) wears a yellow dress trimmed with black
lace, more *décolletée* than any other in the room, and there is a
provocative contrast between this costume and the simple
sweetness of her beautiful skin, eyes and face. Again the likeness
to her brother is noted, rather more emphatically. It is surely
this likeness that gave Tolstoy the clue to his eventual process?
Anna must not be introduced until we are entirely familiar with
her brother: it is through him that we may first perceive and
understand her. The peculiar advantage for Tolstoy of leading
off with Stiva Oblonsky is that his nature, and the predicament
in which it has placed him, require no preamble or filling in of
background. In a flash we know what he is, and like all his
friends and colleagues—even the Tartar waiter who brings him
oysters—we stand and regard him with smiling indulgence. His
physical charm affects people like something solid. Tolstoy
makes us virtually of one flesh with him—it is as if we ourselves
were waking up on the morocco couch in the dressing-room
after a delightful dream—so like those in *War and Peace*, so

unlike the terrible dream his sister will have at the end of the book.

> There was a dinner party in Darmstadt—no, not in Darmstadt but somewhere in America. Oh yes, Darmstadt was in America, and Alabin was giving the party. The dinner was served on glass tables, yes, and the tables sang *Il mio tesoro* . . . no, not exactly *Il mio tesoro*, but something better than that. And then there were some kind of little decanters that were really women. . . .

With him we suddenly recall the terrible fuss the night before, when Dolly found out about the governess, and "there happened what happens to most people when unexpectedly caught in some shameful act". He had no time to assume the expression suitable to the position he was in and "involuntarily (reflex action of the brain, thought Oblonsky, who was fond of physiology) he smiled his usual kindly and therefore silly smile".

When he first hit on the idea of opening with Stiva, Tolstoy presented him at a cattle-show in a Moscow park, where Ordyntsev (Levin), "an agricultural expert, gymnast, and athlete", with "a Russian face", is showing some of his stock. The two were to welcome one another and talk about Kitty. The final version, showing Stiva waking up, dressing and going to the office, came later; and later still the opening epigram about happy and unhappy families. The strength of the first chapter is that it presents a man ideally suited to the scenic method, and who gives that method an absolute initial justification and authority which will never falter throughout the book. Not the least of Stiva's functions is to make us feel that we know everyone, and that everything about them is quite clear. Particularly everything about his sister.

Another role of Stiva's is no less important. It is to identify us, at the outset, as if it were in play, with the situation of an adulterer. The immediate and involuntary sympathy that we feel with him—perhaps identification rather than sympathy, for it is something physical rather than moral—will stay with us in all such situations throughout the book. It makes us realise, too, that what to one person (a participant, not a spectator) is merely unfortunate and a bore, can to others be deadly. Not only is nothing permanent in the world of *Anna*

Karenina—nothing is seen in the same way by any two people. Anna cannot regard her brother's disgrace with the same disgust and misery as Dolly, not because she has an instinctive sympathy with it but because she is seeing it from a different angle. Anna herself will be subject to the sympathy of Dolly and Kitty at the end of the book, when just before her suicide they remark to one another how attractive she is, and yet how pathetic. The solitude of the point of view is unobtrusive, frightening, sublime. With Stiva, Tolstoy raises to its highest art his practice of letting the individual appear in the light of his own point of view. Though his sex-life is presumably more complicated and sordid than that of any other character, it seems innocent to us because it seems so to him. Like an Elizabethan shepherd he gives a ballet girl a coral necklace, "and contrived, in the midday darkness of the theatre, to kiss her pretty face". More we do not see.

The scenic role of Stiva answers the criticism made, among others, by Percy Lubbock in *The Craft of Fiction* and by Arnold Bennett.[1] For the former it is the presentation of Anna that is the chief flaw in the book, "a flaw which Tolstoy could not have avoided if he was determined to hold to his scenic plan". But, as we have seen, Tolstoy has a horror of backgrounds: they smell not only of 'the novel' but of what I have tried to suggest by using the term 'pastoral'. However much Tolstoy may intervene and take charge in his own person, he never tries to take charge of a character's past life.

In *War and Peace* and *Anna Karenina* there are no exceptions to this. Tolstoy seems instinctively to feel that a character's past life is a kind of reality, a reality which the author has no right to possess himself of. A novelist should not have it both ways, owning both past and present: Tolstoy confines himself to what he can make of a character from the moment he creates him. It takes a Tolstoy to do this, but as a method it is surely self-justifying? Dostoevsky's method, oddly enough, is not dissimilar, though it is a dramatic and not a scenic method, and his references to the past ("that was before we knew what had

---

[1] "It is easy to show where very many of the great novels, e.g. *Anna Karenina*, fail in technique, and where they could have been improved if the author had had the advantages of Flaubert, Maupassant, or even Chekhov" (*Journals*, 1924).

taken place when X was at Y", etc.) are not intended to fill out a character but to contribute to the general dramatic atmosphere. There is a sense, indeed, in which both novelists resemble Shakespeare here: all three giants can afford to ignore the lesser writer's necessary claim to every sort of access to character and motive. Shakespeare's characters, as I suggested earlier, are so full of life that they appear to have a past and a future which are no part of their creator's intention or requirement. So have Tolstoy's.

"The method of the book," writes Percy Lubbock, "does not arise out of the subject: in treating it Tolstoy simply used the method that was congenial to him without regarding the story that he had to tell." It is quite true that in starting so much with the idea of the novel, and using one of the oldest plots in the game, Tolstoy lays himself open. Granted the premise of *The Craft of Fiction*, Percy Lubbock's criticism is cogent enough, though it reminds us of eighteenth-century objections to Shakespeare's violation of dramatic rules.

> He began it as though Anna's break with the past was the climax to which her story was to mount, whereas it is really the point from which her story sets out for its true climax in her final catastrophe. And so the first part of the book is neither one thing nor another. . . . Tolstoy did not see how much more was needed than a simple personal impression of Anna, in view of all that is to come. Not she only, but her world, the world as she sees it, the past as it affects her—this too is demanded and for this he makes no provision. It is never really shown how she was placed in her life and what it meant to her: and the flare of passion has consequently no importance, no fateful bigness. . . .

"To the very end," he sums up, "Anna is a wonderful woman whose early history has never been fully explained."

But even on the ground of technique the critic has chosen, this is not quite true. What is Stiva for? His past we know as instinctively as his present. We have also the Princess Barbara, Anna and Stiva's aunt, and she too—though the most minor of characters—is instantly visible and comprehensible. Dolly, "who knew she had been all her life a hanger-on of rich relatives", dislikes her, and is shocked to find her staying with Anna when Vronsky is "a perfect stranger to her". Her presence suggests the sort of background which Anna had known well when young. Tolstoy's worldliness is absolutely comprehensive, with the confidence that suggests an understanding all the more complete for being tacit. (It is very different from Proust's.) Clearly the Oblonsky family, a little like the Kuragins in *War and Peace*, although of the very highest society (it is the first thing Vronsky notes in Anna) did not have the sound and solid traditions taken for granted in the Rostov, Levin and Shcherbatsky families. They lived by wit rather than by custom. We can see Stiva living like this all through the book up to the moment when—his sister dead—he sends a triumphant if belated message to Dolly that he has managed to get the lucrative appointment to some board of directors. Equally clearly, the Vronsky family resembled the Oblonskys rather than the others. Vronsky's mother is a splendidly and chillingly accurate portrait—a woman of the world with the cold good sense to see that affairs are all very well but that this kind of passion may ruin her son. Nothing is more revealing than the impression we get of her feelings about Anna after their night train journey together, when Vronsky meets his mother at the station. She likes Anna, but instantly grasps her status as a threat, not—as she herself has been—as a woman who likes affairs, but as a woman who unknowingly believes in passion.

Stiva married into a sound and stable family, and it is his salvation. However much he may deceive and impoverish Dolly he is secure because of her; nor does he fully realise how much his unchanging status and popularity owe to the stability of his family relations. His sister was much less lucky. She has no more natural talent for home-making than her brother, no doubt because in the family there was no instinctively learnt tradition of home. Clearly that family found her a good match— rather a dull man, but perfectly presentable, and destined for the highest office. No doubt Princess Barbara, and others of the family too perhaps, saw excellent opportunities of sponging and place-seeking. And Anna—warm, hopeful, impulsive, and ready to please—would be perfectly willing. Ambitious and able, Karenin is a man without background: Anna must make the home, which she can't do. Nor can she after she has gone off with Vronsky. Dolly spots at once that Anna is like a guest in her own house, just as she once spotted that the Karenin household was not really like a home, and that Anna made rather too much of her role as a mother. It is Vronsky who runs everything, gives a considering glance at the table, catches the butler's eye. Vronsky, we remember, has never known family life. Now he is selfconsciously and rather pathetically playing at it, with no one to embody for him how it naturally and simply happens.

In an early draft the pair marry after Anna's divorce, and have two children. Interestingly, Vronsky was given in this version a much more stable family background; and for the same reason he was presented as genuinely in love with Kitty and about to propose to her. Tolstoy portrayed, too, his chagrin that his children by Anna cannot be brought up as he was—he has cut himself off from the roots that should have grown through him into a new generation family life based on the old. If Tolstoy had held to the plan of their remarriage the pair would have remained separated by their different family backgrounds, because they had sought to unite themselves solely by passion. With this as their visible and necessary tie, the background of neither could have helped them, and the discrepancy between the two would have eventually turned things bad.

Such things, it seems to me, are present and visible in the novel, and provide a history as we understand a history in life: not something simply told to us, that is, but to some extent found out and deduced for ourselves. If Tolstoy "did not see how much more was needed", may it not have been because he assumed the reader would provide it? He may have been wrong in assuming this, but it is one of his most mesmeric characteristics that he writes about Moscow and Petersburg social and family life as if it were a universal thing, and as if his readers would understand what he understood in it. Possibly Homer made the same assumptions. Certainly Balzac and Proust did not. They are showing us over their acquired territories: Tolstoy belongs to his. If Balzac had been a banker he would not have wanted to explain to us all the processes of banking; if Proust had been a duke it would not have occurred to him to conduct us with such relish through all the tones and nuances of the French aristocracy. In Tolstoy's hands Moscow and Petersburg family life becomes a universal thing. Irrespective of social level some families are like this, some like that: and the conventions of collective existence in each powerfully affect the fates and fortunes of individual members, when these go on to lead their own lives. Jane Austen, like Tolstoy, took this for granted. In *Mansfield Park* she shows us nothing of the Crawford's upbringing, but she makes quite clear what effect its shortcomings had on the crucial decisions of their adult lives.

If the Rostovs are such a solid family, it may be objected, what about Natasha's signal lapse from virtue? Yet Natasha was a girl, and behaved as any spirited girl might have done—the impress of family backbone appears later in life. If Pierre had turned out as unintimate and unattentive as Karenin, Natasha would not have been likely to go off with another man. 'Principle' shows itself not in the way you make your bed but in how you lie on it. But in a sense all this is by the way. Anna is of course not the product of a bad or broken home. In suggesting how much we may be said to know about her early history I wished only to show that the accusation of a gap, a Tolstoyan hiatus, is not really justified. The real significance of our impression of a gap, though, lies in the fact that Anna comes to feel it herself.

She cannot review and consider her life calmly—*therefore we must not.* She does not know herself what she has done or will do; she does not know "how she is placed in her life and what it means to her"; she takes it for granted until the crisis comes, and after that she cannot reconstitute it. This is part temperament, part upbringing. She has her brother's power of living in the moment. If we knew about her previous life we should know (as of course Tolstoy knows) what she might do. She must be continuously immediate, terribly and exhilaratingly so. And so successful is Tolstoy here that we feel that most other comparable heroines in fiction are in some curious way *safe.* Poor Eugénie Grandet, poor Emma Bovary and Isabel Archer and Lily Dale!—but the reader cannot quite escape the impression that they have nothing to worry about. They are so snugly placed in their novels. Indeed many persons in life, too, seem placed there like these characters in novels, and can, as it were, present their past and future in the midst of their present experience, but not Anna. If the Crawfords may be a minor English analogue for Anna's family side, the only one for the immediate *apparition* of her is Catherine in *Wuthering Heights*.

And perhaps Shakespeare's Cressida. Both have a presentness, a momentariness, about them that can be shocking and unnerving. "Anna, is this you?" asks Karenin, echoing Shakespeare's Troilus—"This is, and is not, Cressid"—as he echoes any amount of shocked and anonymous incredulity in real life. Tolstoy brings home to us the serio-comic way in which we do keep other people in our everyday consciousness by feeling them to be fixed in life as if in a book. We assume that they will continue to do what we are accustomed to them doing, as we assume that Pip has great expectations, and that King Lear will always divide his kingdom between his three daughters. Living, in fact, depends on this process.

> Karenin was being confronted with life—with the possibility of his wife's loving somebody else, and this seemed stupid and incomprehensible to him, because it was life itself. He had lived and worked all his days in official spheres, which deal with reflections of life, and every time he had knocked up against life itself he had stepped out of its way. He now experienced a sensation such as a man might feel who, while quietly crossing a bridge over an abyss, suddenly sees that the bridge is falling to pieces and that he is facing the abyss. The abyss was real life; the bridge was the artificial life Karenin had been living.

It is a good example of Tolstoy's closeness to the reactions of his characters. Whether or not in his daily routine he has been 'living' is neither here nor there. The important thing is that he is now confronted with a terrible and unexpected situation which he instantly feels to be 'real life'. He is as unaccustomed as most people to "putting himself in thought and feeling into another being". (In Dolly's daydream of taking a lover, she imagines with relish the amazement and incomprehension of Stiva, who takes her as much for granted as Karenin takes Anna.)

Anna is in a similar state: she is amazed at her own reactions, her newfound impenetrability and refusal to be understood. We can no more 'see' her than Karenin can. Coming back from the party where she has met Vronsky again (the same party that figures in the two possible opening drafts), "her face shone with a vivid glow, but not a joyous glow—it resembled the terrible glow of a conflagration on a dark night". This is one of Tolstoy's best similes, and it shows us how right he was not to retain those first physical impressions of Anna—embonpoint, shoulders, air of *jolie laide*, etc. The more she is in love the less she is visible, to us and to the other characters.

She begins to be a centre of isolation and unreality. So she becomes for Kitty, who admired her so much and imagined her at the ball in a lilac dress. But she appeared in black, which at once seemed right, and now her shoulders and hair can be described (though it is not her but a Madame Korsunova who is the most *décolletée* woman present) and there is something brilliant and pitiless about her. Kitty cannot talk to her any more, nor she to Kitty. The hand on Vronsky's shoulder is not the "small energetic hand" which had comforted Dolly. In the morning the children had adored her, but the next day they seem to have forgotten their new aunt and are quite indifferent about her.

Again Stiva acts as a kind of index to her. When Vronsky first meets her he smiles involuntarily at her charm, as everyone smiles at Stiva. They will always go on smiling at Stiva but Anna has become different, and at the ball Vronsky has a sub-missive, dog-like look. Her whole being now seems indeter-minate, like fire or water: the stability of others, Stiva, Karenin, her maid Annushka ("dozing, her broad hands, with a hole in one of the gloves, holding the red bag on her lap") enable us to perceive and inhabit the strange element. Returning to the country after his failure with Kitty, Levin cheers up and reflects that "he was himself and did not wish to be anyone else". It is the great Tolstoyan resource and comfort, the *samodovolnost* of *War and Peace*, but with Anna it has quite disintegrated. "Am I myself, or another?" she wonders in the train. The train, the storm, the shrieking snow, whirl her away from her pleasure in her travelling arrangements, the pillow from the little red bag, the paper-knife, the English novel.

Anna read and understood, but it was unpleasant to read, that is to say, to follow the reflection of other people's lives. She was too eager to live herself. When she read how the heroine of the novel nursed a sick man, she wanted to move about the sick-room with noiseless footsteps; when she read of a member of Parliament making a speech, she wished to make that speech; when she read how Lady Mary rode to hounds, teased her sister-in-law, and astonished everybody by her boldness—she wanted to do it herself. But there was nothing to be done, so she forced herself to read, while her little hand toyed with the smooth paper-knife.

The ball, the storm, and Anna's return to Petersburg, are breathtaking in their assurance. Metaphor, insight, and the objectification of a state with which he was himself becoming more and more familiar—they were never combined more felicitously in his art. And all these climactic scenes are shot through with humour. Anna may have been triumphant and pitiless at the ball, but as she reads her English novel, or notices her husband's ears on Petersburg station, she is touching and comic. Yet the climax of the seduction is the end of life flowing like a fountain or blazing like a fire: it is like the constriction of the black bag, the confrontation of death. Everything shrinks to one fact.

"It's all over," she said. "I have nothing but you left. Remember that."

The despair of the discovery remains with her to the end, however great her subsequent joy, possessiveness and pleasure. She compared herself to a starving man given food, and we remember this when Levin is compared to a starving man in a toyshop. Yet Tolstoy's fear of sex, as of death, does not obtrude: the discovery of what they have done is the lovers' alone, and we completely accept that what Tolstoy tells us is their own reaction.

What does obtrude a little are Tolstoy's novelish devices. The storm, the journey, and the meeting with Vronsky and then Karenin, are no more like a novel than the English novel Anna reads on the train resembles *Anna Karenina*. They are an onrush of life and power. Not so the omens—the man killed on the line

as Anna arrives in Moscow—or the schematisation of 'the peacemakers'. Admirably done as is Anna's intervention with Dolly
on her brother's behalf, Tolstoy is surely pulling the wires
when Anna urges Dolly to remember that men, however dis-
gustingly they may behave with actresses and governesses,
never lose their reverence for The Home. Nor does it seem
other than contrived that when he meets Anna again in Petersburg Vronsky should have been engaged on rescuing two comrades from a farcical situation. "Blessed are the peacemakers, for
they shall be saved," said Princess Betsy, remembering she had
heard someone say something like that. The humour is engaging, but the atmosphere of Biblical quotations seems to close in
on us—"He saved others . . ." and "Vengeance is mine: I will
repay". It is left to Stiva to appear wholly himself in the bene-
ficent role, and that because he might do as much damage as he
does good. At his dinner party he seems strangely like the hero
of the novel, getting Levin and Kitty engaged at last as simply
as he gratifies Karenin and "kneads all that society dough till
the drawing-room was in first-rate form".

Almost any party demonstrates an aspect of Tolstoy's Law—
his clear stream of narration and comment always seems more
full of meaning than his deliberate effects, however just and
masterly these may be. Kitty struggling with a pickled mushroom as she asks Levin if there are bears on his estate, and the
same Kitty after marriage tidying up the dying Nicholas and
making him comfortable; Turovtsin, who helped Dolly when
her children had scarlet fever, laughing so much that the thick
end of his asparagus falls in the butter sauce; Stiva laying his
hand for a moment on the hotel waiter's head—these facts seem
more meaningful, as well as more vital, than the metaphoric
pattern, the omens, and the peacemaking parallels.

More meaningful, too, than the wider parallel between
Levin's ideas and convictions and the multifarious action of the
novel which invisibly and silently corroborates them. In *War
and Peace* there seems no predetermined connection between
events and Tolstoy's views about them. Event and view only
finally coincide in the triumph of the marriage sequence at the
close. In *Anna Karenina* their coincidence is already implied at
the beginning. When we are informed that Levin thought of

family life as the thing that really mattered, and imagined the family scene in his home before he imagined the woman who would share it with him, we feel that—through him—conception and view is anticipating character and actuality. Levin should expand and not contract the scope of the book. On the whole he does, and so earns his decisive role: the shooting, the mowing, the wedding, the elections, are all excellent, assimilated into the flow and yet far enough from the tragedy to relieve us from it, and contrast truly with it. None the less it is the function of Levin as unconscious arbiter, in whose attitude solutions are already present in schematic form, that is a more serious danger to the scope of the novel than is Tolstoy's use of the scenic method. In spite of its omissions that method enlarges and expands, and nothing that expands can go wrong in Tolstoy— the longer he goes on and the more he gets in the better. It is contraction and symbolic schematisation that are the dangers.

But we can become aware of these as much through the original participants of the novel as through Levin. Pivotal episode as it is, in that it precipitates Anna's confession to her husband, the steeple-chase at Krasnoe Selo is not quite the self-justified thing we should expect, when we consider the status of other such great scenes in Tolstoy, like the two hunts in *War and Peace* and the two shooting-parties in *Anna*. The trouble seems to be that Tolstoy tried to make it too symbolically decisive, too eloquent of the relations between Anna and Vronsky. Literal genius as he is, Tolstoy's symbolic touch is far from delicate, far from being the sort of poetically instinctive thing that it can be in Turgenev at his best, or in novelists otherwise as dissimilar as Hardy and D. H. Lawrence. Dr F. R. Leavis has indeed compared the scene unfavourably with episodes in Lawrence's novels, concluding that while the latter have an instinctive psychological relevance to the author's intention, Tolstoy is easily seduced from the current of his novel by anything fashionable, of the *beau monde*.

So much the better for Tolstoy, given the kind of writer he is, and would that it were so here. Lawrence's imagination can be reserved to him: it does not make a good stick to beat Tolstoy. Tolstoy himself said that he had no imagination, and his enormous literalness does seem to leave our ordinary use of the word standing. Not for him the almost unconscious creation of symbolic atmosphere that we associate with a vivid literary imagination. The railway and the storm in *Anna* is only a partial exception. The suicide of a despairing woman under a train was the occurrence from which the novel began; making the lovers' first meeting in a railway station was a logical step which would be equally effective in any other writer—it is not specifically Tolstoyan. The linkages by means of metaphor are almost a substitute for the symbolic imagination, as if Tolstoy felt that a novel—"the first I have attempted"—required something of the sort. They are inherently clumsy, like the Dickensian touches he sometimes falls back on when a scene is antipathetic to him, or an individual physically unattractive—the divorce lawyer who catches moths, or Karenin's habit of cracking his finger-joints. These are neither imaginative nor literal.

The early drafts leave us in no doubt that Tolstoy intended a symbolic parallel between the fate of Anna and of Vronsky's mare in the steeplechase. Indeed both have the same name—Tania. In the final version the parallel is no longer emphasised, but it is still there, and it collides in an agreeably but unintentionally comic way with the superb literalness with which Tolstoy describes the mare and her trainer.

> Frou-Frou was of medium size and by no means free from blemish. She was slenderly built. Her chest, though well arched, was narrow. Her hindquarters tapered rather too much, and her legs, especially her hind legs, were perceptibly bowed inwards. Neither fore nor hind legs were particularly muscular, but on the other hand she was exceptionally broad in the girth, now that she was lean from her strict training. She appeared all the more narrow in build because so deep in the breadth. But she possessed in the highest degree a characteristic that made one forget all her defects. This was her thoroughbred quality—the kind of blood that *tells*, as they say in English. The muscles, clearly marked beneath the network of sinews stretched in the fine mobile skin as smooth as satin, seemed hard as bone. Her lean head with the prominent bright and sparkling eyes, broadened out to her muzzle with its wide crimson nostrils. Her whole appearance, particularly about the head, was spirited and yet gentle. . . .
>
> As soon as Vronsky entered she took a deep breath, and turning her prominent eyes so that the whites became bloodshot, looked

from the other side of the box at the newcomers, shook her muzzle, and stepped lightly from foot to foot.

"See how nervous she is," said the Englishman.

"You darling!" said Vronsky, going up to the horse and soothing her.

But the nearer he came the more nervous she grew. Only when he reached her head did she suddenly calm down, and the muscles under her fine and delicate coat vibrated. Vronsky stroked her firm neck, adjusted a lock of her hair that had got on the wrong side of her sharply-defined withers, and brought his face close to her dilated nostrils, delicate as a bat's wing. Her extended nostrils loudly inhaled and exhaled her breath; she set back one of her finely pointed ears with a start and stretched out her black firm lips towards Vronsky, as if wishing to catch hold of his sleeve. But remembering her muzzle she jerked it, and again began stepping from one of her finely chiselled feet to the other.

This is, as Chaucer would say, the most *horsely* of horses. It is a superlative instance of the power of Tolstoy's creations to be "the thing they are and not another thing". And it shows us why Anna and the mare cannot be metaphorically related. The early versions present an elementary but effective dramatic relation which Tolstoy entirely removed in the final text, while involuntarily retaining the ghost of the old identification. His first idea was that Tania the heroine should be virtually responsible for the disaster which overtakes her namesake the mare and Balachev (as Vronsky was first called). She is determined to watch the race, but she has had a terrible dream about her lover's fall at the main obstacle, and therefore she stands with a friend beside the smaller jump at the end of the course. Balachev sees her as he approaches and it unnerves him. His jump is a little premature, and in an elaborate passage Tolstoy describes—more convincingly than in the few oddly perfunctory words of the final version—how the mare slips on a broken turf as she lands, tries to change feet and recover herself, but falls heavily, breaking her spine. Tania runs up and asks Balachev if he is hurt. He limps off without replying.

The symbolic significance is graphic and clear. Tania has helped to lose Balachev the race: she will now ruin his life and that of her husband, and destroy herself when she sees what havoc she has caused. The relation of heroine to horse does not matter, because both are so closely involved with the rider in the drama of his fall. The final version is not so graphic, but it is far more effective psychologically. It is in keeping with the tone of personal relations throughout the book, for instead of bringing the lovers together it emphasises their isolation from each other. The point (implicit in the fine description) is that—so far from there being any resemblance—Frou-Frou and her fate belong to a different world from Anna and hers. In the excitement of the race Vronsky has entirely forgotten about Anna, a kind of forgetting which in the later stages of their relationship will call forth her most demonic jealousy. Vronsky's failure and disappointment are wholly his own: Anna's anxiety and relief are wholly hers. Tolstoy conveys their separation in the mere account of Frou-Frou and her trainer, and in Vronsky's preoccupation with his horse and his rival, but he also underlines it by a simple narrative device. He describes the race twice: first as Vronsky rode it, and then from the point of view of Anna and Karenin as spectators. Such drama as remains is now not between the lovers but between the wife and the husband, who observes her terror at the news of Vronsky's fall and her indifference to that of the others.

Through the early versions Vronsky evolves always in the direction of greater self-possession, of tranquil uncommitted aplomb. He evolves, in fact, to become *incapable of a dramatic relationship*. The early Vronskys are passionate and vulnerable, as capable—significantly—of a dramatic and sympathetic relation with Karenin himself as with Anna. Their dramatic potential shows even in their appearance—young Balachev, as well as being bald and blue-chinned, wears a single silver ear-ring: it is an old family custom. One cannot imagine our Vronsky doing anything so *outré*. Balachev-Vronsky is not unlike Mitya in *The Brothers Karamazov*—his passion has the same directness and unintimate animal facility. The dramatic triangle of the steeplechase is repeated in that between himself, Anna and Karenin. But in the final Vronsky, Tolstoy has returned to something much more like a subtle and intimate version of 'the superfluous man'.

The advantage of this Vronsky, in terms of a high challenge to the author, is that he is the last person apparently to go overboard in the way he does. The passion of Balachev-Vronsky for Anna is just what we would have expected, and any interest it had would be collective and dramatic rather than intimate and psychological. But as novel readers rather than dramatic participants we are, so to speak, much more like the final Vronsky than the earlier one, and more ready to enter fully into his motives and feelings. Tolstoy makes us feel that if *we* were to go overboard with Anna we should do it like this, that we should be as adroit, as collected, only realising after each step had been taken how deeply we had committed ourselves. It is because we are so close to him when he has his moments of stocktaking, sitting down in a clean shirt the morning after the steeplechase to square up his debts and consider his relations with Anna, that we still feel close at the climax of his humiliation with Karenin when Anna is so ill, and even in his attempt at suicide. Tolstoy's secret here is to compel a naturally undramatic character to participate in drama against his will. Instead of being the natural outcome of character and the climax of Anna's situation, illness and Vronsky's suicide attempt is unexpected and without a sequel, for (Tolstoy implies) it has no lasting significance for the personalities involved and for daily life as they have to go on living it.

The final Vronsky has no self-destructive impulse. His *samodovolnost* has about it an alert and instinctive decorum which makes him liked and admired: and he is not adroitly calculating—indeed he fails to calculate in his military life the results of having turned down an important post. He assumed his lack of vulgar zeal would commend itself, and was chagrined to find himself misunderstood: instead of respecting in him the higher self-seeking, his superiors assumed he was not interested, and were quite prepared to leave him to go his own way. He meets Anna at the moment when his role of disinterest has begun to pall.

Tolstoy the analyst could not have described a love-affair without an element of calculation in it—that is why the dramatic spontaneity of the early Vronsky-Balachev had to undergo modification. There is nothing repellent in the calculation; it is simply human and does not make Vronsky unsympathetic, but it indicates why he would be more successful in the role of lover than in that of husband. He wants to do everything properly, but he supposes that doing things properly in love requires the jockey's, the general's or the gambler's powers of skill and concentration. Although he does not confide in them, he feels that the only two of his friends who would understand him are the gambler Yashvin, and the successful commander Serpukhovskoy. Both would grasp the seriousness of the business, the *intentness*,[1] and would realise from their own philosophy that this is his way of fulfilling himself, or risking everything.

But when he is left alone with Anna he finds there is nothing left for this power of intentness to accomplish. He had been flattered that Serpukhovskoy thought him a necessary man, but now he has become a superfluous one, whose only function is to continue to tell Anna that he loves her. In the end he grimaces with pain at the very word 'love', and at Anna's incessant and bitter repetition of it. The careful and methodical side of him, to which love—like power or war—had seemed to offer a high challenge, must now devote itself to estate management and local politics, and even these activities are poisoned by the aftermath of his *coup de main*. He hankers for any ordinary occupation away from Anna. "The innocent mirth of the elections, and this dismal burdensome love to which he must return, struck Vronsky by their contrast. But he had to go, and he took the first train that night for home."

Solipsism in *Anna* is as joyful as in *War and Peace*, as shiningly serene. In the first half of the novel, at least, the solipsistic man is happy and therefore right. But instead of being a part of the natural order of things, this rightness conceals a strange irony. When Anna and Vronsky are happiest in their love they are alone: we never see their happiness together, as we see that of the married couples at the end of *War and Peace*. Vronsky is happiest on his own when he is going to see Anna, not when he is with her.

He put down his legs, threw one of them over the other, and

[1] An admirer of Stendhal, Tolstoy would naturally tend to make Vronsky as a lover not wholly unlike the classic Stendhalian type.

placing his arm across it felt its firm calf, where he had hurt it in the fall the day before, and then, throwing himself back, sighed deeply several times.

"Delightful! O delightful!" he thought. He had often before been joyfully conscious of his body, but had never loved himself, his own body, as he did now. It gave him pleasure to feel the slight pain in his strong leg, to be conscious of the muscles of his chest moving as he breathed. That clear, cool August day which made Anna feel so hopeless seemed exhilarating and invigorating to him and refreshed his face and neck, which were glowing after their washing and rubbing. The scent of brilliantine given off by his moustache seemed peculiarly pleasant in the fresh air. All that he saw from the carriage window through the cold pure air in the pale light of the evening sky seemed as fresh, bright and vigorous as he was himself. The roofs of the houses glittered in the evening sun; the sharp outlines of the fences and corners of buildings, the figures of people and vehicles they occasionally met, the motionless verdure of the grass and trees, the fields of potatoes with their clear-cut ridges, the slanting shadows of the houses and trees, the bushes and even the potato ridges—it was all pleasant and like a landscape newly painted and varnished.

When he sees her, "a thrill passed like electricity through his body, and with renewed force he became conscious of himself, from the elastic movement of his firm legs to the motion of his lungs as he breathed, and of something tickling his lips".

Vronsky's self-sufficiency at this moment is outrageous, sublime; he can no more deny it than Stiva could prevent that stupid kindly smile ('reflex action of the brain') coming over his face at a most inopportune time. For the men in *Anna* it is the body that leads and the feelings that follow; the state of one's own body, not other people's feelings, tells one whether an experience is good or bad. For Vronsky, the sign and seal of love is this extraordinary increase in his *samodovolnost*. It is not Anna but *himself* who is aware of the joyful tickling of his moustache. *Samodovolnost* is a far more shameless thing in *Anna* than it was in *War and Peace*, and it seems likely that, even at its most apparently serene, there is now in it a sharp element of self-hatred. *Anna*, as Dostoevsky remarked, is by no means an innocent book. Tolstoy was well aware of the destructive potential of this joyful solipsism.

We already know how much Anna is irritated by Vronsky's calm happiness. The cold fresh summer day, so enchanting to him, is for her malignant and disintegrating. She wishes Vronsky to confer on her the same joyful unity that he feels himself, but she knows that he will not and cannot. How could there be unity between two persons in such entirely different *physical* states? She must tell him that her husband now knows.

> If at this news he would say to her, firmly and passionately, and without an instant's hesitation: "Give up everything and fly with me!" she would leave her son and go with him. But the news had not the effect on him that she had desired: he only looked as if he had been offended by something.

She thinks this cold severity is aimed at her, but it is only caused by his gravely satisfied contemplation of a duel with Karenin. Worst, of all, she realises that his reaction to the news is not spontaneous.

> She understood at once that he had already considered this by himself, knew that whatever he might say he would not tell her all that he was thinking, and that her last hopes had been deceived. This was not what she had expected.

Reactions in Tolstoy are not spontaneous—only physically involuntary. Like Stiva, Vronsky cannot keep a certain look off his face, the look with which he imagines himself confronting Karenin's pistol. Even his solicitude irritates her, for it is without intuition. He supposes that telling her husband was agonisingly difficult, but that, as she dryly tells him, came of itself. Yet this failure to meet each other is not insisted on: there is one deeply moving moment when sobs choke her as she says she is proud of his love, and "for the first time in his life Vronsky too felt ready to cry".

Anna goes back to Petersburg and another misunderstanding occurs. Karenin is fresh from his triumph at an important committee meeting, and the last thing he wants is a showdown. All he requires for the moment is that everything should remain outwardly the same, so that he can at least enjoy his political victory. Anna says timidly that their relations cannot be the same, and, too late, realises that her husband is not referring to their going to bed together, but only to the proprieties being observed. He rubs this in with hatred and sarcasm, and her humiliation is complete.

In the next chapter we are back with Levin and his ploughs and hayfields, and we begin to realise that his nature obeys the same laws as Vronsky's, and Stiva's. His spells of euphoria are perfectly his own, without relation to what is going on around him. When he is gloomy he feels the peasants misunderstand and dislike him; that they break his farm implements on purpose and have no wish for improvements of any kind. When he is cheerful he sees a wonderful future for his new system and ideas. He is feeling happy about his book when his brother Nicholas arrives, dying of consumption. At first he feels ashamed to remain happy when his brother is dying, but Nicholas reminds him of death as malignantly and incessantly as Anna will remind Vronsky of love, and with the same result. His brother at once attacks the ideas of his book, not because it is bad but because it is written by a man who will going on living, while he himself must die.

> "You do not want to establish anything. You simply want to be original, as you have always done, and to show that you are not just exploiting the peasants, but have ideas!"
> "You think so? Well then, leave me alone!" said Levin, and he felt that a muscle was uncontrollably quivering in his left cheek.

Life is telling death to leave it alone, as self-sufficiency will tell love to do so. But in the night Levin gets up, and looks in the glass at his teeth, his hair and his arms. "I am working; I want to do something, and I had forgotten it will all end in death."

I have remarked how Tolstoy's enormous vitality continually displayed itself in his way of narrating by two 'positives', where one might have expected a positive and a negative. Thus Prince Andrew cannot find his former love for Natasha, but in its place is a new, sober and perturbing sort of tenderness; or Levin himself does not feel the expected love for his newborn child but rather a "new and distressing sense of fear", and "the consciousness of another vulnerable region". These are new and vital discoveries which will in turn give place to further discoveries. In *War and Peace* life and death are themselves such positives. Andrew seems to go from one to another as he does from one phase of experience to another. Death is described almost as a different aspect of life. But in *Anna* death appears as a true negation, which cannot be faced because it offers nothing imaginable to experience. And love itself is not very different.

Levin's period of euphoria, as he waits to engage himself officially to Kitty, is just as solipsistic as Vronsky's in the carriage on the way to Anna. But because his love is secret and self-created, Vronsky's happiness begins and ends in his own body, while Levin's joy is shared (as he thinks) with everyone he meets. His self-preoccupation has not only a public licence but the property of making others happy, as young Rostov's happiness infected the German inn-keeper on whom he was billeted, as if both wanted to exclaim: *"Vivat die ganze Welt"*. The waiter at the hotel seems to respond to Levin's joy, "as men get infected by others' yawning". And Kitty's parents are infected too. "The old couple seemed to have become confused for the moment, and did not know whether it was they who were again in love or only their daughter." The idea of 'infection' in this marvellous and moving passage seems to correspond closely to Tolstoy's formula of how we are 'infected' by good art. The artist's joy in creation is solipsistic, but we share in it with him if what he describes is universal and necessary.

Levin's meeting with Kitty is attended by the same kind of misunderstandings and failures of communication as that of Anna and Vronsky, but they are completely swallowed up in the human and social necessity of their coming together. They are in love because it is necessary for them to be so in order to fulfil their lives. Both are convinced it was certain to happen, and Kitty thinks she is telling the truth when she says: "I always loved you only, but I was carried away". Natasha might have said the same to Pierre. Whatever she felt for Andrew or Kuragin, or Kitty for Vronsky, cannot afterwards be called love because it came to nothing. Even more unblushingly calm is the disclosure by Tolstoy that deep in Kitty's heart "was the fear and humiliation of being an old maid". Levin apprehends this, but instead of reflecting that this motive might be more important to her than his own personal charms, "he too felt the fear and humiliation". It infects him as his joy in the betrothal infected others. There is a touching irony in the fact that Levin loves

Kitty more, through sensing that she does not love him so much as a person but as a means to an end; while Vronsky does not sense Anna's desperate hunger for him personally, but sees himself playing a role—that of the dignified lover facing the injured husband's fire. It is Vronsky's impossible task to embody love, while Levin has only to be its vessel and representative.

Anna has to keep the word love because it is all she has, a hard object to fling in Vronsky's teeth, until it becomes identified with the death she will also fling at him. The account of her consciousness in the carriage and train at the end is strikingly similar in tone to those of Vronsky in his carriage and Levin's night before the betrothal. In order to kill time, Levin goes with Koznyshev to a Moscow town council meeting.

> What seemed remarkable to Levin was that they were all perfectly transparent to him that day, and that by means of little signs which he had never noticed before he recognised the soul of each, and clearly saw they were all kind, and—in particular—were all extremely fond of him.

Anna has the opposite experience. From the depths of her despair she can see equally clearly that they are all vile. "That man wants to astonish everybody and is very well satisfied with himself". She knows that Vronsky will not be unfaithful to her, or go off with the young Princess Sorokina, but this makes no difference. She sees that Vronsky wants to relax, to be kind and familial, but for her that would be hell, "for where love ceases, there hate begins". She realises her compulsive need to make Vronsky suffer for the suffering he has caused her.

Tolstoy accepts with his usual calm the human urge to repay in kind. After his rejection, Levin was ashamed to find how agreeable it was to hear that Kitty was ill "and was suffering—she who had made him suffer so much". Anna's impulse is the same as that of her persecutors. Karenin "does not acknowledge it to himself", but he wishes her to suffer, and under the influence of religion and Lydia Ivanovna he can make this desire respectable. Lydia Ivanovna herself, who claims that she can "understand immorality but not cruelty", achieves her own purpose in her reply to Anna's request to see her son, the purpose "which she had hidden even from herself". "Her letter wounded Anna to the depths of her soul."

Vengeance is one of Tolstoy's fictional themes, but he does not overdo it. He does not forget that most human beings are incapable of feeling one thing for long, even the desire to get their own back. He makes us realise how dependent most novelists are on the obsessiveness, or at least the unusual single-mindedness, of their characters. He makes us wonder whether George Eliot's Tito Melema and Rosamond Vincy, or Henry James's Gilbert Osmond, would have been *quite* so unremitting in their selfishness or their vindictiveness. The impulse to please, to make up for things, to provoke confidence and grati-tude, simply to tease or be teased—even the selfish and the vindictive must feel this at times. And Anna's nature is not selfish or vindictive. The most touching thing on her last drive is when she sees an absurd name—Tyutkin—over a hairdresser's shop. "*Je me fais coiffer par Tyutkin*—I shall tell him that when he comes back she thought, and smiled." But then she remem-bers she has no one now to share something funny with. The touch both emphasises the imminence of catastrophe and de-prives it of inevitability. They might have made a go of it. Anna might have acquiesced in Vronsky's diminished passion; her 'demons' would always have come back, but there is much in life she enjoys and could go on enjoying, and she recognises this up to the last moment.

What crushes Anna most at the end is not, in fact, her sense of the impossibility of life with Vronsky, but her sense of isolation. And the chilling thing is how completely and how casually Dolly and Kitty, who are genuinely attached to her, have come to accept that isolation. It is her sense of being out-cast from the kind of society in which she is most naturally at home, and where at the beginning of the book she was at home, that gives Anna her final despair. When Anna leaves them at the end, Kitty and Dolly—as they pass on to their preoccupations—remark how charming she is.

"But there is something pathetic about her, terribly pathetic."

"Yes, but today there is something peculiar about her," said Dolly. "When I was seeing her out, there in the hall, I thought she was going to cry."

It is the tone of this exchange which is most final. Ordinary society has not so much excluded Anna as simply failed to see how much she needs it. She has become accepted as being a different sort of person, and to her this is the final loneliness.

Yet Tolstoy does not attempt to convince us that isolation is the human fate, or that love as Anna and Vronsky experience it is necessarily a matter of isolation and misunderstanding. At no point, either, are we asked to accept anything definitive about passion, nor are the numerous contrasting patterns of love required to imply a judgment on the central one. Levin, Kitty and Dolly may sometimes appear as ideal figures, full of the unsought wisdom of the ages, but they are disposed—as it were helplessly—among others, of their kind, who are the same and yet different. There is Stiva; Koznyshev and Varenka, disappointed and yet relieved after their failure to get engaged in the mushroom wood; the egregious Sappho Stolz and Liza Merkalova, as assertively alive as the main characters, and living endorsements of Princess Betsy's dictum—"You see, a thing may be looked at tragically and turned to a torment, or looked at quite simply, even gaily".

The sensations lead and the emotions follow. The difficulty of coming to any conclusions about life is that the body does not remain in the same state for long enough. When Anna is ill she feels love and admiration for her husband, as if her dream of having two husbands who both loved her had come true: when she recovers he excites in her only repulsion and fear. And Karenin himself recovers from the forgiveness, the dignity, and the simplicity which the strain of her illness had produced in him. Rage, sorrow, confession, repentance are almost equally gratifying and cathartic to the body, like sneezing, sweating or shedding tears. Before the climax Karenin goes to Anna carrying his rage like a cup he is anxious not to spill; when she is ill he prays that the pleasure of forgiving may not be taken from him, and he feels "a sense of joy at the greatness of his own humility". When he is gloomily contemplating Anna's newly born daughter "suddenly a smile, wrinkling the skin on his forehead and making his hair move, came out on his face".

Vronsky's move to shoot himself is like a gesture of physical exasperation. "With a strong movement of his whole hand, as if

to clench his fist, he pulled the trigger." The attempt at suicide
made in that gesture is caused by the torture of his humiliation.
He and Karenin have changed roles. It is himself, and not the
deceived husband, who turns out to be ridiculous. Powerful
emotions—hate, love, forgiveness—are not only good to feel in
themselves, they confer dignity on the person who feels them.
For Tolstoy—so unlike Dostoevsky here—shame and humiliation do not. For both Vronsky and Levin it is not the best and
the worst things in their lives that they remember but the
moments of stupidness, awkwardness. "Most terrible of all was
the ridiculous and shameful figure he had cut. . . . 'Take away
his hands,' Anna's voice is saying. Karenin pulls away his hands,
and he is conscious of the shame-suffused and stupid expression
of his own face."

But for Vronsky, too, the anguish does not last. He and Anna
both recover; they meet again; they are as they were before,
and so is Karenin. So exultant, so exhaustive is the narrative
that we have no feeling of anti-climax, no impression of point-
lessness; nor do we feel that Tolstoy has wished to make some
point. He never suggests *himself* that strong emotion is physical
in its origin, and therefore ephemeral, and in a sense without
moral significance; that Vronsky, Anna and Karenin feel so
differently about each other and their situation when in a
heightened physical state, but that they are returned unchanged
to the 'coarse power' of habitual personal and social need. It is we
who receive this impression amongst others, not he who appears
to give it. We cannot draw any conclusions about the trio from
their behaviour here, nor make any generalised deductions from
it about human nature. It is a good example of the indirection
of Tolstoy's grasp, and his power of imitating the deceptiveness
of life itself, making his whole picture—like that of Mikhaylov
when his guests are studying it—"come alive with the inexpressible complexity of everything that lives".

Formal ideas about our emotional states—like the James-
Lange theory of their identification with their physical expression, or the rather similar theories of Sartre—cannot, of course,
suggest life in this way. Indeed Sartre's fictional exemplifications
of his theory remain precisely that: by maintaining his ideas his
characters forfeit the possibility of total life. Life deceives as

Tolstoy does: it suggests explanations only to contradict them, unintentionally as it seems. Few persons were more spontaneous in their affections, more rooted in their devotion, than the Countess Rostov. Yet we found her at the end of her life putting aside the miniature of the dead Count which Pierre has brought her, because she did not want to feel grief at that moment— the moment in her daily routine when she was accustomed to feel irritation or a desire for chat. So far from giving us a gloomy impression of the conditions of living, this is curiously exhilarating and enlarging. Sometimes we cannot avoid being ourselves, sometimes we can. Karenin has always led a mental life, outside the physical world, looking askance at the robust calves of the footmen, thinking "how strong and healthy they all are physically". When the catastrophe occurs and 'real life', as he thinks of it, breaks in, he suddenly experiences the intense enjoyment of physical emotion and this gives him a sort of moral grandeur. He is a different man.

It is because of this absurd and marvellous complexity that we can accept so easily the intrusion of Tolstoy's own explanations. He is obviously telling us himself that what made Karenin's new moral fineness and calm impossible for long was the 'coarse power' of social pressure. ". . . The very thing that had been a source of suffering to him had become a spiritual joy . . . but as time went on he saw that however natural his position might appear to him at the time, he would not be allowed to remain in it." This suggests that Karenin has found, what Tolstoy himself always wanted to find, a clear and simple solution to his troubles, and that only society prevents it. Tolstoy calmly ignores the fact, so abundantly clear from the previous pages, that Karenin's own nature, necessarily complex as it is, would soon disrupt his present calm without any help from society.

The stasis in which he does eventually repose, with the help of quack religion and Lydia Ivanovna, is that of a very ordinary hypocrisy and self-righteousness. It seems to be something of a relief to Tolstoy to get him settled in this way, for he has shown every sign of being a fascinating and uncontrollable figure. Though his disposal is convincing, he is disposed of: he is removed from the area of the novel in which development takes place, and in which the involuntary revelations of Tolstoy's analytic art can still intrigue and disconcert us. He might be said to be carried forward into the pages of *Resurrection*, for he becomes the type of figure we meet with in that novel.

His disposal was important for the final version of Tolstoy's plot. His refusal to divorce Anna has no effect on the outcome. Anna has refused the offer of divorce when he was in his forgiving mood because she needed—if she were to escape—to think of him not as she did when she was ill but as she had done during the first period of her love for Vronsky. If he had forgiven her and wished her well, Anna could not have shaken him off as one might shake off a drowning man. "That other one was drowned; of course it was wrong, but it had been the only way of escape."

Tolstoy had originally planned that she should feel remorse for "that good man", her husband, and that this would help to destroy her subsequent marriage to Vronsky. She would have felt guilty towards both men, and tormented by the continued presence of both in her life. In this version Karenin must remain capable of the exalted mood in which he forgave Anna when her daughter was born. That mood, must in fact, be a reaction based not on the physical temperament, of which Tolstoy is a master, but on the oddities of the psyche, where he is far less at home. The triangle would persist with its three sides in a highly dramatic relation to each other, and Karenin in the role of Dostoevsky's "eternal husband". Karenin haunts the new *ménage*. In spite of the pain it gives him he goes out of his way to see the pair at social gatherings. Vronsky is not happy, and goes into society by himself. Distracted and jealous, Anna reflects that there is nothing for her but to enjoy the so-called pleasures of life, and thinks even of running away with Yashvin, whom she knows to be secretly in love with her. Karenin, having heard talk at a party of murders inspired by jealousy, buys a pistol. He goes to see Anna and urges her to return to him, not for his sake or hers, but because they have broken the sacrament of marriage. Christ has saved him, by enabling him to pardon her, and will save her too. He bursts into tears. At this moment Vronsky comes back from the ballet. Karenin rushes out. Anna says to Vronsky: "He has come as a spiritual director, believing me to be unhappy". "That's very decent of him," sneers

Vronsky, and goes on to accuse Karenin of false emotionalism and hypocrisy. Anna defends him passionately, and there is a violent quarrel which leads to Anna's suicide.

The interest of these early scenarios is their resemblance to Tolstoy's plays, particularly to his last one, *The Live Corpse*. Significantly, both the *idea* of the novel's early drafts, and of the play, resulted in an externalisation of character—we can no more imagine Tolstoy entering into these persons than he could enter the persons initially conceived of in terms of appearance— the buxom sloe-eyed *jolie laide*, and her bald blue-chinned lover. Moreover, the scenario shows him taking the emotions seriously, as it were, and resolving the plot by means of them. The dramatist cannot afford to question the absoluteness of the emotions out of which his drama is concocted. Henry James's great 'scenario' novels—*The Wings of the Dove* and *The Golden Bowl*—require a necessary faith in the permanence of states like love and forgiveness—these things cannot be allowed to disappear or modify under examination, because the drama depends on them for its poignancy and point. Similarly, in *The Live Corpse*, which uses a variant of the triangular situation of the early *Anna* scenario, Tolstoy accepts the scenario convention in order to secure a dramatic effect and also score a forensic point about marriage as a social institution. Karenin the virtuous lover of *The Live Corpse* (the coincidence of names reveals the relation to the *Anna* scenario) is simply 'in love' with the married heroine. The nature and quality of this love cannot be analysed and hence this Karenin cannot acquire true Tolstoyan life as a character. The 'live corpse' himself, the heroine's erratic husband, Fedya, wishes to disappear in order to leave her free to marry her virtuous lover, and in order that he himself may live with a gipsy girl. And again, this determination is not an aspect of his character but a necessity of the plot: he is assumed to give the 'truth' about himself when he states that he hates his wife because he has done her harm, and loves the gipsy because he has given her money and done her good.

In the completed *Anna* there are no such truths, only people. Their full realisation by Tolstoy deprives of relevance all the novelist's willed conceptions and plottings, all the dramatist's confrontations and planned crises. For the last time in Tolstoy's art the work comes clean away from its shapings and intentions, as the statue from the marble. For the last time we feel a total difference in kind, and not merely in the degree of development, between the conception and the completed work. Its final self no longer seems to belong to Tolstoy, nor to be capable of being affected by him. The characters "do what is in their nature to do": they are invulnerable to the author's powers of choice. Unthinkable for Anna to contemplate an affair with Yashvin, or for Karenin to visit her and urge her return to him—unthinkable because such elements of the accidental and unpredictable would send them back to the tentative beginnings of Tolstoy's process, from which our knowledge of them, as people, has so completely emancipated them.

In Dostoevsky's method the scenario holds good to the last— the end of his novels is as provisional as the beginning. Shall Raskolnikov commit suicide, or become a new man in Siberia? Shall Alyosha retain his purity or find a new humanity in the sins of the flesh? Dostoevsky has no answer to these queries. He finds his characters in a newspaper paragraph, and ultimately he returns them there, to the news item and the full stop, the unexplained and the inexplicable. How Raskolnikov became human, Dostoevsky tells us, would require another novel to reveal, and that novel is never written. The end of *Resurrection*, as we shall see, is of the same kind. Of its hero we are told that "everything he did after that night had a new and quite different meaning for him. How this period of his life will end, time alone will prove." Possibly, but not to Tolstoy or to us. It is a real goodbye, of the sort where the plans made to meet again only confirm the permanence of the separation. But we do not say goodbye to the characters of *Anna* with any sense of expectation or query, for their modes of being have become assimilated to our own.

VI

Anna Karenina and *What is Art?*

"The sense of shame is lost, the sense of aesthetic shame. I wonder if you know the feeling? I feel it most strongly when I read something that is artistically false, and I can call it nothing else but shame."
TOLSTOY TO GOLDENWEISER, 1901

THE meeting of Vronsky and Anna in Italy with the Russian painter Mikhaylov is particularly interesting for the light it throws on Tolstoy's views on art at the time, and on the relation between the artist and society. Mikhaylov, a self-educated painter of considerable talent, is probably modelled on the painter Kramskoy, who did a portrait of Tolstoy and with whom he became very friendly. The introduction of the theme of art at this moment in the lovers' relation has a special significance, because their lives are no longer given but chosen; no longer taken up with involuntary emotion and event. They have, in a sense, stopped living, and so have leisure for art.

The timing of the incident reveals what Tolstoy was afterwards to state theoretically in *What is Art?*—his distrust for art which is not an involuntary and necessary part of the life of the individual and society. Italy is an aesthetic *enclave*; it symbolises the status of art as a fashionable upper-class amusement. "Being a Russian and an intelligent man," Vronsky cannot feel for sightseeing "that inexplicable importance the English manage to attach to it"; even though the Palazzo they have rented contains a fine Tintoretto—"one of his later period". The information comes from Golenishchev, the eternal parasite on art, who "never missed an opportunity of instilling into Mikhaylov a true understanding of it". He thinks Vronsky has talent, "his conviction being supported by the fact that he required Vronsky's praise for his articles and ideas, and felt that praise and encouragement should be mutual. Tolstoy's analysis of Golenishchev is deadly but not unfair. No doubt he is a man of genuine sensibility who can distinguish the good from the bad, but his power of doing so has been fatally compromised by his own social and personal needs, the chief of which is the need to avoid recognising his own sterility. Vronsky, on the other hand, "left off painting without any explanations or excuses" when he became aware he had no talent for it, and this is of a piece with his experience as a lover—he feels he has no real talent for that either, and finds it impossible eventually to disguise the fact. Anna's refusal to face this fact torments and embitters her until she cannot leave love alone any more than Golenishchev can leave art alone.

Tolstoy's central conviction that bad art is an affair of the will is expressed more powerfully in the narration of *Anna* than in his theoretical statements. Such artistic activity—whether as producer or spectator—means that one's life is not proceeding along natural, simple and inevitable lines. To amuse oneself with art is like amusing oneself with food, or with sex, and making a diversion out of something that should be an essential. Vronsky discovers "the eternal error men make in supposing that happiness consists in the gratification of their wishes": art, like happiness, is not a question of gratifications but of necessities. And it is through the essential that art and life coincide; soldiers sing songs and tell stories as a part of their way of life; a Vogul audience groan, weep and shout with joy at a dramatic representation of a hunting scene. Pozdnyshev, in *The Kreutzer Sonata*, makes Tolstoy's general point specifically about music.

> When a march is played the soldiers march to the music and the music has achieved its object. A dance is played; I dance, and the music has achieved its object. . . . Music . . . otherwise is only agitation, and what ought to be done in that agitation is lacking.

Passivity,[1] instead of participation, leads to the abuse of art and to its decadence. Karataev, Natasha and 'Uncle' sing like birds: in "an unendurable scene", as Tolstoy calls it, Wagner imitates birdsong.

There is a remarkable analogy, whether or not Tolstoy intended it, between his conception of what is bad in art and his presentation of what happens to Anna and Vronsky's love.

---

[1] Tolstoy's argument is strengthened today by the denaturing which art undergoes when packaged for passive consumption by a television audience.

Anna's passion was spontaneous, but the things that woman's love needs to perpetuate itself as necessary and good—family, home, husband—are lacking. Anna has no time for the English novel she tries to read in the train to Petersburg, because her excitement over Vronsky makes her want to live; but later we see her living with Vronsky very much the kind of life which that novel described as fashionable and offered as a distraction. Mikhaylov is silent about Vronsky's pictures because as a true artist he is bewildered and repelled by the atmosphere with which art is surrounded by those who want to use it as a distraction. For him, Vronsky is like a man who in the presence of a lover caresses a big waxen doll. The striking and sinister metaphor cannot but infect our idea of Vronsky as a lover as well as an artist. When Dolly goes to stay with Anna and Vronsky she is somewhat in the position of Mikhaylov—she is repelled by what she instinctively feels to be an imitation of family life and affections. Love is mocked as art can be mocked; as the life of the intellect is mocked for Levin by the intellectual dilettante Sviyazhsky, and as the love of country is mocked by the Pan-Slav enthusiasts.

But because *Anna* puts Tolstoy's view of art into a deeper and closer relation with the rest of life than does *What is Art?* it also reveals the inherent objections to that view. The novel does not deny that the love of Anna and Vronsky is still alive at the end, still capable and potential, and this fact dissolves dogma. What seems bogus and dead can still come alive—as his picture did for Mikhaylov—and display "the inexpressible complexity of everything that lives". Because this is so, it is not meaningless for Anna to interest herself in the groom's little girl and to plan a book for children, or for Vronsky to build a hospital and take part in the local elections. Because she no longer has the inevitabilities of a woman's life (Tolstoy brilliantly and convincingly suggests their loss in the fact that she cannot love her daughter by Vronsky as she loved her son by Karenin) it does not mean that affection and interest cannot revive in Anna, as art renews itself in new ways in new societies. Being itself a work of art the novel admits this in a way that *What is Art?* does not. In the later treatise Tolstoy merely asserts the comparison that "real art, like the wife of an affectionate husband, needs no ornaments . . . counterfeit art, like a prostitute, must always be decked out".

Tolstoy frequently compares counterfeit art to eating for gratification, but Stiva's mere presence contradicts this in the memorable scene where he and Levin have lunch together. He lends a scene which might have been—on Tolstoy's theory must have been—pretentious, gluttonous and mechanical, his own individual zest and spontaneity. He is a living proof that art can be a relaxation, a lightness that infects us with gaiety and spontaneous pleasure. It is the same with Sviyazhsky, who according to Levin/Tolstoy represents counterfeit intellectual activity, the wish for knowledge as an amusement and distraction. But the novel admits, and admits with authority, that Sviyazhsky is not 'placed' by Levin, who cannot "get beyond the reception rooms of his mind"; that he has "other bases of life which Levin could not discern"; that he has the mysteriousness of human individuality which, like the individuality of art, cannot be categorised and dismissed just because it is not understood. It continually happens in novels and plays that a character is not created enough to make the author's point of view about him convincing[1]; Tolstoy is the rare example of the opposite taking place. The reality of his characters breaks the dogmatic pattern into which they were made to fit, and suspends the judgments prepared against them.

Anna Karenina does not only contain its own qualification and contradiction of Tolstoy's attitude to art—it also gives unexpected support to the examples of good and bad art that Tolstoy chooses. When we read *What is Art?* we may assent to many of his general propositions, but we are staggered by the apparent perversity of his taste. *Hamlet* and *Lear* are notorious instances, but even more disheartening is the offer of Hugo, *Uncle Tom's Cabin*, his own stories *God Sees the Truth but Waits* and *The Prisoner of the Caucasus* (his only works of good art according

---

[1] E.g. we do not believe enough in Kipling's soldiers to accept their creator's conception of military life. The same is true of Pinter's play *The Homecoming*, where the contrast between ways of life depends on a true realisation of the individuals which is not achieved. This criticism does not of course apply to either Shaw's or Tolstoy's own plays, where the characters are not intended to be fully realised and, as it were, topographically true.

to Tolstoy) and of the crudest kind of *genre* painting. He singles out for special praise a sketch by Kramskoy (the Mikhaylov of *Anna*)

> showing a drawing-room with a balcony past which troops are marching in triumph on their return from the war. On the balcony stands a nurse holding a baby, and a boy. They are admiring the procession of the troops, but the mother, covering her face with a handkerchief, has fallen back on the sofa sobbing.

In spite of the different moral, this sounds horribly like the modern Russian *genre* painting *The Letter from the Front*, said to be Khruschev's favourite. But when with Anna and Vronsky we suddenly catch sight in a corner of Mikhaylov's studio of his picture of two boys angling, we are, like them, completely won over by it. Tolstoy makes a picture seem good which cited as an example in *What is Art?* would seem awful, and the reason is that he can make the picture alive for us in the novel by the element of *participation*. We are vividly aware of the attitudes of the three spectators, of their ennui with Mikhaylov's big religious work and their need to say something intelligent about it; of their attempt to express appreciation by means of the word 'talent', "which they understood to mean an innate . . . capacity, independent of mind and heart, and which was their term for everything an artist lives through"; and of how their bogus appreciative vocabulary is extinguished by spontaneous delight at the sight of the angling picture, which Mikhaylov has forgotten all about, as he has forgotten "the sufferings and raptures" he went through while painting it. The point is not that the painting is 'good art'—the novel does not pronounce on this—but that it gives these people whom we know real pleasure instead of merely engaging with their aesthetic expectations; that it leads us, therefore, into a true and penetrating study of the relation of artist, art and spectator. Tolstoy has made it come alive "with the inexpressible complexity of everything that lives".

It is precisely the absence of this life which condemns the examples thrust down our throats in *What is Art?*. Tolstoy had little experience of pictorial art and less education in it. He saw it in terms of the bad painting of his own time, but given this

large limitation (of which he admittedly seems unaware) his
taste is singularly just. He preferred the bad picture with feeling
to the bad picture with none. Though he might not have cared
for Piero della Francesca, and still less for Cézanne, he none the
less urges upon us the considerations in art which makes those
artists great; the dependence of skill upon 'mind and heart';
the true invitation to the whole of human experience. He detests
art that stops short at beauty, or indeed that stops short
anywhere.

All treatises on art are unsatisfactory—the issue is at once
too simple and too complex for any theorist to do justice to—
and Tolstoy's is no exception. What he says is profoundly true,
but it is not the sort of truth which can be set out in the way he
chooses to do so. As polemic, the effectiveness of *What is Art?*
lies not so much in its positive assertions as in its rejection of
much that was taken for granted in the aesthetic theories of the
time, particularly as these relate to the story and the novel.
Tolstoy explicitly rejects the Kantian isolation of art as the
realm of decoration and play, and all the nineteenth-century
doctrines of art for art's sake which stem from it. He points out
that the word for beauty in Russian, *Krasotá*, applies only to
what is seen, so that it makes no sense to speak of beauty in an
action or a novel, or even in poetry or music. The interchange-
ability of words meaning *good* and *beautiful* in Western languages
has, he implies, resulted in the notion of some sort of beauty,
verbal or aesthetic, as the goal of art.

The admired literature of the nineties could hardly defend
itself against a charge like Tolstoy's. Even Wagner and Ibsen—
to say nothing of Maupassant, Huysmans, Mallarmé, Rilke,
Bryusov and the symbolists—they *are* inferior to great writers
and for the reason Tolstoy gives, a lack of that wide and involuntary humanity which unites the writer's consciousness with the
human experience that "knew the thing before but had been
unable to express it". We are reminded of the eighteenth-
century pre-Kantian view of art here—"what oft was thought
but ne'er so well expressed"—and we remember the reaction of
Vronsky to Anna's portrait by Mikhaylov (where the general

point is characteristically sharpened by Vronsky's unconscious assumption of his superior background and culture.)

> "One needed to know and love her as I do to find that . . . expression of hers," thought Vronsky, though he himself had only learnt to know it through the portrait. But the expression was so true that it seemed both to him and to others that they had always known it.

Tolstoy perceives with great clarity the connection between 'art for art's sake' and the new morality associated with Nietzsche and his followers. "It is said that art has become refined. On the contrary, thanks to the pursuit of effects, it has become very coarse." Art for art's sake aims at the pure 'effect', but because art cannot but mirror the religious feeling of the age, the new aestheticism has become the prophet and religion of a new barbarity; and this applies not only to trivial works like the *Contes Cruels, Salome,* Andreyev's *The Red Laugh,* and so forth, but to such otherwise dissimilar writers as Flaubert, Kipling and Gerhard Hauptmann. Tolstoy detests the notion of the *Zeitgeist,* and with some justification sees the new aestheticism as pandering to it and dependent upon it.

Even when the moral is supposedly good, the craze for what Tolstoy calls "physiological effect" vitiates it—the writer is concerned not to infect the audience but to play upon their nerves, as at the climax of Hauptmann's play, *Hanneles Himmelfahrt.* It is instructive to compare Tolstoy's caustic comments on this piece, in which the part of the ill-used girl might have been expected to arouse his sympathy, with the enthusiastic preface he wrote for a German novel—Von Polenz's *Der Büttnerbauer*—with its similar part of a meek and injured wife. In the play there is "no infection between man and man" but only a deliberate attempt to excite the audience. The novelist on the other hand "loves his protagonists", and in an equally pathetic and terrible scene compels the reader not only to pity but also to love them.

Irrespective of the merits of the actual play and novel, Tolstoy's criteria are cogent. He considers the play form more subject than the novel to the crudity of the author's intention and desire for effect, and it is notorious that he considers Shakespeare as guilty in this respect as Hauptmann. As in the case of pictorial art, it is his lack of knowledge that is at fault here rather than his critical sense. He supposes that Shakespeare, like other playwrights, is chiefly concerned to secure an effect, and he denounces such an intention untiringly. "You see his intention," he observes of a new composer, "but no feeling whatever, except weariness, is transmitted to you." And again—when attacking Kipling and Zola—"from the first lines one sees the intention with which the book is written, the details all become superfluous, and one feels dull". When praising Chekhov's story *The Darling* he asserts that Chekhov intended to make fun of 'the darling', "but by directing the close attention of a poet upon her he has exalted her". The best books, the most full of infectious feeling, are those in which the author's intention is lost sight of, or even contradicted by, the close attention or 'love' which he devotes to his characters. Tolstoy is here implying a criticism of himself and revealing why we feel as we do about Stiva or about Anna.

Only once does he come near to perceiving that Shakespeare might have the same gift of 'close attention', and that is when he observes that Falstaff is his only non-theatrical character, the only one who does not behave like an actor, "He alone speaks in a way proper to himself". It is an illuminating comment. Again we feel that the novel, and in particular the naturalism of the Russian novel, is being called in to condemn the theatre. Falstaff is the only occasion when Shakespeare, like a novelist, set out to do one thing, and by becoming involved with his hero, did another. Such is Tolstoy's view, and he implies that Falstaff moves us for this reason, and that Lear and Cordelia do not move us because they are not seen in this way and not, as people, involuntarily loved. For this to happen they must be seen (like Falstaff) as if in real life and surrounded by the complex detail of real life.[1] Tolstoy is of course committing here the common critical fault of attacking a work because it has not the form that he prefers and refusing to understand the form

---

[1] Essays by Professors Wilson Knight ('Shakespeare and Tolstoy') and L. C. Knights ('*King Lear* as Metaphor') are illuminating on the question of Tolstoy's presuppositions about character and naturalism in Shakespeare. L. C. Knights also compares the 'realistic' method of Turgenev's *nouvelle, A King Lear of the Steppe*, with the 'metaphorical' method of Shakespeare's play.

in which it is actually written. And even on his own ground he is wrong, for the most obvious thing about almost all Shakespeare's characters is how continuously—and often, in terms of dramatic requirement, how unnecessarily—like 'real people' they are! Had Tolstoy known it, Shakespeare was really on his side.

Moreover, his criticism of *Lear* indicates not, as Tolstoy holds, what is wrong with the play, but what is remarkable and unique about it. It is true that Lear and Cordelia are actors whose parts are almost impossible to present and sustain, and that when Tolstoy speaks of "Lear's terrible ravings which make one feel as ashamed as one does when listening to unsuccessful jokes" he describes with uncomfortable accuracy the kind of embarrassment we feel at pretentious acting and an insensitive production. But we never know where we are with the play, as Tolstoy wished always to know where he was. Edging bathos and weird farce, it confounds our instinctive desire (which in Tolstoy had become an obsession) to see life steadily and whole. There is no clarity or security in which close attention might be paid to the individual—indeed the most unnerving thing about the play is the irrelevance of the character indications that do none the less appear, to be burnt up in the human reduction. Edmund's flashy comprehensibility gets us nowhere, nor does the puffing humanity of old Gloucester so brilliantly hit off in the opening scene—a scene that might well prelude a different kind of work altogether. Strangely enough, the openings of *Lear* and of *Anna* are by no means so different: we feel we know Gloucester as we know Stiva, but it would be unthinkable for Stiva to surrender his personality in some extraordinary metaphorical climax, to be blinded and driven to despair for his misdemeanours with governesses and ballet girls. For Tolstoy this would indeed be a flagrant case of a character being made to "do what was not in his nature", or to suffer what was not. But it is at once Tolstoy's strength and limitation that he will not relinquish his grasp on the individual nature—he cannot tolerate the thought of a total human reduction. On the retreat from Moscow Pierre still remains Pierre, and hence there is 'nothing terrible': Father Sergius cannot renounce his pride and desire to excel; and in spite of his moment of impersonal greatness Karenin cannot shake off his old persisting self.

This is certainly true of human beings in society as we usually
know it. But in *Lear* Shakespeare presents us with another truth,
no more profound but equally convincing. He could have understood and rendered Auschwitz in art: Tolstoy could not have
done. When men are indistinguishable in animal evil and animal
suffering, love and goodness seem no longer qualities connected
with the whole complex of a personality but as graces entering
as if from outside. Tolstoy's final charge against Shakespeare
—curiously echoing Dr Johnson's less censorious comment—is
that his reader "loses the capacity to distinguish between good
and evil". His plays, and plays generally (Tolstoy specifically
includes his own) have "no religious basis", and because they
depend on effect and sensation "even lack any human sense".
One sees what he means, but 'human sense' is not everything,
and religion—in Tolstoy's use of the term—most certainly is
not. In his passion for common sense and common virtue he
turns his back on the extreme situation which deprives us of
personal differentiation, of the habit of being ourselves. For
Tolstoy "the capacity to distinguish between good and evil"
must come out of close attention to the individual self. In
Shakespeare it can also come from prolonged exposure to his
poetic art, and from the range of apprehension—in the widest
sense religious—with which he can infect us as Tolstoy cannot.

There is much to be learnt from Tolstoy's dislike of Wagner
and Shakespeare, though in both cases what really counts is his
refusal to educate himself into their created medium. When
Tolstoy says that from the first reading "I was at once convinced that it is obvious Shakespeare lacks the main, if not the
only, means of portraying character, which is individuality of
language"—one can only suggest that he should have read more
Shakespeare and learnt more English. If all art were simple,
transparent, and international it would not even be necessary to
attack Shakespeare and Wagner—they would hardly have been
heard of. Tolstoy's method of attacking them is the same: he
describes the action of *Lear* and of *The Ring* in his Masonic
"making it strange" language, a kind of seemingly guileless
esperanto, so that the whole complex appeal and participation
through music and language is lost. When he tells us that though
Lear may sound absurd in his version it is even more absurd in

the original, he speaks truer than he knows: but the real absurdity of *Lear* is that of life, not that of basic English. None the less, Tolstoy did show up the chorus of nineteenth-century European pedants who proclaimed Shakespeare's beauties and profundities without any regard for the living complex of linguistic and national sensibility in which they have their being: just as he showed up the *Ring* worshippers who went into mass hypnosis at Bayreuth without any understanding of what Wagner was trying to accomplish in the tradition of Germanic self-awareness and Germanic dream. By being deliberately insensitive himself, Tolstoy revealed the insensitivity of those who profess to adore the great, but this is not the same as revealing that the great are not great at all.

"Great works of art are only great because they are accessible and comprehensible to everyone." By insisting on this principle Tolstoy asserts that a Vogul hunting-mime is far superior as art to *Hamlet*. The mime may indeed be true art, but its level of operation is sufficiently summed up by Henry James's comment on the puppet show: "What an economy of means—and what an economy of ends!" Moreover, 'everyone' is not—though Tolstoy would no doubt like to have him so—in a fixed state of being but in a state of becoming. His level of participation rises with education, becomes more complex and more demanding. "Groaning, weeping, and holding their breaths with suspense", the primitive audience of the mime were clearly participating much more than the average audience of *Hamlet*; but one can be sure that they would respond to *Hamlet*, in so far as they understood it, with just as much interest and enthusiasm, and more so as they got to know more about it. The trouble with drama is not the art but the audience, and the uneasy and pretentious relation between drama and audience—the desire to shock and be shocked—which Tolstoy saw as characteristic of nineteenth-century drama, and which he would recognise in drama today. That is why he returns, perversely, to the most primitive audience/drama relation. He ignores the fact that the Vogul audience would have delighted in the climax of *Hanneles Himmelfahrt*, and by their delight would have purged it of those elements of invited embarrassment and planned sensationalism which he rightly detected in the relation between Hauptmann and his audience. The gruesome thing about modern Shakespeare productions is precisely the mutual wish to shock and be shocked, to give and take gimmicks, but that is not Shakespeare's fault, though Tolstoy said it was. His real target, to a greater extent perhaps than he realised, is not counterfeit art that has been mistaken for great art, but the bad taste that has become accepted and standardised between producer and consumer. This is why much of what he has to say about art is so relevant today.

Unexpectedly, *What is Art?* is an assertion of the solitude of good art in the modern age. It leads us back, deviously but unmistakably, to Tolstoyan solipsism. Tolstoy's shame before the speeches of Lear, or before a performance of Beethoven's Ninth Symphony, reveals an overwhelming fastidiousness, a refusal to find the communal art of his own day anything but false, coarse and embarrassing. His solution—a return to primitive mime and to communal story-telling like that of Karataev in *War and Peace*—is of course a hopeless one, and there is no reason to suppose Tolstoy did not realise it. He disliked public art as much as public government, and the television age would not have given him cause to change his mind about either the one or the other. Tacitly he accepts the novel—the most private form—as the form in which good art still appeared in the modern age, and again and again in his criticism he makes things easy for the novel, allowing it a degree of sophistication which other forms—poetry, music, drama—are not allowed to share. Chekhov's *The Darling* and Von Polenz's novel are cases in point: can Tolstoy really have thought that his hypothetical 'everyone' would grasp the issues that he draws attention to in them, the grounds of appreciation which he indicates? The great irony is that he did not perceive how, with the decay of public art, Shakespeare's works—by one of those transformations of form in time of which supreme art is capable—had come to exhibit themselves, and to be treated, as the most comprehensive of novels—or non-novels perhaps, like *War and Peace* itself. The great unadmitted and perhaps unconscious assumption and conclusion of *What is Art?*—all the more evident from his rejection in it of his own best work—is that art is the novel, Tolstoy's novel.

VII

Resurrection

"The state is a conspiracy for the purpose not only of exploiting the citizens but of demoralising them as well."

TOLSTOY. Letter to BOTKIN in 1857

I

A T the end of *Resurrection* the scenario alternatives with which it began are still alive and kicking. Will Maslova marry Nekhlyudov, or the convict Simonson, or neither? All the possibilities are equally acceptable, for Maslova is too external a character for it to matter one way or the other: we have not acquired enough interior awareness of her in the course of the book to know ourselves what she will do without Tolstoy telling us. We cannot assimilate Maslova. Such assimilation involves the immense domesticity and worldliness of *Anna*, and it is this which Tolstoy has given up. As if in compensation he sharpens his power of external description. We can see Maslova very clearly; in her convict dress at the beginning of the novel; as a young girl playing hide-and-seek beside the patch of nettles in the garden of Nekhlyudov's aunt. We see the slight squint in her shining black eyes, and her "small energetic hand" (the same hand as Anna's—"the dusky broad little hand, with it's energetic cross vein", of Tolstoy's Aunt Tatiana, with which all his important female hands are identified).

Nekhlyudov we have already met before, in *Boyhood and Youth*. After a long lapse of years Tolstoy is able to return to him and make him the hero of a novel without, strangely enough, any need to change the main features of his character as they were perceived for us by the 'I' of the early work, Irtenyev. It is not Nekhlyudov who has changed but the narrator. It is a remarkable instance of the way in which all things seem contained in Tolstoy, as in the sea; in that great continuum we view the same things again from a different angle and through different eyes.

In the course of *Resurrection* we learn that Irtenyev is dead—
a symbolic death if we like to call it so, for Tolstoy wishes to
extinguish an aspect of his younger self, but also a technically
necessary one. Irtenyev's eye must not be allowed to rest on the
new scene. For him, as we have discussed before, the crucial
thing was to be an *understander*. Tolstoy observes in *Youth* that
the function of mutual understanding was to act as a criterion
for what is false or true in youthful experience:

> Two people of the same set or family who have this faculty always
> permit an expression of feeling up to a certain point, beyond which
> they see only empty phrases. They both see at the same moment . . .
> where enthusiasm ends and pretence begins, yet it may all seem
> quite different to people with a different scale of apprehension.

For Tolstoy at this time sincerity was a function of this sort of
family relationship, which Irtenyev has with his father and
brother, and even with a friend, Dubkov, whom he doesn't much
like. "Dubkov fitted in well with our circle and *understood*.
Dimitri Nekhlyudov however, though far more intelligent, was
obtuse in this respect." In the world of *Boyhood and Youth* this
is a damning verdict. Nekhlyudov is absurd, not endearingly
absurd inside the family circle, as Pierre is in *War and Peace*,
but with the hopeless absurdity of an outsider, placed by the
absolute adjudicative power of the family *understanders*.

Seen with the secure family eye, his intently awkward
démarches have something of the same ludicrousness as those of
Widmerpool in Anthony Powell's *The Music of Time*. Particularly embarrassing to Irtenyev are his attempts to live by the
will, "past the point beyond which one can see only empty
phrases". In *Youth*, Nekhlyudov takes up the poor student
Bezobedov, whom he does not like and with whom he has
nothing in common. "I wondered how he could bear the continual strain he put upon himself, and how the wretched
Bezobedov endured his uncomfortable situation." This is very
like the Nekhlyudov of *Resurrection*, but there we have no
Irtenyev—"self-satisfied and with a quiet consciousness of
power as a friend of the family"—to watch him as he comes back
after seeing off Bezobedov, who has at last managed to escape.
"He was smiling a faintly complacent smile and rubbing his

hands together, partly because he had maintained his character for eccentricity, I suppose, and partly because he was at last rid of boredom." Nekhlyudov's sister Varya explains to Irtenyev why she thinks her brother is so much in love with *auntie*.

> Dimitri is an egoist . . . in spite of all his cleverness he is very fond of admiration. . . . *Auntie*, in the innocence of her heart, is prostrate with admiration for him and has not sufficient tact to hide it, so the result is that she flatters him not hypocritically but sincerely.

Maslova is less articulate than Varya, and has not got Tolstoy's youthfully exuberant analysis behind her, but she none the less perceives in Nekhlyudov's obstinate attachment to her a comparable motive—the desire to appear remarkable in his own eyes and "to use me spiritually as he has done physically".

There is a striking contrast between the continuity of Nekhlyudov's character, and the change in attitude towards its characteristics. He has not that "self-derision truly Russian" which goes with family understanding, and which Pierre and Levin possess. (Pierre is in fact very largely a composite figure of Irtenyev and Nekhlyudov.) But by the time of *Resurrection* Tolstoy has come to see self-derision as the final refuge of *samodovolnost*. The humour of Pierre and Levin is banished, and without humour and self-derision in Tolstoy it is much harder to know people and to feel instinctively what is going on. The decisions of the will, once so humanised and penetrated by a sense of the ludicrous, are now respected. Continually we are reminded of the joy and peace which Nekhlyudov feels in having made up his mind, and nothing disturbs these for long. Tolstoy, as if nervously, keeps us away, and this again reminds us of Irtenyev's discovery when he got to know Nekhlyudov and the latter determined that they were to be great friends. Intimacy proved a strain, because the complete frankness which was supposed to be a sign and guarantee of it began to make both parties uncomfortable. Irtenyev is surprised that his friend does not seem to notice what the source of the discomfort is. But Nekhlyudov is not a noticer, and that is one of the troubles in *Resurrection*. Little of Tolstoy's detail and perception seem to pass naturally through the hero, as they pass through Pierre and Levin. He is the kind of character who in Tolstoy is observed

and not observing—a Tolstoyan object not a Tolstoyan subject
—and hence his place in the centre of the book is distinctly
awkward.

II

But it is an awkwardness which brings its own oddly impressive rewards. The most moving things in *Resurrection* move us
not because they are incarnated in a character, as in the big
novels, but because they are open, plain and impassive. We
remember Dostoevsky's comment that *Anna* is by no means an
innocent book. By contrast, both *Youth* and *Resurrection* are
innocent: the first because it indulges the happy conceit of
analysis and 'understanding'; the second, because it takes
Nekhlyudov, the original object of this understanding, and pled-
ges to him and his project a complete and unquestioning loyalty
and obedience. One has the unconscious innocence of a clever
young man, the other that of a determined convert, and Tolstoy
seems in some sense to acknowledge this by making Nekhlyudov
the common factor in both.

Stiva, the centre of worldliness in *Anna*, knows what to do at
the end of a convivial gathering, like his lunch with Levin, where
confidences have been exchanged in a congenial atmosphere,
and yet where the aftermath of the champagne produces a sense
of estrangement rather than intimacy. He knows that matters
should at once be broken off, on a light-hearted note, and cheerfully resumed on some later occasion. It is this saving kind of
knowledge of which the youthful pair in *Youth* are ignorant, and
which the mature Nekhlyudov of *Resurrection* would despise.
Stiva can do, and does, a great deal of good in his own world.
He can make others happy, and everybody is glad to see him.
In acknowledging his gifts and his graces Tolstoy puts aside
the innocence of analysis and the innocence of uncompromising
severity. In an imperfect world the imperfect Stiva is an agent
of light, and in recognising this Tolstoy recognises on a typically
though equivocally heroic scale the necessary imperfection of
things. Such an admission is the essence of worldliness. But what
if Stiva, in the course of his judicial duties which he discharges
so fairly and so well because of "his complete indifference to the
matter he was engaged on, in consequence of which he was

never carried away by enthusiasm and never made mistakes"—
what if Stiva had been confronted with Maslova's case? Tolstoy
does not broach the possibility, but he dare not introduce anyone
like Stiva among the various officials before whom the case
comes.

In forsaking worldliness Tolstoy also closes his eyes to the
kind of justice which it may be capable of administering, even
in a corrupt society. Brilliantly he shows how individual inertia
and ineptitude reinforce official rigidity at each step of Maslova's
case. If they had done this, and had not forgotten to ask that. . . .
But he does not distinguish between the system and this given
case. Is the system, corrupting and deforming the individuals
who attempt to work it, always unjust, or has an exceptional
miscarriage occurred here? It is a point of some importance, but
Tolstoy ignores it. He has to, because he believes all govern-
mental procedures to be inherently bad. The information about
these procedures which he acquired for the occasion, and deploys
in such detail, emphasises the underlying anomaly. He did a
great deal of research. He found out about senatorial protocol,
and what clauses in the penal code dealt with homosexual
offences; what kinds of shirt convicts wore, and what was the
official attitude towards prostitution in the prisons. The Tolstoy
archives in the Tolstoy museum in Moscow contain long lists of
such queries.

Yet all these details are useless if no distinction is to be made
between the bad and the less bad, between the attempts at
improvement and the mere barbarism of traditional power.
Moreover, two kinds of knowing are involved here. The growth
of detail in *War and Peace* and *Anna* is an organic one: from the
early sketches Tolstoy advances towards a copious and absolute
authority of presentation like a tree reaching its full girth and
height. Things are as he says they are, not because he has found
out about them, but because he has drawn instinctively upon his
matured awareness, that vast and privileged awareness which
his family and position, as well as his own being, had conferred
upon him. Knowing in *Resurrection* is by contrast a process of
accretion; new material is added on to the true episode which
Tolstoy had been told, and which he had decided to make the
centre of a novel. He saw that this process of knowing things

by finding them out was close to the process of *invention* which he had always distrusted. "All untrue, invented, weak", he wrote in his diary about *Resurrection*. "It is hard to put right a spoiled thing."

A third way of knowing, which he admired but could not follow, is that of Herzen in his *Memoirs*, or Dostoevsky in *The House of the Dead*. These writers had acquired their knowledge of prisons involuntarily; they had become authorities by necessity, not choice, but it was a knowledge that set them apart and placed them, as narrators, in a privileged position. Though neither boast of their prison experiences, there is about them an involuntary suggestion of the expert, retailing wonders a little *de haut en bas*. (The remarkable thing about *The House of the Dead*, indeed, is that there is so little of this—instead we have the unexpected humility of Dostoevsky before his own powers of survival and even of enjoyment.) Tolstoy's instinctive knowledge, on the other hand, is of the kind which wonderfully takes for granted the same Olympian powers in us: his simplicity and transparency seem to assume that we know all about this too, whether it is being in love or in a battle, gambling, dying, giving birth, or ordering a dinner at the English Club. Only in his early work—the *Sevastopol Sketches* and *The Cossacks*—does he exhibit the third way of knowing, with the result that we have the not wholly persuasive feeling of being told the *truth* about war ("the hero of my tale is truth") as if it were something we had not suspected before.

The fact that he did not know them, but had only seen them, gives the mature Tolstoy his strange and singular honesty about horrible or repulsive scenes, an honesty shared by few other novelists. He takes them seriously, to a degree that made the idea of their imaginative transformation into art repellent to him. It was partly for this reason that he objected so strongly to the transformation of degradation and horror into dramatic art in *King Lear*. He reacted similarly to the inspired imagination of Dickens's horror grotesques, and to the dreadful and comic suffering of Mrs Marmeladov in *Crime and Punishment*. There are some things, he seems to feel, which the highest imagination can only insult by its attentions. Gorky reports Tolstoy as saying that one should not write about such things, and then changing his mind and asserting that it was necessary to write about everything. The probable implication is that they should be recorded, but not novelised or presented imaginatively as art. In an early sketch for *Resurrection* Nekhlyudov offers some novels to Maslova, with a view to improving her education, and she refuses them because "all that is insignificant compared to my life". Tolstoy's animosity towards Maupassant is largely directed at his attempts to give art the significance of 'my life', in Maslova's sense, by exploiting its most sordid aspects. The horrors in *Resurrection* are those of an eye-witness report or a White Paper.

The source of Tolstoy's knowledge was in himself, and this knowledge finds its natural outlet through his characters. The vice and misery which so much shocked him when he explored them in Moscow were seen, but not in this sense known—they cannot be effectively rendered through a character but only noted directly. The fire of Moscow, or the bombardment of Smolensk, achieve their effect through the response to them of Pierre and Alpatych, but this function of character is excluded by Tolstoy from *Resurrection* and from his later stories. Although the nominal eye-witness is Nekhlyudov, no one embodies in himself the *knowledge* of that scorching day in Moscow when the convicts are marched to the station, or of the scene in the Siberian prison where a young boy lies in an overflow of stinking ordure with his head pillowed on a man's leg. And yet, as I have suggested, these and other moving things in the book are moving in what is for Tolstoy an entirely new way. They are distanced, undogmatic, and in a queer way almost tentative; in place of the old confident transparency we have a simple determination to show things that exist as they are.

Details play hardly any part in these passages, and their presence often seems strangely lifeless and unnecessary. In the great sequence of the convicts' march to the station it is of no interest to hear that the police have orange-coloured lanyards on their revolvers—it is a touch of a kind used by inferior writers to build up a significant scene, and Tolstoy himself seems to throw such things off with irritability, as if they got in his way. No more effect is created by the care with which he had got up (as we learn from the archive) the causes and symptoms of sunstroke. But at the end of the sequence, when the convicts on the train are discussing seats, water, provisions—too preoccupied to care that five of their number have died on the way—we have received an overwhelming impression of the whole scene in terms of human suffering and human indifference. 'The system'—'*It*'—as Pierre thinks of it in *War and Peace*—is far more graphically realised in this sequence than in the comparable set piece of the incendiarists being shot, and the reason seems to lie in Tolstoy's removal of character and individual response. There is no one we know to enliven the scene for us with anthropomorphic vividness and urgency. Nekhlyudov, hot, discouraged, weighed down with lassitude—and in any case alien to us and outside us—is the correct recorder of such an event, in which there is neither sympathy nor cruelty but only the weight of a meaningless activity that has to be got through, like the hours and the weather. The system comes to seem an aspect of inertia and isolation, of the refusal of himself by the individual, in which corporate life habitually takes place.

Equally impressive is Tolstoy's account of the fight between the women convicts. In these prison scenes he does not attempt any 'inner' knowledgeability, and the quarrel is quite empty of the sort of authenticity which Dostoevsky or Gorky would have given it as eye-witnesses (or which Kipling would have given it as a pretended eye-witness). It is based on nothing more than a second-hand account given to Tolstoy of how the women fought over any vodka they had illicitly acquired. But the repellent red-haired woman who is the opponent of Maslova's friend, is unexpectedly admitted by Tolstoy, after her defeat, into the memorable bond of his physical understanding, the same clear intimacy in which we meet Natasha and Anna and Dolly. After they have settled down for the night Maslova hears "a strange sound proceeding from the other end of the room".

> It was the smothered sobbing of the red-haired woman. She was crying because she had been knocked about and had not got any of the vodka she wanted so badly: also because she remembered how all her life she had been sworn at and mocked, offended and beaten. Trying to comfort herself she brought back to mind her love for a factory hand, Fedka Molodenkov, her first love, but then she

remembered too how that affair had ended. Drunk one day, Molodenkov had for a lark smeared her with vitriol in a tender spot, and while she writhed in pain he and his companions roared with laughter. Remembering this she pitied herself, and thinking no one heard her she began to cry as children cry, snuffing with her nose and swallowing the salt tears.

The pity we feel, and the absence of any determination to make us feel it, comes from Tolstoy's involuntary tenderness for the body and for its attempts at self-recompense.

Yet this physical tenderness for the red-haired woman, whom we do not meet again, does not extend to Maslova herself. When Tolstoy notes that she now needs vodka and tobacco before anything, he does not sympathise with the fact. She is too selected and hypothetical a character to receive that tenderness (which is never sexual: it is for creatures who have bodies, like men). And Tolstoy refuses to help Nekhlyudov understand Maslova. Looking at him with "her unfathomable squinting eyes", she is as much a stranger to him at the end of the book as at the beginning; and this is highly effective, for he is concerned not with knowing her but with the narcissistic act of making atonement to her.

Tolstoy himself inserts an explanation of what chiefly shocks Nekhlyudov about her—her acceptance of her status as prostitute. Prostitutes are as self-satisfied as everyone else, because their experience makes them aware of their important role in society—all men desire them. This is as sweeping as Tolstoy's assertion that Maslova has now become disgusted with the whole business of sex, for good. No wonder it is of no importance what she does at the end of the book, for Tolstoy can only settle her fate by further arbitrary decisions—indeed he is said to have played a game of patience to decide whether or not she should marry Nekhlyudov, and the cards decided against. The story seems unlikely, for in fact Tolstoy settles the matter rationally enough; but he is only concerned with plausibility, there is no question of the characters "doing what they have to do". His own rejection of sex puts him in a fix, because he must wind up the tale without it, and his two great novels are both, as it were, consummated through its power.

In the earliest scenario the pair do marry, and eventually

escape from Siberia to London, where Maslova helps Nekhlyu-dov with his work on Henry George and the single tax system. In the novel Tolstoy evades this banal consummation, and the sexual problem, by inventing Simonson, the kindly cranky political prisoner who loves Maslova platonically. He considers persons like himself to be "human phagocytes", whose mission it is to help the weak and sick parts of the social organism, and he feels that his love for Maslova would not hinder this activity but act as an inspiration. Like Nekhlyudov he is *seen*, but he is not allowed to appear absurd. He is a Tolstoyan crank, whom the master presents so that his ridiculous side is most obvious, and yet dares us to laugh at him.

> In his rubber jacket, and wearing overshoes fastened with string above his worsted stockings (he was a vegetarian and did not use the skins of slaughtered animals). . . . Simonson stood by the porch jotting down a thought that had occurred to him. This was what he wrote: "If a bacterium observed and examined a human nail, it would pronounce it inorganic matter; and thus we, with reference to the globe, examine its crust and pronounce it inorganic. This is incorrect."

Why does Tolstoy record this? To 'place' Simonson, as he would have been placed in the two earlier novels, or because the thought seems to him arresting, i.e. because it is a 'real' thought of his own.[1] It is an instance of the curious relation between Tolstoy and his characters in *Resurrection*, a relation that when we are used to it is far from alienating; it is, indeed, illuminating and almost genial. We have something of the same kind when Nekhlyudov's sister, Nataly—herself an excellent minor figure —comes to see her brother when he is away and examines his rooms.

> She noticed in everything the love of cleanliness and order she knew so well in him. . . . On his writing-table she saw the paperweight with the bronze dog on the top which she remembered; the tidy way in which his different portfolios and writing materials were placed on the table was also familiar. . . .

[1] He did in fact say something rather similar in a conversation reported by Goldenweiser.

It might be Karenin's table, and yet Nekhlyudov, like Simonson, is not placed or judged in the pathos of this vulnerability.

This new toleration does not apply to the idea of the family, and to its linchpin of *samodovolnost*. Nekhlyudov feels only repulsion for his sister's husband—"that hairy self-assured man"—and when he hears she is to have another child "he felt a kind of sorrow that she had once more been infected with something bad by this man who was so foreign to him". Nataly, the happy mother, is seen in bondage: Maslova, destined to become the admiring helpmate of a crank, and a woman emancipated—surely—against her own nature, is seen as redeemed.

None the less, there persists even here the odd wistful geniality which helps to make the latter part of the book so moving. And something more: a kind of subtlety which, though it is not at Nekhlyudov's expense, shows that his relation to Tolstoy can be more interesting than that of author to hero-spokesman. The granddaughter of the General, on whom Nekhlyudov calls in a Siberian town, takes him to see her children; and the sight of them, and of the mother's pride ("this one's quite a little Siberian") touch him deeply. "I want to live! I want a family, children, I want a human life!"—this thought wells up in him as he sees Maslova for the last time. With her, or with someone of his own kind? Though Tolstoy leaves the question open, the preceding scene has given a strong hint. Yet in his mind Nekhlyudov equates the scene of family happiness with the performance of Beethoven's Fifth which he had heard at the General's house, and which had given him "a feeling of perfect self-satisfaction, and a tickling in the nose, so touched was he with his many virtues". The world of art and the world of the family offer the same insidious incitement to complacency, and both must be rejected. It is at this point that Tolstoy's relation to his hero assumes something of the old sly diplomatic *mensonge*. For is it a relief or a deprivation to lose Maslova? Perhaps both. But there is no doubt that Nekhlyudov finds it easier to reject the vision of family happiness with her and to equate it with the 'unreal world' of art and music, because Simonson's love and regard have now deprived him of the warm feeling of self-sacrifice on her behalf, "and therefore lessened its value in the eyes of himself and others". No one will admire his fidelity and his wish for atonement so much if Simonson wants to marry her *voluntarily*. Yet this does not alter the respect for Nekhlyudov which the power of Tolstoy's conviction has compelled us to share: he *does* wish to atone, and in his way he has come to love Maslova—the vanity which has given him the resolution to change his life has done much good to many people.

But none of the old diplomacy is used on Maslova's motives—her treatment remains doctrinaire. Tolstoy can do no better than to assert that she leaves Nekhlyudov at the end because she loves him, "and thought that by uniting herself to him she would be spoiling his life". Tolstoy was not wont to let the idea of 'love' conclude matters as glibly as this and without further examination. We remember Kitty's 'love' for Levin, which also fitted in with everything she hoped and expected from life. In fact Tolstoy must know how insuperably difficult it would be for Maslova to love her pursuer and benefactor, how much easier and more natural to spend her woman's nature on the stranger Simonson, who likes her for herself. The fact that Tolstoy insists on his apparently touching but in fact dead conclusion makes the last meeting of the pair less moving than it might have been.

III

The absurdity which Tolstoy admires and endorses both in Nekhlyudov and Simonson consists in their power to simplify, to see the rational and beautiful world that might be, and the criminal senselessness of the one that exists. The simplicity of this knowledge is compared to the white night over Petersburg, and contrasted with the corrupt and soothing darkness of the earth, the darkness of ignorance in which life proceeds on the assumptions of class and the assumptions of the body. In *Resurrection* the two are almost the same, and if we abandon one we must abandon the other. Nataly, once full of goodness and inspiration, has ruined herself by 'sensually loving' a bald hairy man of no ideas or enlightenment. The great Tolstoyan body has become a fraud, the mere instrument of social pretence and frivolity. When Nekhlyudov looks at Mariette "the veil of charm was not removed, but it was as if he could see what lay beneath". Missy, whom he thinks of marrying, is beautiful, but with a beauty corrupted by her class . . . "he saw the way her hair was crimped, the sharpness of her elbows, and, especially, how large her thumbnail was and how like her father's" (to this are the great family resemblances of the early novels reduced). We remember how Anna, in her revulsion and extremity, mentally undressed the hunchback lady at the railway station and was horrified by what she saw. It is natural for Nekhlyudov mentally to undress the guests, and to reflect that one must have a stomach like a melon and arms like pestles, while the thought of Missy's mother is too horrible even to contemplate.

All physical being is now not of the body but the *corpse*, the huge corpse of the merchant who is the most powerful presence at the trial of his supposed murderers.

> The indefinite loathing that Nekhlyudov felt was increased by the description of the corpse. Maslova's life, the serous liquid oozing from the nostrils of the corpse, the eyes protruding from their sockets, and his own treatment of Maslova, all seemed to belong to the same order of things. . . .

No wonder the corpse, whose internal organs are exhaustively catalogued, is so gigantic—it is the corpse of all the physical living in Tolstoy, and the post-mortem on it is necessarily macabre. There is no resurrection of the body. Nor, when it is dead, does Tolstoy give it decent burial; its stench poisons the air of the whole novel.

We must escape from its repellent miasma, from the frivolous 'grand monde' of Korchagin and the rest, into the 'vrai grand monde' of the people, and into the 'new and beautiful world' which Nekhlyudov thinks he has found, the luminous clarity of the white night. It is presided over by Mary Pavlovna, the revolutionary girl who detests the whole idea of sex "as something repugnant and offensive to human dignity", and has never experienced it. She is in some ways the most terrifying figure in Tolstoy's novels, for she is regarded without the faintest shadow of equivocation. Only in one revealing metaphor, drawn from the old unregenerate world, does Tolstoy compare her search for opportunities to serve others to 'a sportsman's search for game'; and this description, with its hint of malevolence, is promptly attributed to a fellow-revolutionary, Novodvorov.

On this character Tolstoy can expend all his old analysis, and for a revealing reason. Simonson and Mary Pavlovna are inviolate because they are pure, sexually pure. Their crankiness is treated with reverence; their fanaticism Tolstoy dares us to laugh at. But because Novodvorov is subject to the lusts of the flesh and seeks every opportunity for a 'free union' with any admiring female fellow-prisoner, his character *as a revolutionary* is taken to pieces by Tolstoy with all his old mastery of motive and insight into self-regard.

> The intellectual powers of the man—his numerator—were great; but his opinion of himself—his denominator—was immeasurably greater, and had far outgrown his intellectual powers. . . . Being devoid of those moral and aesthetic qualities which call forth doubts and hesitation, he very soon acquired a position in the revolutionary world which satisfied him—that of leader of a party. Having once chosen a direction he never doubted or hesitated, and was therefore certain that he never made a mistake. Everything seemed quite simple, clear, and certain. And the narrowness and one-sidedness of his views did make everything seem simple and clear—one only had to be logical, as he said. His self-assurance was so great that it either repelled people or made them submit to him. . . . Although in principle he was in favour of the woman's movement, in the depths of his soul he considered all women stupid and insignificant except those with whom he was sentimentally in love. . . .

We almost have the feeling in *Resurrection* that Tolstoy would have to prefer Robespierre, the sexless man of power, to the libertine Danton, so emphatic is his criterion that power and influence over their fellows should only be exercised by the sexually pure.

In the early scenarios for *Anna* Tolstoy had found himself in a dilemma over Karenin which sheds light on the theme of *Resurrection*, and on Tolstoy's determination to end it in accordance with his own will and convictions rather than let his characters "do what they have to do". Tolstoy wished Karenin to be a good and saintly man who would forgive his wife and renounce her to her lover, but he knew that Karenin could not change himself and abandon the body, and hence could not but appear pathetic. Tolstoy was haunted by the pathos of the good Karenin, since he could only concur in the general verdict on it.

Because Karenin continues to live in the physical world, and be subject to its needs, he can only be pitied and perhaps laughed at, not admired. Tolstoy cannot evade the logic with which Anna in this version wonders before her suicide whether she will go back to Karenin. He is good—he has been good to her—she is filled with reverence and even with love for him—"but at the moments when he wants me, when he comes in with his smile and his dressing-gown . . .". Tolstoy was playing with fire here, and he took the other way out. Karenin cannot be saintly but only human. His moment of clarity and forgiveness, when "all seemed simple and natural" cannot last long; he goes back to his body, to being himself.

The artist who created *Anna*, like the artist who created *Measure for Measure*, is profoundly sceptical of the results of human endeavour to achieve freedom from "the wanton stings and motions of the sense". So, indeed, is the Tolstoy who had just written *Father Sergius*. But the obstinate premise of *Resurrection* is that we can achieve 'freedom of thought', which emancipates us from the body and its satisfactions. The phrase is from *Anna*, and occurs twice in the same context. Grinevich, Oblonsky's colleague, is deprived of 'freedom of thought' by his long, carefully kept fingernails[1]; and Levin by the white bosom of his friend Sviyazhsky's sister, revealed by her square-cut bodice. They are unable to insulate their minds from the *samodovolnost* of their bodies. But it is precisely this inability—which in the genius of Tolstoy becomes his unique power of equivocation, of rendering with transparent simplicity the complex servitude of experience—that makes him more lifegiving than any other novelist. 'Freedom of thought', in the sense that Tolstoy means, is not the artist's state of mind. Instead it means the death of the novel; for the power to isolate one idea from the flux—and hold it with total confidence—makes the novel unnecessary, merely a symptom of what Tolstoy in *Resurrection* calls "the usual sophism which goes to prove that a single human intellect cannot know the truth".

The truth is within you, when the life of the body has been

[1] Tolstoy was very likely remembering, unconsciously, Pushkin's comment in the first chapter of *Eugene Onegin*, "One can be an effective man and yet be concerned with the beauty of one's nails".

put aside. One of the most queerly impressive things in the book is Nekhlyudov's encounter with the old man on the ferry.

> "I have no kind of faith, because I believe no one, no one but myself. . . . I have given up everything; I have no name, no place, no country, no anything. I am just myself."

We can hardly help seeing in this apparition the aged Tolstoy. His solipsism is still gigantic, but it is based now on spiritual determination, not on physical experience. And where his physical solipsism had in some marvellous way united us with him in art, this determination divides. But the solitary old man does not care: in a sense his conviction is as intransigent as the revolutionary Novodvorov's, and as "certain that he never made a mistake".

Even so, the reality of the world of *Resurrection*, and its lasting capacity to absorb and to move us, seems to remain outside Tolstoy's conviction and his determined 'freedom of thought'. The reality of the book is in its presentation of the corpse that a corrupt social order has made of the life and enterprise of the body. Its prophecy and warning—as meaningful now as then— is the need for the individual to stand against 'the quiet self-assurance', the mortal mechanical inertia of the official order of things—Maslova's trial, the scene in the fortress of Peter and Paul, the convicts' march across Moscow. More powerfully than any possibility of rebirth for the individual we have in these scenes an apprehension of death in society.

VIII

The Caucasus

It is full of the stir of life—so distant from our dead pleasures, so foreign to this empty existence.

PUSHKIN, *The Gipsies*

As if we were no longer able to write long poems on any other subject than ourselves!

Eugene Onegin

I

THE form of *The Cossacks* gave Tolstoy a great deal of trouble. He worked on it intermittently for ten years, between 1852 and 1862, interrupted by his service in the Crimea and his visits to Europe, and he eventually completed it in the year of his marriage and a year before he began *War and Peace*. At one time he had serious thoughts of attempting it as a poem, though so far as is known he only tried to write verse once in his life and then only in a letter. Pushkin's dramatic poem *The Gipsies* would certainly have been in his mind, and he may have intended to naturalise it from his own personal experience of Cossack life, as he did with Pushkin's verse tale *The Prisoner of the Caucasus* in a story of his own with the same name. This naturalising process would involve the removal of all Byronic romanticism and poeticism, and their replacement by a copious simplicity of detail which would indicate the real contrast between the frivolity of civilised existence and the simple natural ways of gipsies or Cossacks. For Rousseau, and for Pushkin too, such a contrast would hardly need detailed proof: for Tolstoy it must be demonstrated by the completely honest and straightforward recitation of experience.

So Tolstoy himself must come in. Although the subject was such a well-worn romantic one, and given a peculiarly Russian status by Pushkin, Tolstoy is to corroborate it personally, both as an author and as an individual. No wonder we are so much aware of *literature* at the back of *The Cossacks*, and this in spite of its brilliant reporting of life in a Cossack settlement. Tolstoy's last stories are preoccupied with the idea of art in the abstract, and with our infection by art in the right ways. *The Cossacks* is preoccupied with more specifically literary problems: in it Tolstoy seems particularly concerned with placing his experience in a literary context, first Russia's and Pushkin's, and later— after he had read Homer—that of the primitive epic.

Childhood, Boyhood and Youth had in a sense also been based on literary models—Rousseau, Sterne and the German writer Töpfer. But the author, the 'I', was already built into those models, so that Tolstoy was able to occupy them from his own overpoweringly personal standpoint with the minimum disturbance. There is no 'I' in Homer, in *The Gipsies*, or in Gogol's pseudo-Homeric tale of *Taras Bulba*, and the intrusion of an 'I' in them is hardly thinkable. In *The Captain's Daughter* Pushkin achieved the feat of making his narrator credible and intimate, while at the same time letting his personality make little impression on the objective precision of the tale. Ensign Grinyov has all the convenience for such a narrative, of a Scott hero, yet he is not—as those heroes so frequently are—either limp or null. Tolstoy's Olenin has the worst of both worlds. He is obtrusive and yet feeble, much feebler than the beady-eyed Irtenyev of *Childhood*, with his relish for analysis and 'mental eavesdropping'. Being Tolstoy, he is with us totally, both as observer and as a physical presence: being a traditional literary *jeune homme*, of the 'superfluous' model, he is supine and uninteresting. Turgenev, always a shrewd judge on questions of presentation and technique, thought him most unsatisfactory.

Are we to have 'The Cossacks', or 'The Cossacks as seen by Olenin'?—that is the question which Tolstoy cannot be said to have resolved. In his first sketch of the work Olenin is a more positive and strong-minded figure, who has lost immense sums at gambling and whose departure for the Caucasus is correspondingly more urgent and necessary. His tailor writes off the large sums he is owed as a bad debt, remarking that the customer was none the less a remarkable young man. The later Olenin merely remembers with shame and embarrassment the resigned look on the tailor's face when he has to ask him to wait a year for his money. The earlier figure is more like Poltoratsky in the

Sevastopol Sketches, or like Captain Butler in *Hadji Murad,* and as such his relation with the Cossacks could have been seen more objectively, but to get closer to Tolstoy's experience the portrait must become more comical and more intimate. As Olenin sets out in the early morning on the first stage of his journey from Moscow he goes past houses he has never seen before, and "it seemed to him that only travellers starting on a long journey went through those streets". We recognise at once Tolstoy's knack of identifying himself and us in the intimate, almost infantile consciousness of the hero, in whose *samodovolnost* we participate while at the same time it amuses and touches us.

> Now and then he looked round at some house and wondered why it was curiously built; or he began wondering why the post-boy and Vanyusha, who were so different from himself, sat so near and together with him were being jerked about and swayed by the tugs the side horses gave at the frozen traces, and again he repeated "First rate . . . very fond!" and once even "How it moves one! . . . wonderful!" and then wondered what made him say it. "Am I drunk?" he asked himself. He had had a couple of bottles of wine, but it was not the wine alone that was having this effect on him. He remembered all the words of friendship, warmly, bashfully, spontaneously (as he believed) addressed to him on his departure. . . . He remembered his own deliberate frankness. And all this had a touching significance for him. "Perhaps I shall not return from the Caucasus" he thought. And he felt that he loved his friends and someone else too. He was sorry for himself. But it was not love for his friends that so filled him that he could not repress the meaningless words that rose to his lips; nor was it love for a woman (he had never been in love). It was love for himself—warm young love for all that was good in his own soul (and at that moment it seemed to him there was nothing but good in it)—that made him weep and utter incoherent words.

Olenin is one of those people whom we get to know so well so quickly that we cannot help becoming rather bored by them. The intimacy is magical, certainly, but Tolstoy has made us too intimate too soon. Amused and fond we may be, but is this the best company in which to meet the Cossacks? It is like Nicholas Rostov's homecoming, with its incoherent ecstasy and self-satisfaction, but from the beginning of *War and Peace* we feel there is going to be more to Rostov. Nor are we trapped inside him and his naïve immediacy: we can wander away and explore the rest of the book on our own, or listen to Tolstoy's comments and assertions about it. But in *The Cossacks* we are trapped. Once Tolstoy has almost involuntarily seduced us into this eager young outlook we cannot get out, or so we begin to feel.

Like Lensky in *Eugene Onegin*, Olenin's mind is full of romantic dreams, "Circassian maidens, mountain precipices, torrents and perils". Sometimes he resists the tribesmen with unprecedented courage, sometimes he fights alongside them. His old friends are with him, his old enemies against him, and— "even the tailor in some strange way takes part in his triumph". Olenin remains a bore; he does not develop, and he does not, as Lensky does, achieve the dignity of the graphic duel. But in this resemblance, and in the closeness to the warm participatory wit of *Eugene Onegin*, we feel the confinement of our first over-intimacy begin to lift. Tolstoy's complete awareness of the absurdity of his hero is perhaps the liberating factor. Certainly, as the Caucasus appear we are no longer irked by the company of Olenin, even though Tolstoy, in a famous bravura passage, shows us the mountains through Olenin's eyes. At his first glimpse he can see nothing in these mountains "of which he has so often read and heard". But gradually their majestic approach penetrates his consciousness and he begins to *feel* them. "From that moment all he saw, all he felt, all he thought, acquired for him a new character, sternly majestic like the mountains. . . . 'Now it has begun', a deep voice seemed to say to him." And for the next paragraph every ensuing thought and impression is ended for him with that awed and ecstatic refrain. . . . "And the mountains!"

To combine what seems the reality of them with Olenin's vision is an extraordinary feat, and one feels no one but Tolstoy could have made the two into one. From now on this dual vision becomes more emphatic and more effective. Eroshka, the old Cossack, and Maryanka the Cossack girl, inhabit and dominate Olenin's consciousness, but they are also solid figures whom we see to the side of and apart from him. Though far from being

the Circassian maiden of his dreams, Maryanka remains for
Olenin on the same feverish plane of enchantment and strange-
ness. Romance is inverted. Coming and going on bare sinewy
feet across the yard, her pink print smock clinging to her powerful chest and buttocks, Maryanka still remains a magical and
unattainable figure—*La Princesse lointaine*—even though every
detail of her physical life is as overpoweringly present as the
smell of "vodka, sweat, gunpowder, wine, and congealed blood"
which accompanies 'Uncle' Eroshka. The personal atmosphere
of these two, and the appearance and feel of the settlement and
landscape, are run together by means of associative zeugma.
The Terek with its creeks and grey sandbanks; the damp forest
and the fresh dung of the hunted boar in its lair under the wild
vines; the feathers and blood of pheasants; the buffalo-cow in
the stillness of the courtyard at night, which "rises with a deep
sigh first on her foreknees and then on her feet, and makes a
steady splashing on the dry ground"—all these are at one with
Olenin's consciousness of Maryanka's deep breathing and the
beating of his own heart.

Through Olenin, Tolstoy inverts the romantic unobtrusively
and with a sleep-walker's calm. Seventy years or so later Yeats
and Joyce were to do the same thing selfconsciously and with a
great deal of linguistic emphasis. But Yeats celebrating 'great-
bladdered Emer' and her fancy man, where he had earlier
written of pearl-pale Niamh and Oisin, is really doing no more
than did Tolstoy in substituting as romantic object the full-
bodied Maryanka for the sloe-eyed Circassian maiden. *The
Cossacks* is the most influential of all Tolstoy's works and the
most potentially suggestive to innovators of a later literary
epoch. It may be difficult for this reason to see it as it was, for
the potent primary material with which it is filled can be, and
has been, vulgarised. It suffers from the results of its own success, for though nothing can be made out of *War and Peace* or
Anna, later writers—Hemingway is perhaps the most notable
example—have learned much from the method of *The Cossacks*.

But in their enthusiasm they ignored Tolstoy's own com-
parative dissatisfaction with that method, and his continual
attempts throughout the tale to achieve an equilibrium between
Olenin's consciousness and objective description. Hemingway

adopts the Olenin style consciousness with total ardour, seemingly unaware of the claustrophobic consequences in the narrative of *A Farewell to Arms*. (Indeed, if we compare the 'heroine' of that novel with Maryanka, we see how completely the consciousness of its narrator has sucked the reality out of his dream princess, compelling her to be what it is enough for him to imagine she is.) Hemingway is quite innocent, too, of Tolstoy's humorously Russian and Pushkinian approach to the consciousness of his hero.

Not that this engaging irony is an unmixed blessing to Tolstoy: it draws attention to the fact that Olenin's range of responses is so limited. This appears at the end of the tale, when the Cossacks have surrounded a party of *abreks*, hostile tribesmen.

> Olenin was much impressed by the place in which they lay. In fact it was very much like the rest of the steppe, but because the *abreks* were there it seemed to detach itself from all the rest and become distinguished. Indeed it appeared to Olenin that it was the very spot for *abreks* to occupy.

It is the same as Olenin's feeling in Moscow that "only travellers starting on a journey went through those streets". We are back where we started.

One method by which Tolstoy tries to evade Olenin is to break off his journey and describe a Cossack settlement objectively, resuming the Olenin sequence when he is at length posted to the settlement. The device looks forward to the scenic method of *War and Peace* and to the brilliant 'peepshows' of *Hadji Murad*, both of which—as I have suggested—have much in common with Shakespeare's open panoramic sequences in the History plays and in *Antony and Cleopatra*. But here the method is not effectual. So fastened are we to Olenin's consciousness that we see the village through his eyes, even though he has not yet arrived. Worse, the exploit of shooting the *abrek* at the river, achieved by the young Cossack Lukashka, who should be the epic hero, is told with the same partial vividness, and the same lack of grasp of the total situation, which would have been shown by Olenin. Olenin seems to stand beside Lukashka and lend him his eyes and ears, and yet when Olenin arrives Tolstoy starts at once to emphasise the main *donnée* of the tale—the gap in vision, habit and expectation that separates him from the Cossacks.

Tolstoy cannot reconcile his emphasis on this gap with the calm omniscience needful to the heroic mode. In *Hadji Murad* this omniscience is complete, as it is in Scott's story *The Two Drovers*, in Merimée, and in Lermontov's *A Hero of Our Time*. Nothing there is puzzling and unexplained because no partial and limiting vision is involved. But in the sequence in which Lukashka goes on duty to the cordon, waits in ambush, and shoots the *abrek*, a great deal remains unexplained. The extraordinary vividness of the description, the night, the shooting, and Lukashka's bringing in the body as his spoil—all this makes a sharp contrast with the lack of information about how it all came about. In Olenin's vision this would be just, for he is the sort of young man who responds all the more vividly to events because he does not know and is not really interested in what lies behind them and why they happen.

Although much less vividly realised, Gogol's description in *Taras Bulba* of the settlement of the Zaporozhe Cossacks makes it much more totally comprehensible than is Tolstoy's community. Gogol tells us, for instance, that though the Cossacks live for booty their way of life is so careless and immediate that they often conceal their plunder and then forget all about it. Granted the difference in time and place, this one touch tells us as much about the Cossack mentality as all Tolstoy's elaboration of example and dialogue. And when the Chechen braves, the *abreks*, cross the river, what do they come for? Obviously to ambush, murder and steal. But the Cossack village remains oddly separated from their presence, as if it belonged to another world; Tolstoy is remarkably vague about its relation to the hostile surrounding country. One feels, too, that the *abrek* who swims across the river does so solely in order that Tolstoy could make a fine set piece out of his killing. He exists not as a participant in the tale but as an object for description and sensation. There is a similar implausibility about the fight at the end, when Lukashka is wounded (perhaps fatally, we never know) by the brother of the man he has killed. The last fight of *Hadji Murad* is told with absolute comprehensiveness and authority, but this skirmish is hopelessly contrived. The *abreks* obligingly wait where they are located, in order that the alarm may be given and Olenin may be in at the death. Clearly they could have escaped without difficulty. As he rides up with them, Olenin asks the Cossacks some question about the attack which to them "appeared quite meaningless", but unfortunately there is no contrast here between things as they really are to the Cossacks and as they appear to Olenin. The whole operation is unconvincing.

It may seem unnecessary to dwell on these points, but I am confident that Tolstoy himself would have agreed with the criticism implied—in all his subsequent work he took great pains over matters of fact and probability. The wide background of *Hadji Murad* is crystal clear: we see exactly why everything had to happen as it did happen. The episodes in *The Cossacks* are too obviously 'invention'—art rather than life. And the fact that it is so makes Tolstoy's lifelike details, for the first and only time, sometimes slightly repellent when he describes death and violence, not 'transparent' but artful. Masterly as is the description of the dead *abrek*, Tolstoy seems to concentrate more on the description than the man.

> Under the red trimmed moustache the fine lips, drawn at the corners, seemed stiffened into a smile of good-natured, subtle raillery.

It is the kind of touch familiar in Stevenson or Conrad (in *Heart of Darkness* the Negro helmsman, transfixed by a spear, gives the narrator "an extraordinarily profound familiar look" as he collapses). After the fight, Lukashka's friend, before coming to help him, "fumbled for some time unable to put his sword in its sheath: it would not go in the right way. The blade of the sword was bloodstained." There is a lingering deftness here, a little Flaubertian. In his later views on art Tolstoy was very severe on this kind of thing, in himself, and others, and perhaps in this sort of context his severity was justified.

The trouble is the detachment of these aesthetic 'notes' from the total situation and a general human response, and the cause of the trouble is again Olenin. By insisting on how cut off he is, Tolstoy cannot logically evade the aesthetic isolation of his perceptions. Since the Cossacks ignore him he decides to take no part in the fight, because he thought his courage already sufficiently proved, "and also because he was happy". (Hemingway often writes like a translation of *The Cossacks*). Lukashka by contrast has "an air of calm solemnity": unaware of himself, he is completely a part of what is going on. Again the point is made, and now Tolstoy prepares to emphasise it still further. The fight, and his violent rejection by Maryanka which follows it, have cured Olenin of that eagerness for the really significant experience ("Now it has begun," a solemn voice seemed to say) which comes from aimless living in the civilised world. Maryanka's final abhorrence for him is intended to show her apprehension of this attitude: the daily realities of her world are for him excitements which may lead to the 'real thing'. And now Olenin sees this too.

> Again, as on the night of his leaving Moscow, a troika stood waiting at the door. But Olenin did not confer with himself as he had done then, and did not say to himself that all he had thought and done here was 'not it'. He did not promise himself a new life.

Unfortunately we have been given the message too often, and Olenin's state of mind no longer interests us much. What moves us more in retrospect are the character sketches, not only Maryanka and Eroshka, but the slighter ones thrown off almost inadvertently in the course of the tale—Olenin's orderly, Lukashka's dumb sister, the Cossack sergeant who spends all his time fishing—these make the point of the tale more effectively than its formal mechanism does. What they say, and the speech they use, is one of Tolstoy's most subtle ways of suggesting the point of his story, and unfortunately we lose here more in translation than we do elsewhere in his novels. The portentous verbiage which the sergeant proudly displays before Olenin can be rendered without much difficulty, but the Cossacks' speech among themselves, which should contrast with that of Olenin and his fellow-officer, is another matter. That the Cossacks should converse *merrily* and call each other *my lad* is hardly convincing, but it is almost impossible to render their colloquial speech into a similar style that retains unselfconscious life. (The word *veselo*, which Tolstoy uses a great deal, usually has to become *merrily* or *cheerfully* in English, but the connotations are disastrously different: we have no suitable adverb that does not sound localised or coy.)

Eroshka's style is similarly hampered, but its essential quality does come over. Olenin is gratified to think that he and the old man are friends and understand one another, but because he thinks this he is wrong. Like Maryanka, Eroshka is a romantic figure with whom he would like to identify himself, but there is nothing there—in his sense—to identify *with*. With Vanyusha, his servant, he is identified, because he never considers him: the pair "are friends without knowing it", and "would have been very much surprised to be told they were". Olenin thinks Eroshka must have some exciting philosophy of life that is probably *it* at last; and he is much impressed when the old man says that "when you die the grass will grow on you and that's all". Later Olenin repeats it back admiringly, but the old man refuses to respond to the phrase in his mouth, and it turns out in any case to be something a Russian captain, killed long ago in Chechnya, used to say. The old man will not even be the 'character' that Olenin wants him to be. He has no philosophy; he talks and exists without meaning as Olenin understands it. *"Karga!"* he says to Olenin, who asks him what the word means. It is a Tartar word meaning 'all right'—"but I just say it so", laughs the old man. *"Karga! Karga!"* It is a word meaning nothing but the moment, as immediate as his smell of vodka and sweat. He is shocked when Olenin asks him if he has killed many people. He has, but at particular moments: it bothers him to consider the notion retrospectively.

When Olenin asks Maryanka to marry him she agrees because the idea means nothing to her, and she bursts out laughing. In the same spirit the Cossacks call Olenin their *kunak*—pal. It means nothing to them to do so as it would not occur to them to address their real comrades as such. But Olenin, taking it all seriously, writes in his diary:

> Many things have I pondered lately and much have I changed, and I have come back to the copybook maxim: the way to be happy is to love . . . to spread a web of love on all sides and take all who come into it. In this way I caught Old Eroshka, Kukashka, and Maryanka. . . .

At this moment the old man comes in, urges him to drink and sing instead of writing, and after a marvellous performance falls down dead drunk. Olenin feels depressed. But the keenest touch by which Tolstoy 'makes it strange' linguistically, comes at the end when Olenin's servant, who prides himself immensely on the bit of French he has picked up from his master, sees Maryanka as she comes into the yard for the last time.

> "*La fille!*" said Vanyushka, with a wink, and burst out into a silly laugh.
> "Drive on!" shouted Olenin angrily.
> "Goodbye. . . . I won't forget you!" shouted Eroshka.
> Olenin looked round. Eroshka was talking to Maryanka, evidently about his own affairs, and neither the old man or the girl looked at him.

Like Pushkin's poem *The Gipsies*, *The Cossacks* is about fate, the fate that life has assigned us without our knowing it or wanting to know it. The heroes of both try to lead a different life in a different community and both fail, though one failure is comical and the other tragic. The humour of *The Cossacks*, relieving the callow egotism of Olenin, is an asset which the hero of Pushkin's poem does not need—with the other characters he is like a point on a diagram, accurately and economically drawn. Entering the gipsy tribe, he extols the simple life to the girl he settles down with, and tells her how corrupted is the society he has left. But the simple life is also innocently promiscuous: helplessly reverting to the standards of civilisation he kills the girl and the gipsy lover with whom he finds her. It is worth noticing that Pushkin's hero does achieve the gipsy girl's love for a time, but—as her old father (a formalised Eroshka) observes—"Who will show the moon her place in the sky and say: stop there?" Tolstoy could not have followed this lead. Either Maryanka must love and marry Olenin or not: the rigidity of the theme, as of Tolstoy's moral attitudes, will not permit any compromise. It is for this reason that he strains plausibility by making Maryanka so chaste and severe, towards Lukashka as well as Olenin. To her friend Ustenka is left the kind of behaviour which is normal, so Tolstoy tells us, among Cossack girls. So that Olenin, in his enthusiasm for Cossack life, has fallen in love with the one girl who happens not to conform to it. What then becomes of the contrast between Cossack life and civilised life, if we find the same variation in individual behaviour in both? It is an interesting example of Tolstoy failing in the kind of plot logic which came so naturally to Pushkin, whose conceptions do not 'grow', but are developed with all the inevitability in the given form.

Tolstoy's kind of inevitability comes from the processes of growth, and with *The Cossacks* there was no room for growth: it could only be subjected to manipulation, and Tolstoy was never satisfied with it. He even manipulates fate—we never feel that Pushkin wanted his hero to fail at being a gipsy as we feel that Tolstoy wants Olenin to fail at living with Cossacks. Only in the growth and scale of his two great novels does his own kind of inevitability really triumph, and it is the method of these novels—but on a miniature scale—which he employs in *Hadji Murad*.

II

As if to emphasise the diminution, Tolstoy clamps this story within the vice of a metaphor—the Tartar thistle which has resisted the cultivation of a field, and which Tolstoy compares, at the beginning and end of the tale, to the old Tartar chieftain whose history he had heard many years before. It is essentially a narrative demonstration; our participation is not invited as it seems to be in the novels: we are to see and not to share. Yet within its artificial clamp the story expands and diversifies with superb power.

It is possible to give a misleading interpretation to its virtues, in order to show how the artist had endured in Tolstoy and how superior the artist was to the moralist and sage. I have already suggested that the parabolic conception of art which he had come to hold had the unexpected effect of making his artistry seem more and not less evident—the smell of art is also the smell of a moral. I have called *Hadji Murad* 'a parable without a point', and this does suggest a reason for some of the admiration it has received. It can be seen as a marvellous aesthetic object from which the perishable matter of assertion and dogma have been drained off. One class of Tolstoy's admirers are delighted that baby and bathwater have at last been got rid of, and that they are left with what they seem to prefer—a strikingly handsome and well-made bath! The philosopher Wittgenstein, though no great admirer of Tolstoy, was a devotee of *Hadji Murad* and praised its clarity and objectivity. But in fact, in spite of its unusual shapeliness and air of art, the story is as full of tendentious Tolstoyan matter as any other of his works, and as impregnated with the continuous and manifold assertiveness of his personality.

If it were not so it would be less remarkable than it is. As history—the history of the Russian penetration of the Caucasus —it has the lightning rapidity and penetration, in example and dialogue, of Shakespeare's *Antony and Cleopatra*—not a work which it would occur to one to praise in terms of simple and impassive aesthetic form.

Instead of a young Russian's attempt to abandon civilisation, it tells the story of an old native chieftain who is constrained to join the Russians. Like *The Cossacks* it ends in failure: Olenin goes back to Russia; Hadji Murad tries to get back to his native village and is killed by his Russian pursuers. Its swiftly alternating scenes are short and dramatic. As in *War and Peace* and *Anna* (the horse-race) Tolstoy does not put them in strict chronological sequence. We leave Hadji Murad, go forward to the Russian fortress to meet the young commandant Vorontsov and his wife, before returning to the Tartar *aoul* where Hadji Murad is still considering how best to approach the Russians. Then Tolstoy abruptly switches the peepshow to Russia and to Petersburg. On the day the soldier Avdeev is wounded we see his family in Russia, his old father threshing rye, and his despised brother—a family man—in whose place Avdeev had gone off to serve in the army. They have not seen him since, "for in those days the conscription was like death". The weight of that comment has got into the details, which are as heavy and unhurried as the blows of the flail (one can learn from this scene exactly how the work on a threshing floor was carried out). The mother's letter, with a rouble in it she had sent him, is returned with the news of Avdeev's death, and the old woman wept "for as long as she could spare time". His widow is secretly glad, because she can now make the shopman, with whom she is living, marry her.

Avdeev's death seems to be based on that of the artillery soldier in *The Woodfelling*, the best of the early army sketches and taken from Tolstoy's own experience. Its 'superfluous details' have a freshness and spring about them—in contrast to the spare and measured weight of *Hadji Murad*—but we note that they give no true perspective and coherence to the tale. There is much detail about the guns, and yet we have no clear idea how the guns were fired or why, as we have none about military matters in *The Cossacks*. The young Tolstoy bounds to and fro, noting peculiarities and recording feelings and smells: the old man goes more sombrely to work but his work is unobtrusively clear and methodical. Not less than that of Hadji Murad himself, the whole of Avdeev's life is before us—clear, mute, and strange—its pattern accepted by all, himself included. It appears in the slow talk of the soldiers, repeating what they have often said before. Sometimes Avdeev got drunk when he reflected on the fate that had brought him here and left his brother at home—"it seems just a piece of bad luck". . . . But mostly he was cheerful.

It is the distillation of a life, but distillation is a chilly process. The death in *The Woodfelling* must be admitted to be more moving. The narrator is close to it, and to the reactions of the other soldiers: it happens, it is not recorded and placed in logical perspective. The soldiers speak of it in the night bivouac "as if it had happened goodness knows how long ago, or had never happened at all". Tolstoy is with them in the fact that they are still alive and have no sense of the history and meaning of a death. The scene is as immediate and transparent as that of the night bivouac and Petya's death in *War and Peace*. But in the novel Tolstoy commands both this immediacy and—by reason of the growth and progress of the work behind him—a mute verdict and a perspective as well. In *Hadji Murad* we cannot have this combination: something must be lost by the art which makes the miniature, and it is the strictness of the art itself which determines what has to go.

Swiftly and calmly Tolstoy numbers the reactions to Avdeev's death, those of his friends, his officers, his family, the clerk who wrote that he had "died defending his Tsar, his fatherland, and the Orthodox faith". Then he closes the ledger. Coldly he takes us to Petersburg and shows us how the news of Hadji Murad's surrender is received; how the war minister tries to discredit the general who made the report, and how the Tsar—his wit sharpened by his ill humour over a ballet girl—detects the attempt. Compared to the Olympian disfavour of this peepshow the sarcasm with which Tolstoy "made strange" what he disapproved of in *War and Peace* seems like the gambolling of a happy innocent. Even his most sustained and vitriolic exercise in "making it strange"—the account of the service in the prison in *Resurrection*—is full of a necessary relish that is not to be found in the method of *Hadji Murad*. And yet we cannot call the story objective—indeed in a sense it is less objective than anything he ever wrote, for it quietly turns into what seems like objectivity all his most ultimate convictions. And this is indeed a triumph for art.

In this way the wickedness of government is displayed with what seems a hopeless tolerance. After our meeting with Nicholas in Petersburg; with Shamyl, the leader of opposition in the Caucasus; and with Vorontsov, the Russian viceroy who is trying to destroy him, we feel convinced of the hatefulness of power and the dreadful helplessness of those who exercise it. Tolstoy does not bother to be hard on the Vorontsovs; both father and son are human, kindly, devoted to each other and their families. He merely remarks of Vorontsov *père:* "he did not understand life without power and submission". Buried in the narrative as it is, the finality of this is none the less monumental, like the moment in *The Bronze Horseman* when the madman makes his submission to the great statue as he finds himself crossing its square.

Tolstoy makes no submission but he seems without hope. Kutuzov and Alexander, even Napoleon and Speransky, had some pretensions to examine themselves and their role as rulers: the terrifying thing about the men of power in *Hadji Murad* is that it has become necessary to them without their knowing it, and they exercise it as unreflectingly as ordinary people run their homes or go to the office. The thoughts of the Tsar (Nicholas I) are totally aimless and incoherent.

"Kopervine . . . Kopervine . . .," he repeated several times (it was the name of yesterday's girl). "Horrid—horrid." . . . He did not think of what he was saying but stifled his feelings by listening to the words.

He thinks of his sister-in-law, one of "that futile class of people who discussed not merely science and poetry but even the ways of governing men", and again overcomes the irritation the thought of her gives him "by whispering the first words that came into his head". Words have become for him a sort of totem, devoid of meaning, and we are reminded of the linguistic contrasts in *The Cossacks* and the silly laugh with which Vanyusha said '*La fille*' and '*La femme*'! That habitual unawareness of what words distinguish and actions signify is the atmosphere of power in *Hadji Murad*.

Returning to his capital the Tartar leader, Shamyl, "does not wish to think at all". He wants only peace and his youngest wife. But because they are "as necessary to him as his daily food" he says his prayers and determines his policy, telling Hadji Murad's son, who is his prisoner, that he will be blinded if his father does not surrender. Leadership in Tartary is the same as in Russia, and Tolstoy makes no contrast between the freedom-loving Tartars and the tyranny of Russia. Simple, economical, and reserved as they are, these political scenes are the most chilling in Tolstoy. They are not ironic—we remember Pushkin's remark that a tone of irony ill becomes power—and again we are struck by the recollection of something sanguine, innocent and joyful in the ironies of *War and Peace*. Tolstoy is never fair in the historians' sense, and probably neither Nicholas nor Shamyl were in fact as he portrays them, but his portraits seem none the less true, as true as Shakespeare's portraits of Octavius and Antony. Though he was so scornful of Napoleon he did not deny him the sympathy of the body; these two men of power receive neither the scorn nor the sympathy: all we know of them is their habitual process of mind, and the presentation of this carries instant and horrible conviction.

Yet some portraits in the story are as life-giving and complete as those in *War and Peace*. We even have the 'double positive' effect of the novel in General Kozlovsky's farewell speech, as we had it in the banquet at the English Club for

Bagration. There is consternation at the thought that the old ass will disgrace himself on the occasion and make the farewell dinner a farce. His speech is indeed deliciously absurd (Tolstoy is as good as Dickens at making it audible to us) but it also comes so much from the heart that the whole company—even the Vorontsovs—are reduced to tears.

Perhaps the most moving thing in the story is the sympathy between Hadji Murad and Marya Dimitrievna, the woman who lives with the drunken major at the fort. Belonging to different worlds, they feel all the same an understanding for one another which has nothing sexual about it, the sort of sympathy which Tolstoy failed effectually to portray in the later scenes of *Resurrection*. And in the most brilliant time shift of the story we are shown in this context the hero's severed head before we are given the climactic set-piece of his last battle.

> It was a shaven head with salient brows, black short beard and moustaches, one eye open and the other half-closed. The shaven skull was cleft, but not right through, and there was congealed blood in the nose. . . . The blue lips still bore a kindly childlike expression.
>
> Marya Dimitrievna looked at it, and without a word turned away and went quickly into the house.

This is very different from the description of the dead *abrek* in *The Cossacks*, for we are involved here in a relation between two people whom we know in and for themselves, though one is now dead. The impassivity of description and the background of individual knowledge make the scene genuinely Homeric—as if between Andromache and the dead Hector—and show us how far are the earlier works, even *War and Peace*, from that particular distinction of style. No general point about war and bloodshed is made: it is done simply through the different reactions of the woman and the men to the sight of the head. The drunken officers want to kiss it, as the head of a hero. Butler, the young lieutenant, follows Marya Dimitrievna to ask what is the matter.

> "You're all cut-throats. . . . I hate it! You're cut-throats, really."
> "It might happen to anyone," observed Butler, not knowing what to say. "That's war."

"War? War, indeed! . . . A dead body should be given back to the earth. . . ."

When Butler goes back to ask the man who brought the head what had happened he hears the account of Hadji Murad's last fight, which completes the tale.

Hadji Murad and *The Live Corpse* were the only two works of Tolstoy's last period which he himself said he valued. They have something in common. Both achieve a dramatic relation between author and hero which is new in Tolstoy's work, and both substitute a technique of dramatic exchange for the usual Tolstoyan assertion. They have been called detached, even serene; but though these characteristics are certainly an aspect of the technique they scarcely describe the real feel of either story or play. In a sense they seem more and not less auto-biographical than the great novels, for we detect Tolstoy in them instead of merely seeing him, as we detect Dickens in his last and seemingly most muted novel, *Edwin Drood*. I have argued that one of the classic formulae of the novel is the author's creation of a world in which to explore his nature and give it play, and that in *Anna* we have this alongside the more straight-forward Tolstoyan mode represented by Levin. In *Hadji Murad* and *The Live Corpse* Tolstoy has cut away all evident connection with himself, but the underlying identification is correspond-ingly more intense.

In both there is what might be called a new kind of 'super-fluous man', a man who has got rid of too much. Fedya, the live corpse, has pretended to commit suicide in order to free his wife and her upright lover from the burden of his shiftless and inconvenient existence. When the deception comes out his wife and her new husband are charged with bigamy, and Fedya only saves the situation by committing suicide in earnest. The covert irony might be that there is no way for Tolstoy to abandon the world without being an intolerable nuisance to everyone: death is the only way out. For Hadji Murad the position is not dis-similar. He too has had to abandon his way of life, and is trusted neither by the Russians nor by his own people. Even his son Yusuf, whom he loves, has rejected his father and given his allegiance to Shamyl. Hadji Murad remembers the tale of the falcon, who was caught by men and then pecked to death by his own kind when it managed to escape back to the mountains. But while he is alive he lives without question or complaint; he knows without misgiving what he has to try to do, and his isolation does not in the least perturb him, even though what is for the Russians simply "an interesting event" is for him "a terrible crisis in his life". He is the final reply to Tolstoy's unending speculation about the ground of belief and action in himself and others.

Of course there is much more to *Hadji Murad* than this transmutation by Tolstoy of his own experience. In *The Live Corpse* there is not—it makes its point and suggests to us a comparison with Tolstoy's own predicament. But the story has a compression normally absent in Tolstoy, and alien—one might have supposed—to his genius. Its apparent simplicity is heavy with many kinds of meaning and with conflicting insights reconciled not—as at the end of *War and Peace*—by the natural growth and fulfilment of living, but by the archaic tranquillity of the narrative form. Over the eight years he worked on *Hadji Murad* Tolstoy must have come to love and to need this tranquillity. It must have been a strange comfort to imagine himself into a man who never agonised over what he should or should not have done, a figure in the creation of whom he bowed before the heroic certainty of a vanished mode of life. Drawing on his own vivid memories, he imagines Hadji Murad as a child.

> He remembered how his mother had shaved his head for the first time, and how the reflection of his round bluish head in the shining brass vessel that hung on the wall had astonished him. He remembered a lean dog that had licked his face. He remembered the strange smell of the cake his mother had given him—a smell of smoke and of sour milk.

And he sees the pictures that filled his mind at the moment of death "without evoking any feeling within him—neither pity nor anger nor any kind of desire". When Tolstoy was lying at the Astapovo railway station he repeated over and over in his last moments: "I do not understand what it is I have to do". Like Hadji Murad, whom he had imagined so well, he had nothing to do but to die.

IX

The *Nouvelle* as Hypothesis

"One cannot create virtues for oneself."

THE MARQUIS DE SADE

1

IF one married, along what lines might the relation proceed? What would happen if one became murderously jealous, or obsessed with desire for another woman? Suppose one were to contract a fatal and painful disease, or gave up the world to become a monk and hermit? These hypotheses are specialised; they depend on the rest of life being left out, so that we can concentrate on one particular possibility and problem. Yet all ask the question which is implicit in all Tolstoy's fictions: how should a man live?

Only one hypothesis became a fact for Tolstoy. He got married, and in some ways his married life resembled his forecast. Yet even *Family Happiness*, no less than the four other stories to be discussed in this chapter, remains an abstract analysis, on the mental plane. In all of them Tolstoy forsakes the life of the body, even though it is problems and predicaments of the body with which most of them are so acutely concerned.

In general the characters in these stories act as Tolstoy's agents, representing his interests as if in some obsessive lawsuit. He does not *imagine* them, as he imagined the characters in his great fictions, and he does not on the whole identify himself with them, as he might be said to do with the hero of *The Live Corpse* and with Hadji Murad. The narrator of *Family Happiness* is the most successful agent, because she benefits from Tolstoy's understanding of a woman's life, even though this understanding has not the marvellous physical quality that it has in the two novels.

In *Father Sergius* the moving power is Tolstoy's own submerged self-awareness, his knowledge that men do not change and that their natures are stronger than their wills; yet this knowledge, which takes us back to the world of *Anna Karenina*, is not exactly what Tolstoy intended to reveal in the story. It illustrates again the truth of his own point about Chekhov's *Darling*, and it is this which chiefly moves us about it, rather than the fact that "the old man wrote it well", as Tolstoy himself remarked, that he strove to fashion it as an infective parable.

The hero's sister, who is "as proud and ambitious as himself", perceives that after the humiliation of finding that his *fiancée* has been the emperor's mistress he decides at once to become a monk "in order to be above those who considered themselves his superiors". His leading characteristic is the desire to excel and to be remarkable in whatever he undertakes, and Tolstoy reveals more subtly than the passion itself the attitude of mind that accompanies it—the need to play the part that is due to him or can be made to fit him. When the society woman comes to his cell to tempt him, he plays that part more easily than he knows or even than the story allows; and at the climax of her temptation chops off his finger with an axe and dismisses her with God's blessing. She is profoundly impressed by his role and responds to it, for both socially and by temperament she is the same kind of person as he. He has shown her the kind of role which she too could play, and she takes the vows of a nun.

The incident and its aftermath bring him celebrity and strengthen his part as the austere and saintly *starets*. But when a merchant's imbecile daughter is brought to him and allures him by her mere gross femininity, he is jerked out of his role. Naked desire leaves him helpless and without any part to play, as abject as Vronsky was when deprived of his idea of himself by the unexpected dignity of Karenin. Like Vronsky, his first urge is to kill himself. But then he remembers Pashenka, a girl he had known as a child, "a thin little girl with large mild eyes and a timid pathetic face", whom he and his friends used to make fun of, and whom he had met again briefly at his monastery after she had become a widow—"still the same, not exactly stupid, but insipid, insignificant, and pitiable". At once he determines to go in search of her. The account of his meeting with Pashenka is extraordinarily moving, like that of Cordelia and Lear.[1] Tolstoy conveys the goodness of Pashenka, and her lack of any sense of herself, as movingly as he does that of Alyosha Gorshok in one of his last and shortest tales. He can describe it, as Father Sergius can play its part. For with the same determination which has dictated all the changes in his life Sergius sets out to be *like* Pashenka, to throw himself into this new role. "I lived for men on the pretext of living for God, while she lives for God imagining she lives for men."

It is at this point that Tolstoy's deep and intuitive grasp of Sergius's nature seems to part company with the desire to point a moral and to emphasise the great change that finally came over Sergius when he saw where his pride had led him. In fact when he stands in his peasant clothes and with bare head before a party of gentry, begging alms on behalf of his fellow-tramps, he is surely as conscious of what his position demands of him as if he were on the parade ground in Petersburg or receiving adoring worshippers in his monastic cell? Even when he ends up working for a peasant in Siberia, there can be no escape for Sergius from himself. The tale inexorably confirms the bonds of nature and personality at the point where Tolstoy requires them to cease and be transcended. It is this which makes its effect on us, and which may have caused Dostoevsky's reported outburst as he read the later Tolstoy—"no no!—it is not like that at all!"

The thankless task of acting as Tolstoy's agent in the story falls with particular weight on Pozdnyshev of *The Kreutzer Sonata*. He is required to express Tolstoy's views, but with a pathological violence and peculiarity supposedly his own. It is as if we knew that Shakespeare hated sex, but not so much as Hamlet does; and was disgusted with human beings, but not in quite so sensational a fashion as Timon. Tolstoy can neither release Pozdnyshev nor conceal himself behind him. The technical flaw in the stories, more marked in *The Kreutzer Sonata* than in the others, is that they employ a mechanism that makes for simplicity and rigidity without any compensatory detachment.

When the 'I' of *The Kreutzer Sonata* objects that if Pozdnyshev's ideas were really practised life would die out, he replies:

[1] In fact Tolstoy may be said to have touched, involuntarily, the heart of *King Lear* later in this story. While life lasts, illusion lasts.

"But why live? If life has no aim, if life is given us for life's sake, there is no reason for living." And "he evidently prized this thought very highly". So in a sense did Tolstoy, but he bestows the overt absurdity of priding himself on such a conviction upon the unfortunate Pozdnyshev. This is not the "self-derision genuinely Russian" which made Pierre so engaging a character and his relation to his creator so successful. The gradual externalisation of Pozdnyshev, as the climax of his story mounts, and his becoming—at the end—so touching a figure, makes this Tolstoyan use of him seem particularly jarring. When Prince Andrew denounces marriage to Pierre, or Levin tries vainly to see what makes Sviyazhsky tick, we are drawn into a real dialogue, an interchange, a familiar discussion —the index of familiarity being that we know Tolstoy will address us soon in his own person. But the dramatic dialogue here is stilted and artificial, and its artifice largely thrown away.

All marriages in Tolstoy, whether described before or after his own took place, are, we feel, the same marriage—not his own, but an archetypal one. He presents the *marriageness* of marriage more directly and exhaustively than any other writer. In *Family Happiness* he envisages it; in *War and Peace* and *Anna* he describes it; in *The Kreutzer Sonata* he denounces it. Everything depends on the point of view; many of the events of the two stories might have happened in the novels—indeed have happened—but they have not been isolated and concentrated on. Andrew and the Little Princess, Pierre and Hélène, Anna, Karenin, Vronsky—they have all gone through the same kinds of disillusionment, rage, disgust, acquiescence, as the characters in the stories, but they were not able to remain in these states of mind for long. Life—the novel—carried them along; dissipating these impressions, creating new ones, and returning them to the first state without their being fully conscious of the repetition. The process of the stories is not a living one in this sense but a mental one. Like so many much more ordinary stories they have a strong element both of nightmare and of daydream in them.

> I think of running away from her, hiding myself, going to America. I get as far as dreaming of how I shall get rid of her, how splendid that will be, and how I shall unite myself with another, an admirable woman—quite different. . . .

Most married men, and women, would have to admit to occasional day-dreams something like those of Pozdnyshev. That is the intended power of the tale—to compel the individual to own up, to confess that his bosom returns an echo, and that there is some force in Pozdnyshev's contention that all marriages are secretly alike. But the accusing finger fails to disconcert us as much as it intends. For one thing, such fantasies are for most people occasional rather than obsessive; and a more serious weakness is that behind Pozdynshev's day-dream is another—that of Tolstoy himself. Tolstoy is letting himself go, and there is an element of self-indulgence in the display. The realism with which he describes the killing is particularly out of place here. The resistance of the corset; the sheath of the dagger dropped behind the sofa, and the reflection "I must remember that or it will get lost"—this is the realism of the self-told day-dream and it is highly imitable. Any competent sensationalist is Tolstoy's equal in this region of the mind.

And yet we still have the old directness—Tolstoy infects us with the terror that the fantasy arouses in him, where for most people it would be a comparatively harmless way of letting off steam inside themselves. We have something of the same feeling of horror in Dickens's description of the murder of Nancy in *Oliver Twist*, and Dostoevsky's of Nastasya Philippovna in *The Idiot*; but Dickens is fascinated rather than appalled—it was his favourite scene for recitation and used to excite him to the point of frenzy—while Dostoevsky's imagination is always on equable terms with every kind of violence. In all three we are aware of the pressure of a preoccupation—not uncommon in nineteenth-century fiction—with murder as a sexual act, but only Tolstoy seems to become fully aware as he describes it of the contrast between the insulated fantasy of the murderer and the outraged *otherness* of his victim. Pozdnyshev's wife is not, as Nancy and Nastasya are, a natural murderee who appears to acquiesce in the atmosphere which the murderer and his creator have generated. It is significant that Norman Mailer's revival of the imagined murder as a sexual act, in his novel *An American Dream*, follows the Dickens-Dostoevsky pattern, not Tolstoy's.

Involuntarily, at the climax, the real argument of *The Kreutzer Sonata* comes out, the argument overlaid by the various diatribes indulged in through Pozdnyshev. Sex is often a hostile act, even in marriage; its consummation resembling murder in its indifference to the reality of another separate and independent being. Jealousy and hatred "have their own laws" and require their climax as inexorably as sexual passion. Only after the climax does Pozdnyshev reach the dazed awareness that his wife is, after all, "another human being".

After the evacuation of Moscow in *War and Peace*, when Natasha gets up in the night to see the wounded Prince Andrew, she says: "Forgive me". "Her face, with its swollen lips, was more than plain—it was dreadful", but Prince Andrew only sees that the jealousy which has obsessed him for months has no connection with the reality of Natasha. When he sees his wife's face, as if for the first time, and bruised and swollen where he has struck her, Pozdnyshev too says: "Forgive me". But she only looks at him "with her old expression of cold animal hatred". The ultimate horror of his act is to have put her beyond the possibility of recognising him, as he now recognises her. At the end of the story the narrator goes up to Pozdnyshev in the railway carriage to say goodbye.

> Whether he was asleep or only pretended to be, at any rate he did not move. I touched him with my hand. He uncovered his face, and I could see he had not been asleep.
>
> "Goodbye," I said, holding out my hand. He gave me his and smiled slightly, but so piteously that I felt ready to weep.
>
> "Yes, forgive me—" he said, repeating the same words with which he had concluded his story.

'Forgive' is almost the same word in Russian as 'Goodbye'. Since his wife's death deprived him of recognition and forgiveness, Pozdnyshev has to ask both of strangers.

The end of *The Kreutzer Sonata* is deeply moving: that of *The Devil* not at all. Whether the hero should shoot himself or his peasant mistress—Tolstoy tried both conclusions—scarcely matters: each is equally plausible and equally unsatisfactory. For Eugene Irtenyev (who is not connected with the hero of the same name in *Boyhood and Youth*) never escapes, as Pozdnyshev does, from the role of a Tolstoyan agent. "If Irtenyev was mentally deranged," Tolstoy tells us, "—everyone is in the

same case." That injunctive 'everyone' disappeared at the end of
The Kreutzer Sonata, where it is the isolation of Pozdnyshev that
stresses itself so movingly. Irtenyev never becomes a person,
but he is far from being an Everyman. He strikes us rather as a
singularly unfortunate being, like an alcoholic. In most people
the temptation to commit adultery, like the temptation to drink
too much, may be given way to at times but is none the less
controllable. In the mood in which he wrote *The Devil* Tolstoy
would rather see Everyman as an alcoholic than as a rational
drinker who sometimes drinks too much.

One trouble with *The Devil* is its length—it is too short for a
proper deployment of some of the material in it. Tolstoy, again
involuntarily perhaps, makes the hero's wife a great deal more
real than he is—*she* is not required to point a moral. But her
presence threatens to build up a solid foundation for life which
is at odds with the cursory speed of the plot.

> However much he had expected from his wife, he had never expected
> to find in her what he actually found. . . . Raptures of love—though
> he tried to produce them—did not take place or were very slight,
> but he discovered something quite different: that he was not merely
> more cheerful and happier but that it had become easier to live.
> He did not know why this should be so, but it was.

This kind of Pierre or Levin discovery, so familiar from the
leisurely transparency of the novels, is discrepant with Irtenyev's subsequent behaviour. Pierre or Levin might have felt an
overpowering urge to ambush a peasant girl—they might have
done so. Natasha or Kitty would have found out; there would
have been an appalling row; thoughts of suicide would have
occurred as a refuge from "the intolerable situation"; but—as
in the Oblonsky household—things would have calmed down.
All Tolstoy's most persuasive work goes to prove that the
necessities of life—like the grove of interbranching oaks to
which he compares Russian life and institutions—are hardly
disturbed by the impulses of the moment. The sudden realisation
that family life is hell, that one wants to make love not to one's
wife but to some attractive girl—in the wide perspective of the
novels such things are not of great importance. But in *The Devil*
Tolstoy is determined to find them so. *The Devil* is the only

work in which Tolstoy's own experience is awkwardly intrusive, and the only one in which we can legitimately call upon our knowledge of that experience to question his art. For if Irtenyev is Tolstoy, and Everyman, why did not Tolstoy himself blow out his brains or those of the handsome wench whose presence distracted him at Yasnaya Polyana? To the saga of his marriage, as of any marriage, these impulses did not in fact make any very decisive contribution.

The crowning falsification in the tale is the determined exclusion of the wife. From being a character of importance and potentiality, Liza is reduced in the end to a mere cypher in a melodrama. "She could not at all understand why it had happened." Tolstoy discounts the whole bulk of the relation between her and her husband, and makes his suicide depend on the chance that he *might* have told her what was wrong "had the nurse not inopportunely entered at that moment". The mishap is far from poignant, and reminds us how absent is this kind of 'it might have been' expedient—Hardyesque 'Ironies'—from Tolstoy's best work, though he makes a more convincing use of it in the early story *Polikushka*.

2

There are often disproportionate elements in Tolstoy's tales, as if a sculptor had had to add diminutive limbs to a great torso. This 'making it small' is one of the troubles in *Family Happiness*. The other is Tolstoy's notion of borrowing from *Jane Eyre*, which he had read and admired, a female narrator. The vitality of Jane Eyre comes from her being so powerfully and exclusively herself; no imaginative transposition is involved. Tolstoy compels his narrator and centre of consciousness to be the kind of ideal girl whom he feels would suit him, while he himself takes up, as it were, the position of Rochester. The result of this cross-relation is that the heroine lacks the naturalness and vigour of Tolstoy's great observed heroines, while the hero is the only one of his spokesmen figures who strikes us as priggish. By relying on a conception from literature, instead of on his own more straightforward creative process, Tolstoy is left with the literature rather than the life of the borrowed idea.

And when the heroine enters high society in Petersburg we are given no real impression of what it is like—there is no room for a Tolstoyan description of the ballroom.

> It seemed to me that I was the centre round which everything revolved, that for my sake alone this great room was lighted up and the band played, and that this crowd of people had assembled to admire me.

It is illuminating that Tolstoy cannot get away with this: it is no use that his object in the story is not a family chronicle but a psychological study—the fact remains that he cannot, as Pushkin or Turgenev could, suggest the whole of a ball by the tone of one sentence. He has to have room—room to enumerate the guests and the dances, the men's calves and the women's shoulders—before the scene can appear before us. Instead of such transparency he tries in *Family Happiness* to give us *atmosphere*—a very different thing. And it was perhaps this poetic atmosphere in the vein of Turgenev which made Tolstoy dismiss *Family Happiness* as soon as it was written with even more than his usual repugnance for one of his completed works.

Yet in fact the atmosphere of this 'foul blot', as he called it, has great charm. We remember the evocation of autumn, with the rowan berries hanging red and wrinkled on the boughs.

> We went along the footpath over the beaten and trampled stubble; our voices and footsteps were the only sounds. On one side the brownish stubble stretched over a hollow to a distant leafless wood, and across it at some distance a peasant was noiselessly ploughing a black strip which grew wider and wider. . . .

In spite of Tolstoy's greater detail and knowledgeability this is similar in tone to the famous evocation of a winter landscape in Constant's *Adolphe*. It has the meticulous delicacy of the *nouvelle* form, very different to the joyous, casual seizure of nature in the rest of Tolstoy, which is like the hero of *Boyhood* seizing the wet branches of wild cherry after the thunderstorm. We have the feeling, as with most successful *nouvelles*, that the writer is fashioning something with a secret and delightful appeal to his imagination, rather than remembering and re-creating out of a full and thoughtless experience.

The hero of *Family Happiness* distrusts the idea of love but would like the calm happiness of family life. Marriage with the narrator, Masha, makes him fall really in love, the kind of love that makes them "laugh with joy at the mere sight of each other". But Masha is young; she wants "personal experience of all the nonsense of life": her husband sees that she must have them and sees, too, that their joyful communion will have to end, otherwise her awakening to the pleasures of society will be too painful for him. He repeats the last two lines of Lermontov's poem *The Sail*.

> But, ever restless, it demands a storm
> As if in storms comes its repose.

Masha does indeed find repose in the excitements of high society, "which became a habit and monopolised my capacity for feeling". Yet her husband's withdrawal of intimacy makes her unhappy, even though she no longer needs and depends on it. She almost yields to the passionate embraces of an Italian count—a remarkably stagey figure. She thinks: "Let more and more storms of unhappiness break over my head". At last, at home in the country again, after an emblematic summer storm, she and her husband have one of the old frank talks, and he tells her that it is no use asking for their old mutual spontaneity back; that "each time of life has its own kind of love", and that they should now be happy in a different way.

By putting himself in the wife's position Tolstoy shows his remarkable powers of intuition and discernment, but he also shows how he would wish her to respond and feel, and he lends her his analytic power for the process. Natasha did not 'judge' her husband, but she did not know she did not: Masha describes how she comes to do so with great precision in order to deplore it. She feels that she and the friend in whom she confides have sat in judgement together on her husband, and that "now each measured the other by the standard of other people". Even before marriage Tolstoy had a remarkable understanding of its most important and precarious intimacies. And of its moments of causeless delight. Masha's feeling in the dark carriage after the wedding that "her love had vanished, giving place to a feeling of mortification and alarm" is a 'double positive' that looks forward to the experience of Prince Andrew and Levin, and so is the moment when after a quarrel they look at each other and burst out laughing. Tolstoy already has the gift of revealing the inside of marriage without any touch of sentimentality or—worse still—of knowingness and self-congratulation.

The achievement of *Family Happiness* is not—for once in Tolstoy—in its characters, who have no chance to come fully alive, but in its analysis of the channels of communication in a marriage. Strangely enough, no comparable study existed in the Western novel, as if such communication could be taken for granted and treated according to well-defined conventions. In Goethe's *Wahlverwandshaften* for instance, for which Tolstoy at one time professed admiration, the modes of communication are laid down like a bureaucratic procedure. The English novel in Tolstoy's time had plenty of married couples who were shrewdly or facetiously observed (the Proudies, the Micawbers) or supposed to be in a state of wedded bliss railed off from the eye of the writer. But the Russians, unconventional in this as in other respects, seemed to come and look at what actually happens with a direct and pragmatic sympathy, as if it were one of the most interesting things a novelist could notice.

Nor was Tolstoy the first to do so. Though serialised in a magazine ten years earlier, Sergei Aksakov's *Family History* had appeared in book form in 1856, only a year or two before Tolstoy wrote *Family Happiness*, and the younger writer may well have experienced the influence, perhaps unconscious, of the unforgettable portrait of a marriage which it contains. Aksakov does not have the Tolstoyan transparency—there is a certain 'creaminess', as Mirsky says, about his happy composed Russian style—but for sympathy and penetration of insight nothing of the same sort, even in *War and Peace* or *Anna*, is superior to his account of the relation of the young couple who were in fact his own father and mother. Though Aksakov makes no secret of the fact, we do not feel *A Family History* to be a memoir, and we remember Tolstoy's comment that none of the notable prose works of the period fit exactly into the fictional or any other category.

The mixture of piety, warmth, and objectivity with which Aksakov describes his forebears is remarkably like that of Tolstoy in *War and Peace*—his grandfather, Stepan Mihailovich, comes before us on the same scale as the Old Prince Bolkonsky—but he shows us the unity and incompatibility of the couple who were his parents not by Tolstoyan analysis but by means of small incidents and observations scattered over the course of a leisurely narrative. And this suggests the eventful uneventfulness of a marriage more realistically than *Family Happiness* does. Though passionately devoted to his lively and intelligent wife, Alexei Stepanovitch possesses "the gold of sensibility but not the small change". He cannot sustain the display of love with which he first threw himself at her feet to swear that "his happiness would consist in the fulfilment of all her wishes". The intensity of his feeling brought it out, but it was not natural to him, and clever as Sofia Nicolaievna was she could not perceive this. The discrepancy between his declaration and his real and habitual nature proved, says the author, as firmly as Jane Austen might have done, "that he could not assure a woman's happiness". But love of power was one of his adored's ruling passions, "and, though she did not know it, helped her to her decision". She is blind to his emotional inadequacy because she feels she can mould him as she wishes.

She is wrong. Although he desires to please her in everything the bent of his nature cannot be changed.

> He was a man unable to appreciate display of feeling, or to sympathise with it, from whatever cause it arose. Thus his wife's power of passionate devotion frightened him: he dreaded it, just as he used to dread his father's furious fits of anger. Excessive feeling always produces an unpleasant impression upon quiet unemotional people: they cannot recognise such a state of mind to be natural, and regard it as a kind of morbid condition to which some people are liable at times . . they are afraid of people with such a temperament. And fear is fatal to love, even to a child's love for his parents. And in point of mutual understanding and sympathy, the relations between Alexei Stepanitch and his wife, instead of becoming closer, as might have been expected, grew less intimate. This may seem strange, but it often happens thus in life.

So it does, but it is extraordinarily rare for a writer to turn such a relation into a work of art. Aksakov's sympathy and detachment are perfect. Sofia Nicolaievna soon realises that though her husband is ready to die for her "she ought not to demand from him what he could not give". But this makes no difference. She cannot cease to demand "a tender and constant observation", and her husband—even after he has come to know his wife and understand her needs—cannot bring himself to supply it. Her warm nature and her yearning for a shared sensibility impel her to extravagantly affectionate makings-up after a tiff which her husband was hardly aware of, and he finds these renewals of love as disconcerting as her reproaches. For many novelists, like Dickens, this would be material for character comedy, seen from the outside; Aksakov's art gives it a truer and more touching humour.

I have mentioned Aksakov's portrait of a marriage because it is a parallel to the married relation in *Family Happiness*. It is more modest than Tolstoy's, not tied to a genre, and concerned with actual and not hypothetical people; and it remarkably anticipates the strength and the method that Tolstoy was to display in his great novels. Indeed we could almost say that the relation of Anna and Vronsky—the similarity is even more marked in early drafts—forms a tragic analogue to that of Aksakov's couple. Aksakov himself had attempted and produced much artificial work based on European models before the influence of Gogol—as we saw in the first chapter—showed him his true subject. *Family Happiness* was also something of a blind alley for Tolstoy. Like Aksakov he needed not the future but the past—his own and that of his family and of Russia—in order to develop his narrative genius.

X

Tolstoy's Legacy. *Dr Zhivago*

One record more, the last. . . .

PUSHKIN, *Boris Godunov*

On and on they went, singing 'Eternal Memory'.

Dr Zhivago

A real work of art, in which the author says what he feels he must say because he loves what he is speaking about. . . .

TOLSTOY, *What is Art?*

A TEST of one kind of great literature is how it makes use of the past and relates itself to it. Of all authors, except Shakespeare, Tolstoy is the most easily and the most comprehensively retrospective. The more one reflects on what constitutes *Tolstoyness*, the more it seems to consist in the immense area of time which, through him, we are continually carrying forward into the future.

This time has little to do with the history of his own life. We are lucky to know so little about Shakespeare: about Tolstoy we know far too much. Chekhov exclaimed at the fact that here was the greatest of Russian writers talking and no one was putting anything down! How different with Goethe, embalmed in the pages of Eckermann and a hundred others, as if such a meticulous recording were a substitute for history. More, in fact, was being put down than Chekhov realised, and illuminating as much of it is, we could well do without it. The great Russians of the nineteenth century had an instinct for what could be done without. Pushkin (who burnt his own) said he was glad that Byron's memoirs had been destroyed. To live and to write one's history as the Russians did as if it were a common familial project, is one thing: to make notes about it, so that posterity may admire and do one justice, is another. It brings up the vexed question of sincerity, that bugbear of the self-explainer, a question that never even occurs to us when reading Pushkin and

Tolstoy. There are no Rousseaus in nineteenth-century Russia, no historians of the self.

Instead they live with and write about their history, neither turning it into 'the past'—into a kind of National Trust—as Scott and his followers did in England, nor converting it into an instrument of policy and advertisement as Soviet writers have done. They see themselves with an extraordinary clarity, yet inside the Russian family there could be no irony because there was no detachment. Tolstoy's irony, his 'making it strange', is a device for dealing with things that are comically or stupidly outside the family. "Where do I have satire?" demands Pushkin in a letter. "There is not a hint of it in *Eugene Onegin.* . . . My embankment would crumble if I were to touch it." Byron is a real satirist, says Pushkin, no doubt because he did not have this "embankment", this passionate identification with the national family life.[1] Both Saltykov-Shchedrin in *The Golovlyov Family*, and Goncharov in *Oblomov*, began their novels with satirical intent; but, as Tolstoy says happened with Chekhov's *Darling*, the heroes of both novels—the unspeakable Judushka and the pathetic Oblomov—end up as known and as naturally loved as other members of the family. One of the rare occasions when Oblomov is really upset and indignant is when his servant compares the way he lives with that of 'other people'.

The imperfective form of the Russian verb describes what is in the process of happening, and we feel this 'imperfective tendency' (as Jane Harrison called it) of the Russian novel when Tolstoy or Aksakov are talking about their parents and grandparents, real or fictionalised, as if they were still alive. It contrasts with the retrospective convention of the English family novel—"Thirty years ago, reader, when this story opens, etc. etc."—which both places the writer outside his subject and yet allows him the licence of a more mellow and leisurely outlook than that of the present time. In more recent family novels the family is seen from the outside by the decamped, the undutiful son or daughter, whose separation and undutifulness consists ultimately in the fact that they are writing about the family as they are. "*Non serviam . . .*" look what I have

---

[1] Significantly, Henry James admitted that the tone of the westernised Turgenev is "not altogether purged of sarcasm".

freed myself from. But family history must be understood on the inside. The intelligence and art involved must not seem self-created and self-hoarded. The analytic intelligence of Tolstoy or Aksakov never strikes us as exclusive but as a part of what it describes, and a part of the latent communal shrewdness which in life may reveal itself only as vitality and action. There is an illuminating comment on this aspect of family life in one of Anthony Powell's novels.

> Individuals born into such a world often gain an unsentimental grasp of human conduct, a grasp sometimes superior to that of apparently more perceptive persons whose minds are unattuned by early association to the constant give and take of an ancient and tenacious social organism.

Certainly a kind of rapid inadvertent perception, which they seem not to bother to register to themselves, is characteristic of the Russian family writers.

The inspiration of history and the family in time, drawn upon by the great Russians, was soon dissipated, and with it the 'Tolstoyness' available to the younger generation of writers. The *genres* of the great nineteenth-century Russian prose works are, as Tolstoy says, entirely their own, but by the end of the century Russian literature has become recognisable to Europeans on an exchange basis. The backlog of European literature has been filled up; parity has been attained and every sort of European novel or poem has its counterpart in Russia. Having caught up with history, the Russian writers find it no longer available to them. Brilliant and effervescent as it can be, Russian poetry and prose of the three decades before the revolution has an air of familiarity about it. All the new techniques of the west are used, often more excitingly and with greater enthusiasm. One thing was different, however. The great giant of the golden age was still there, almost as if Shakespeare had survived to read Carlyle, Swinburne and Shaw. In *What is Art?* Tolstoy twice mentions Kipling—about whom the new men like Gumilev and Kuprin were enthusiastic—and mentions him with the disfavour we should expect, but it seems as singular that the author of *Puck of Pook's Hill* should have been known to the author of *War and Peace* as that a poem by Count Robert de Montesquiou —the Charlus of Proust—should have been quoted by him as an example of the decadence of modern verse.

In a sense his continued presence on the scene itself inhibited the possibility of learning from him. In *Sanin* Artsybashev employs something of the *Resurrection* technique; Andreyev coarsens the stark simplicity of the later stories and accentuated the perversity with which their moral is rammed home. Dostoevsky was undergoing the same sort of vulgarisation. In Sologub's novel, appropriately entitled *The Little Demon*, his colossal degradations are reduced to a total pettiness and malice without scale or function; and innocence is presented with a furtive sexual excitement which parodies its source. Andreyev's story *In the Fog* parodies the sexual obsession in *The Devil* and *The Kreutzer Sonata* in a similar way. Travesties and curiosities as these works seem now, they none the less made the same impact on the Russian reading public as their great predecessors had done.

More complex and interesting is the relation between Chekhov's stories and Tolstoy's. Chekhov's *My Life* is the story of a Tolstoyan. In it Chekhov describes with a simplicity that carries total conviction the forlornness of taking up a position outside society instead of working in it and through it; he implies that the search for truth is ultimately less important than the need to do one's duty and get on in the world. There is no hint of criticism of Tolstoy's ideas in the story, but it is one of the best imaginative apprehensions of the gap between those ideas and the world as it is. It is also genuinely inspired by Tolstoy, in that Chekhov has imagined himself into the Tolstoyan awareness and submerged in it his own personal tone.

What that tone usually is, and how it differs from Tolstoy's, can be seen in the contrast between Chekhov's tale *Sleepy* and Tolstoy's equally short and simple *Alyosha Gorshok*, written several years later and possibly with the Chekhov story in mind. The little servant girl in *Sleepy*, who drudges all day and is expected to rock the baby at night, finally kills it in order that she can lie down and sleep. It is a clinical story: Chekhov does not create the little girl as Tolstoy creates the individuality of the young peasant drudge Alyosha Gorshok, so we have no means of knowing whether killing the baby was a likely thing for her to do or not—the act is related to her situation and not to herself. Chekhov is the dedicated doctor, summoned to the story as if to a case.

In the composition of *Alyosha Gorshok*, and in his comments on *The Darling* Tolstoy reveals the difference between his narrative instinct and Chekhov's. Tolstoy was a divided man, and all his most searching critical comments take this division in the artist for granted. That is why he assumes that Chekhov in *The Darling* set out to do one thing and did another. Had Tolstoy himself written the story this might well have been so, but Chekhov, reasonable sensible and straightforward as he is— the nicest of all authors—regards his characters more as patients to look after than as people to explore and know. He is far more detached than Tolstoy.

Tolstoy on war seems imitable, perhaps because he had him-self borrowed a method here from Stendhal, a method taken up again by Hemingway and others—including Isaac Babel. And both Babel and Hemingway spoil the method by the deadpan glee with which they use it, like little boys hinting they have seen nastier things in the woodshed than any other little boys. Apart from this, the panoramic size of *War and Peace*, with its short chapters and interwoven fates and families, was and is the model for innumerable Russian novels about the two wars and the civil war. Tolstoyan techniques are standardised by the practitioners of socialist realism. "But what they derive from their great predecessors," observes Professor Gifford, "affects only the surface."

> The rendering may look similar, but you cannot have a living relation with the past unless you engage with it unreservedly. . . . Soviet novelists do not risk their own assumptions when they resort to Pushkin and Tolstoy.[1]

This is certainly the reason for the lifelessness of these novels. We look in vain for any trace of Tolstoy's own most vital if

[1] Professor Henry Gifford, *The Novel in Russia.*

unadmitted process—the subversion by the material and the characters which he creates of the ideological position from which the author set out. However much the Soviet author sees he cannot examine it with 'close attention', for he already knows what is there before he begins to write.

Yet even indifferent Soviet novelists can see and describe natural objects with something of the precision and delicacy of Tolstoy and Turgenev, rather as mediaeval authors continued to etch in the details in the garden of the rose, or eighteenth-century poets those of parks, houses, journeys. There is a strange gap between this almost finicky descriptive precision and the coarse political decorum of characterisation and narrative. In Sholokhov's novels the sky above some revolutionary tableau is minutely described; a drizzle makes the dry sand between railway sleepers look like a face pitted by smallpox; rifle shots sound like the splitting of acacia pods. But beside this evidence of the seeing eye and the sensitive ear we have passages of complete inanity. "Their comrades took their rifles and cartridges: dead men have no need of weapons." Even a war reporter would have shrunk from writing down the second half of that sentence, which is as far as possible removed from the epic simplicities of Tolstoyan description. It is meaninglessly rhetorical, with a rhetoric that has seeped in from politics.

Dr Zhivago is not very obviously in the tradition of Tolstoy. With its elaborate images and correspondences, its complex and detailed working out of parallels in Christian liturgy and mythology, it seems at first a novel wholly from the symbolist era, the era of Blok and Bely, with whom Pasternak had been associated when young. And before 1914 it would indeed have been one, had Pasternak written such a book in such a time. It is because history seems to seize him, rather than he it, that his novel transcends the disabling limitations of the 'poetic' novel and achieves a true and involuntary historical status. As Tolstoy did not choose his period and made no headway when he tried to do so—with the history of Peter the Great or of the Decembrists —so Pasternak's vision of history grew up in him like a necessity. Dr Zhivago feels that an august and terrible role has been thrust upon him, and for his creator it was a Tolstoyan role— the presentation of a hero, like Tolstoy's Pierre, through whom the significance of an extraordinary epoch can be apprehended in relation to all that is most enduring and precious in life.

Do we feel, as Tolstoy required, that we are recognising a universal truth in Pasternak's novel, that we "knew the thing before but had been unable to express it"? Not entirely perhaps. Zhivago is a poet; most of us are not poets. How then does Zhivago's experience become universal for us, as universal as Tolstoy's "relations of married couples, of parents to children, of children to parents, of men to their fellow-countrymen . . . to the land"? Pasternak's answer is that in the time in which he writes the poet has become Everyman, the representative of enduring human truth, and that we cannot but feel this when we recognise—through Zhivago—this truth in ourselves. Indeed Pasternak makes the most explicit Christian parallel between Zhivago in us and Christ in us, between the Garden of Gethsemane—"the vastness of the universe was uninhabited, and only the garden was a place of life"—and the poet's saving conviction of what is most real in life on earth. In Zhivago's most moving poem *Gethsemane*,[1] from which that quotation comes, Christ tells his disciples that "the Lord granted you to live in my days", and so certain is Zhivago of his role that their friendship for him is, he sometimes feels, the only thing that will be remembered about his political friends.

It is a measure of the remarkable power of Pasternak's novel that we come to accept this amazing, and as some would feel even blasphemous, egotism, without amusement or distaste but with a kind of participatory awe. In the face of what has happened to Russia, in the face of political abstraction and pitiless theory, the detachment of a poet, which in the old days would seem a matter merely of aesthetic preference, can become a path to salvation. By being himself, and by his insistence on the sacredness of the individual, Zhivago undergoes the role of saviour. At a time when Yeats wrote

> *I think it better that in times like these*
> *A poet's mouth be silent, for in truth*
> *We have no gift to set a statesman right—*

[1] The poem is an impressive example of the continued life and inspiration in Russian poetry of the language of the Russian Bible. It has the same timeless power here as in Pushkin's poetry (*The Prophet*) and in Tolstoy's *Confession*.

Zhivago must show forth 'the hard gem-like flame' of personal experience as the light of the world. In his poem *The Twelve*, Pasternak's friend Blok had imagined Christ in the forefront of the revolution, and leading twelve red guards, his disciples, through the streets of Petrograd. *The Twelve* is an effective rather than a moving or convincing poem. Pasternak's conception of Christ, and of the Calvary of Zhivago, may be as subjective and as symbolic as Blok's but there is in it a far more profound and imagined sense of history. Blok's Christ is not only subjectivised but officiously modernised: Pasternak's Christ figure shows the survival and the resurrection of life which is outside political movements. Zhivago is not against the revolution—far from it—but he must go down into the tomb and rise again because of the kind of death it brings.

It is hard to say what Tolstoy would have thought of the method and direction of Pasternak's symbolism—probably he would have disliked it for reasons I must return to—but the assurance and inner conviction of Zhivago are strangely like that of the old man on the raft in *Resurrection* who says "I believe no one—no one but myself". And Tolstoy's sense of history, as it creates and sustains our human imagination, is very like Pasternak's. Both see history as stillness neither in the past nor the future, an abiding place of the human spirit into which flows the stream of events, and it is this which is so movingly conveyed in the last lines of *Gethsemane* when Christ says

> *And to me for judgement, like barges in a convoy,*
> *The centuries shall come floating out of the darkness.*

Its symbolism is only a part of *Dr Zhivago*. The scope of the book is not constricted by it, and indeed I am not sure that we lose a great deal—any more than we do in *Ulysses*—from an unawareness of how complex and multiform the symbolic pointers are. In one respect they do weaken its total reality. We can accept Zhivago's growing awareness of a divine analogy in his creative role at this time, and still think of him as an ordinary human being whom we have come to know and love; it is when a corresponding role is taken for granted as the whole reality about his mistress, Lara, and other characters, that we begin to feel a lack. They have no intimate life, no true individuality: our sense of them is solely what they mean to Zhivago—there is no way of telling what they might mean to themselves. The ego-centricity of Tolstoy wishes to encompass that of other people: Pasternak's wants only to give them their parts in a symbolic drama. For the symbolist there can be no saving failure of intention, no involuntary switch of insight of the kind that Tolstoy, as we have seen, had such an eye for.

Tolstoy would have been impatient with the modern technique of taking and allotting *roles* in life, and would probably have considered it a social expedient of an anonymous and undifferentiated society in which the unit of true and unconscious individuality—the family—no longer counted for so much. It is instructive to compare the roles which Pierre plays in *War and Peace*—the enlightened disciple, the saviour of his country against Napoleon, etc.—with the symbolic roles of the cast in *Dr Zhivago*. Pierre's are comic, delightfully so: he achieves his *reality* without knowing it, in the family, the goal of *War and Peace*. But in the world of *Dr Zhivago* the family has utterly broken down, and its characters can only find themselves and their meanings in the ancient pattern of nature, mythology and legend, as waifs or wise women, Judases and Magdalenes, wood spirits, town hermits. Find themselves?—not quite: the parts are found for them by the author, as in Tolstoy they did not seem to be. The method of Dr Zhivago is openly authoritarian, as if the breakdown of the family meant the end of its instinctive give and take of individual freedom, in art no less than in life.

But if we sometimes feel this about the method we do not feel it about the language. Symbols apart, description is freedom-giving here as it is not in other Russian novels since the revolution. Pasternak attempts to call everything by its right name, to identify everything alive, without reference to the system which has to maintain its reality by its rigidity, its power to convince that what it says is there, is there, and what is not, not. The whole texture of the novel is unassumingly alive in this way, and though the characters cannot exist outside their author's intention, the warmth of feeling and the play of language seems untouched by it. Every page reveals this, and one can quote almost at random.

The falling snow could be seen only beyond the far end of the roofs; seen so far away it looked almost still, sinking to the ground as slowly as breadcrumbs, thrown to fishes, sink through the water.

It is 'superfluous detail': there is no particular point in it, and yet here there is every point.

Freedom, too, is in the form. *Dr Zhivago* does not fall into the category of the symbolist novel, or into any category. As Tolstoy said of the best Russian prose works of the nineteenth century that they belonged to no recognisable genre, so Pasternak's seems to have been called into being by his unique need. Like *War and Peace* it is indifferent to the spectacular set piece, the 'epic' effect; Pasternak celebrates the events of the revolution with the same eager detachment, the same grasp both of the individual and of the public event, with which Tolstoy celebrates 1812 or Shakespeare the English wars. The veterans of 1812 were not pleased with Tolstoy. His version of the heroic episodes is in fact, "a mockery of their whole world, an insult to it", as Zhivago is told that his very existence is to the Party men. Prince Hal might have had the percipience to feel the same way about Shakespeare. This is where true history comes in, the place at one side that art creates, and that shows great events in the perspective of unchanging human psychology. So far from "distorting Soviet reality", Pasternak will one day be seen to have celebrated it. The European reader today even feels a certain envy for the people and the events that can be described like this: to have called forth such a complex vitality in art is like an election of grace.

One wonders how such an account as Pasternak's of the clandestine political meeting in White-dominated Siberia, in Chapter 10, could be interpreted as dangerous, negative and falsifying, any more than Tolstoy's account of the rivalry of the Russian leaders in 1812 could be; or Shakespeare's scenes of the rebel discussion in *Henry IV*, or of the quarrel between Brutus and Cassius in *Julius Caesar*. Reading such a scene we remember again Pushkin's disowning of any satiric intent. The thing is done from the inside, not from inside the Party but from inside Russian life and human nature. It is as far as possible removed from the portentous malice, the negative flourish, with which

Conrad describes similar revolutionary meetings in *The Secret Agent* and *Under Western Eyes*, or the way in which Arthur Koestler manipulates the confrontation of old and new style revolutionary in *Darkness at Noon*.[1]

These scenes of joyful humour, of participatory zest in the vagaries of men as well as in the unchanging background of nature, are not rare in *Dr Zhivago*. Yet though there is never any drop in the confidence with which they are set forth, many scenes and episodes are on nowhere near the same level of artistic achievement, but are frankly object lessons transposed into incident and description. Such is the account of the attack on the partisans by the white cadets, and Zhivago's rescue of one of them. The actuality of the business seems to be ignored by the author here as it is ignored in similar accounts in the fiction of 'socialist realism'. And though he theorises and pronounces as simply and naturally as Tolstoy, Pasternak cannot have Tolstoy's air of total individuality, of being on his own. Zhivago is supposedly isolated, a solitary voice, but in fact the age, with its primal ideological division, puts him inevitably on one side and against another.

Pasternak's contemporary, the poet Mandelshtam who disappeared in the purges, said in a poem that his age was like a once supple beast with a broken back, looking behind at the tracks left by its paws. Pasternak's novel is maimed in this way, maimed by the incurable division to which it seeks to give the novelist's and the historian's sanctification and meaning. Paster-

---

[1] Gletkin, the new Soviet man who interrogates in the novel the old revolutionary intellectual Rubashov, is a classic example of how a point can be falsified, even in a sense sentimentalised, by the author's stopping up what Nietzsche called "the conscience of the ears", by his refusal to pay close attention to the evident truth of his character. Gletkin is made to 'understand' Rubashov's position, and suggest that though he must be sacrificed now for the benefit of the Soviet State, history will eventually rehabilitate him. This has indeed occurred, but not through the Gletkins' doing. The foresight, the historical delicacy, wished by his author upon Gletkin remains intolerable, since it is clear that his monolithic strength depends precisely on the fact that he is not interested in matters like history but only in his place and his power in the system which has produced him. The moving thing about him and Rubashov is, or should be, that there can be no communication between them, but this does not suit the author's desire to produce an 'illuminating' dramatic exchange.

nak is compelled to call in nature as a third force; to make everything he values testify on his behalf. "Only nature," he says, "had remained true to human history", and he organises her for the struggle as sweepingly as the revolutionaries had organised their own resources. The birds, the waterfalls, every twig, icicle and rowan berry, are pressed into his partisan movement; lined up on behalf of "the nature of life itself "against the power of the abstract word.

The art of Russia's Silver Age—a period of elaborate symbolist techniques—lends itself all too easily to this kind of struggle. The use of the waterfall is an example. On the train journey to the Urals Zhivago wakes up at dead of night and hears some party officials talking on the platform. But their discussion, though in the usual sort of inhuman jargon "such as is rejected by life itself", seems uncannily quiet and considerate. There is a waterfall near by; "the incessant noise of the falling water dominated every other sound and created the illusion of quietness". So far so good, but we are not yet finished with the waterfall. Under its influence some of the forced-labour contingent on the train successfully desert, and in the morning Zhivago reflects that "they just ran away—like the water". Nor can one feel happy about the symbolism of the tram, airless, ramshackle, on the verge of breakdown, in which Zhivago takes his last journey and from which he forces his way out to die in the street. To this has come the Russian *troika* in its wild career? In the milieu of pretended reality a symbolic pattern cannot tell the truth, even though it misleads more subtly than the pastoral tone of socialist realism. We see it coming and feel "that distrust and resistance always evoked by an author's evident predetermination" which Tolstoy mentions several times in *What is Art?*

It is this aspect of the book which is presided over by Zhivago as a poet, and which is logically vindicated by his role. It is the way in which a poet might see not only his own life but life itself: chance contact, event and experience are unconsciously given shape and pattern in the creative matrix of his consciousness. In a sense, indeed, Zhivago is a poet in order that the rest of the characters should not have to be characters, as we apprehend them in life, but aspects of coincidence, fate, desperation and delight, as they impinge on his working mind and heart.

And yet we may feel that the best and most memorable things in the novel are not directly concerned with Zhivago and with his inevitably localised poetic consciousness, but are more like Tolstoyan or Shakespearean 'peepshows', reminding us—if they remind us of literature at all—of much wider and more multifarious kinds of creativity than are accessible to the hero. We feel then that the perspective of the novel is wider than that of Zhivago himself, as *War and Peace* is wider than the consciousness of Pierre and Andrew. We feel this in the account of the murder of Commissar Gintz, and in frequent episodes on the Urals journey. The waterfall is Zhivago's, but other incidents are as transparently from life as the incidents of Pierre's march from Moscow, where his heightened awareness of things is complemented by a continual sense of objective reality. One such "peepshow" occurs when the driver refuses to go on, and the armed sailors who rule the train attempt to coerce him.

> The snow round the head of the train was lit up at intervals, as if by a bonfire, by fiery flashes from the engine. By this light several dark figures were now seen running to the front of the engine.
>
> The first of them, presumably the driver, reached the far end of the running board, leapt over the buffers, and vanished as if the earth had swallowed him. The sailors who were chasing him did exactly the same thing: they too leapt and vanished.
>
> All this aroused the curiosity of several passengers, including Zhivago, and they went to see.
>
> Beyond the buffers, where the track opened out before them, they were met by an astonishing sight. By the side of the permanent way the top half of the driver's body stuck out of the deep snow into which he had fallen. His pursuers stood in a semicircle round him, like hunters round their quarry. Like him they were buried in snow up to their waists.
>
> "Thank you, comrades!" the driver was shouting. "A fine sight, sailors chasing a fellow-worker with guns!"

What matters is the humour of the thing. The significance of the snow, the natural force which in this absurd way prevents bloodshed, is in the narrative, and is not drawn into Zhivago's alignment of nature. Indeed this simplicity and mute humour reflects to some extent on Zhivago himself, rather as Pierre's dreams and meditations are lent a kind of saving absurdity by the actual episodes of the march, and those of Andrew, on the summer retreat, by his glimpse of the two little girls stealing the plums.

In one significant episode at the end of the novel Pasternak himself seems to say goodbye to the metaphorical structure which has served him in it. It vanishes in the light of common day when we find that the daughter of Zhivago and Lara, left behind in Siberia, has grown up a *besprisornaya*, one of the millions of lost children who wandered over Russia after the Revolution. Two of Zhivago's old friends come across her near the front during the Second World War and hear her terrible story. The way she tells it, her way of speaking and her unconscious acceptance of total change and of the new order of things, is done with great subtlety and compassion, and established her as a much more individually alive figure than her mother was—as if Lara had lived in an age of metaphor and she in one of simple reality. And indeed the contrast is emphasised in the reflection of one of Zhivago's old friends.

> Take that line of Blok's, "We, the children of Russia's terrible years": you can see the difference of period at once. In his time, when he said it, he meant it figuratively, metaphorically. The children were not children but the sons, the heirs of the intelligentsia, and the terrors were not terrible but apocalyptic—that's quite different. Now the figurative has become literal; children are children and the terrors are terrible. There you have the difference.

"Now the figurative has become literal." In the interrelation of the two, and in this final admission, appears the triumph of Pasternak's method. We may remember how Tolstoy, in *Master and Man*, made an implicit contrast between Pushkin's poem about a snowstorm and the real thing. The imagination is powerless before what actually occurs. The impending storm of the revolution, hailed by Blok, belonged to the world of his imagination, not to the world of fact; and before the facts of the great change Blok had become dumb, and died dumb. The resurrection after the darkness of the tomb, which Zhivago dreams of, is itself a metaphor, to which an age convinced that it is self-made, and not reborn, may remain totally indifferent.

Pasternak faces, as Tolstoy did, the need to reconcile the fact of what has occurred with the human imagination of it, to build up a sense of the past which is also a sense of the present and of what the present will always need. The horror of brute fact must be overcome, but not dishonestly overcome by the whole-sale conversion of it into legend or into some official history. And Pasternak shares with Tolstoy the power of transforming and humanising the actual and the terrible, not by shutting himself away from it but by remaining unexcited by it. Neither has an ambiguous relation to violence, or gives way to the novelist's temptation to dispense it as an earnest of truth. It is goodness in which they are interested, and *Dr Zhivago* is im-pregnated with goodness, almost involuntarily as it seems, yet as if its author never doubted that our "perceptions of the mean-ing of life", in Tolstoy's phrase, depend on our recognising it. The main thing about Zhivago is not that he is a doctor or even a poet, but that like Pierre and Levin he is a good man—a good man buried alive in an age in which men have "come to them-selves half-conscious and with half their memory gone". It is his task to show how they can be made whole again.

INDEX OF PROPER NAMES

INDEX OF PROPER NAMES

Fictional characters are not included. Titles of books are indexed under the name of the author except in the case of Tolstoy, whose works form separate entries.

INDEX OF PROPER NAMES

INDEX OF PROPER NAMES

INDEX OF PROPER NAMES

INDEX OF PROPER NAMES